THE KNOWING HEART

THE
KNOWING
HEART

A Sufi Path of Transformation

Kabir Helminski

SHAMBHALA
Boston & London
1999

SHAMBHALA PUBLICATIONS, INC.
Horticultural Hall
300 Massachusetts Avenue
Boston, Massachusetts 02115
http://www.shambhala.com

© 1999 by Kabir Helminski

9 8 7 6 5 4 3 2 1

FIRST EDITION
Printed in the United States of America

♾ This edition is printed on acid-free paper that meets
the American National Standards Institute z39.48 Standard.
Distributed in the United States by Random House, Inc.,
and in Canada by Random House of Canada Ltd

Library of Congress
Cataloging-in-Publication Data
Helminski, Kabir, 1947–
The knowing heart: a Sufi path of transformation
/ by Kabir Helminski. — 1st ed.
p. cm.
ISBN 1-57062-408-9 (alk. paper)
1. Sufism. I. Title.
BP189.H45 1999   98-31122
294.4′4—dc21   CIP

Dedicated to those anonymous friends
who recognized my longing as their own,
without whom I could not have learned
what little I know of the Heart.

Contents

Author's Note

Quotations from the Qur'ān appear in italic type throughout the book, and most translations of the Qur'ān are from Muhammad Asad, *The Message of the Qur'ān* (Gibraltar: Dar al-Andalus, 1980), although sometimes I have translated anew to bring out the necessary meanings.

Extra-Qur'ānic divine sayings transmitted by Muhammad (Hadīth Qudsī) and traditional sayings of Muhammad (Hadīth) are in Roman type.

Citations to the *Divan* of Rūmī are indicated by a *D* (e.g., "Rūmī, D 1652"). Citations to the *Mathnawī* are indicated by an *M* (e.g, "Rūmī, M, I, 3665–66").

A simplified system of transliteration is used, with macrons indicating long vowels. Thus, for example, *murīd* is pronounced *mureed*.

Unless otherwise noted, translations are my own.

ACKNOWLEDGMENTS

With profound gratitude to these beloveds and elders who lived to share the Truth and were part of the living transmission for me. It is inevitable that their voices should mix with mine in this book: Refik Algan, Assad Ali, Andac Arbas, Metin Bobaroglu, Sefik Can, Tosun Bayrak, Daud Bellak, Suleyman Dede, Cahid Gözkan, Bilal Hyde, Feridun Özgoren, Selim Özich, Feisal Rauf, Abdul Aziz Said, Hasan Shushud, Ahmed Tijani, Yannis Toussulis, Murat Yagan, Celalettin and Faruk Celebi, the Celebi family, and my wife, Camille.

THE PROCESS
AND THE
COMPLETION

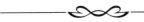

A Lover's Tale

A STORY

Attributed to Shaikh Ibn al-Arabī

ONE DAY, ONE OF GOD'S LOVERS GOES TO THE HOME OF his shaikh. The shaikh begins to speak to him about love. Little by little, as the shaikh speaks, the lover begins to melt, becoming more and more subtle until he just flows like a trickling stream. His whole physical being dissolved in front of the shaikh, until there was nothing but some water on the floor.

Just then a friend of the shaikh enters the room and asks, "Where is that fellow who just arrived?" The shaikh points to the water on the floor and says, "That man is that water."

This kind of melting is an astonishing transformation of state. The man lost his density in such a way that he became what he originally was: a drop of liquid. Originally he had arrived at human form from water, for as God has said: "*We created all of life from water.*"

This lover merely returned to his original essence, the water that is the source of life. And so we may draw the following conclusion: A lover is that being by whom everything is brought to life.

3

The Postmodern Situation

T HE REAL AND ESSENTIAL NEEDS OF THE HUMAN BEING
have not changed very much over the centuries. Eight hundred
years ago, the theologian and mystic Abū Hamīd al-Ghazālī
asserted: "Human perfection resides in this, that the love of God
should conquer the human heart and possess it wholly, and even if it
does not possess it wholly, it should predominate in the heart over the
love of all things."

To grasp his statement, we must understand that this word *God* has
the following synonyms: Reality, the Source of Life, the Most Subtle
State of Everything. The love of God is the love of the greatest Truth.
This quest concerns Reality, not religion. The "love of God" is our
essential relationship with what is most real.

What has changed over the centuries, perhaps, is the form and pressure of those forces that could displace the love of the Real, the love
of God from the heart. And what may change further is that human
beings may lose the whole notion of love of God as the criterion for
human perfection and well-being.

To be a Sufi is to be a lover, but not just any kind of lover. We
need knowledge to know what to love and what love asks of us, in

order that we might become love itself. Mevlānā Jalāluddīn Rūmī[1] says: "There is no greater love than love with no object."

There was once a time, perhaps, when people felt themselves to be part of a cosmic order that offered a straight path to salvation, truth, or enlightenment. In that time before spiritual truth was marginalized, the Divine love and mercy were extended to anyone, no matter what his or her circumstances, who fulfilled the necessary moral and religious duties. Almost every person could find in his or her own humanness the precondition of hope.

We live in times of spiritual uncertainty and great contradictions. We witness signs of cultural collapse and long for a vision of hope. The situation for many in the postmodern era is that all religious truths seem to be relativized; no religion seems absolute anymore. In this situation, even a life of faith and morality is no assurance of salvation. We live with unnamed anxieties and guilt. An undercurrent of shame and unworthiness moves just beneath the surface of our busy lives. We try to find cosmic satisfaction in a lifestyle, a career, a self-image, or a romantic relationship. Some employ therapists to attain self-acceptance, forgiveness, and understanding. Although liberated from divine judgment, we are haunted by existential guilt that refuses propitiation.

Furthermore, there is no shared cultural myth, no unifying vision to bind us together with the wider society. The servitude to religious forms and strictures is quickly disappearing, to be replaced only by a worship of the self or a compulsive escape from the self. The worship of the self conceals itself in many forms: fashion, fitness, career. The escape from the self is served by vast industries that more and more shape our lives: professional sports, alcohol and narcotics, gambling, mass media, and the entertainment of sex and violence. All that unifies us is a synthetic, dollar-driven "culture."

Many attempt to construct their own personal spiritual worldview

---

[1] Rūmī (1207–1273) is one of the greatest saints and literary figures of all time. He lived most of his life in Konya, which is in present-day Turkey. In Islamic cultures his poetry is read more than any other writings except for the Qur'ān.

through a sampling of what the great traditions have to offer. These words, spoken by a nurse, seem to sum up the experience of so many people: "I have looked at many of the world's spiritual paths, and they all seem to be saying pretty much the same thing. I haven't been able to commit to any one of them, and it is difficult to remember the sacred in the midst of daily life."

THE KINGDOM OF THE "I"

What is it that we are searching for? Our situation as human beings is that we live in a world of pain and death. No amount of pleasure can negate this reality. Our means of pleasure is the body, and the body is subject to satiation, sickness, and death.

Even if we no longer fear the punishment of hell, we have to somehow deal with our own animal self. We try to know which of our desires can lead to a real and perhaps lasting well-being. We try to know when and how much is enough; and yet this animal self has endless desires. Repression, or at least self-discipline, is an inevitable condition of our situation. Our very identity, our ego-self, is a complex of psychological manifestations arising from the body and related to its pleasure and survival. There is a terror in living with a body that is irrational, fallible, and, finally, mortal.

We have no cultural and spiritual value systems to reconcile us with the body. We serve the body but we do not teach it how to serve. We worship the body, but we do not sanctify it. Our cultural value systems today are among the least spiritual ever offered to a human community. Basically, the meaning of life has been reduced to an unconscious operating mode: get a job that will enable us to buy what we want, pass through life with a minimum of pain and discomfort. The fulfillment offered to us is the fulfillment of being good and intelligent consumers, effective seekers of pleasure. We will have to repress many of our desires in order to eventually satisfy a few of them.

Yet there is still this problem of our existence. Even if we are free to fulfill our desires, we still lack something to fulfill and give meaning to our lives. Even if we have removed God the Judge, we have a feeling of existential contraction, unworthiness, guilt, and sin.

This existential contraction is the "I" itself, cut off from the spiritual dimensions of Reality. Effectively, in our everyday waking existence, this is all that we know and are. We become this "I" that seeks pleasure and avoids pain. Our capacity for pleasure is, however, limited and our confrontation with pain is inevitable. To protect ourselves we unconsciously try to make ourselves the Absolute Ruler of our own psychological and material realm. We create a kingdom with boundaries and defenses. We strive to consolidate our powers so that we can acquire what we want and keep out what we don't want. This is the business and strategy of the "I." And yet even from a materialist perspective, this kingdom has all the substantiality of a spider's web. Despite our pride and careful efforts to spin this web, fate can brush it away without resistance. It is no wonder that we who depend on the material world for our sense of security and well-being live in a perpetual state of fear and contraction. Even when we are attaining our desires, and so have experienced what we call "happiness," we cannot help but question whether this is real, and how long it will last.

What are we to do with our consciousness, our will, our love? These are the choices that variously confuse, distract, and oppress human beings.

> This human face is a shape
> tethered in the stall of pain:
> part god, part angel, part beast . . .
> a secret charm, rarely released.
>
> —RŪMĪ, D 568

Our "I" is our relationship to the world; and as long as this relationship is characterized by a self and world, we are in duality. This is our relationship with reality. Our resistance, expectations, complaints, and desires fly off at a tangent from what actually *is*.

The vast majority of human beings are living in a state of alienation from spiritual reality and from their own essence. Instead of living life directly and knowing themselves directly, all experience is filtered through layers of mental and emotional conditioning in the form of subjective distortions, defense mechanisms, cultural prejudices. This total mechanism of distortion we take to be ourselves. We are living in a "virtual reality" of our own creation, but because we have always been in costume, always wired to the program, always turned toward the screen of fantasy, we have not known *ourselves*. In the best of these times people's minds are filled with everything but the truth: images from consumer culture, manufactured desires, superstitions, hallucinations, beliefs, allergies to beliefs, the clichés of neurotic individualism. In the worst of times, human minds may be occupied with mass psychoses of nationalism, fanaticism, racism, tribalism, or religious fundamentalism.

THE PURIFICATION OF CONSCIOUSNESS

Because of these constant distractions, human beings cannot know the present moment and the truth it contains. A spiritual education and transformation would first of all have to minimize our subjective distortions, or, in other words, increase the objectivity of our consciousness. Since distortions exist in every area of our lives, the reeducation must be applied to every area of our lives. Meditation alone would not be sufficient. We must also bring a new consciousness into all our relationships and activities.

The full human reality includes the transpersonal reality, but because we have become fragments, we exclude true reality. We focus on parts. We take the individual human person as the ultimate unit of reality and ignore the fact that a common life and consciousness flows through each of us. We can recognize ecologically that all of life is interdependent—that water, minerals, light, and other energies all cooperate to allow a living thing to exist. But when it comes to ourselves, we fantasize our unique psychological independence, denying that we are dependent on an Unseen Reality and a common human transpersonal dimension. We try to live as if we are alone.

Furthermore, we exist in a psychologically fragmented state, a state of continuous inner conflicts among the parts of ourselves. We have lost the principle of unity within ourselves. We are not only psychological polytheists, worshipping gods of our own creation, we are "polyselfists," because we have many selves and have not known our *essential self.* We know the social selves, the selves of desire; we are preoccupied with the self-cassettes, the self-scripts of conventional society. Because we are thus fragmented within ourselves and in conflict within ourselves, we exist socially as fragments in conflict with each other with little hope of achieving anything but temporary reconciliation based on these conflicted, fragmentary selves. In contrast to this, when people allow their false separation to dissolve, as is sometimes possible in music or lovemaking or sincere worship, a truer individuality emerges and a harmony between *these* individualities is possible. When one whole human being meets another whole human being, there is no antagonism. Even if there is difference, there is respect, because the wholeness of one is not in conflict with the wholeness of the other.

According to the testimony of the most mature human beings, we have the potential for knowing all of Being, all of Reality. We can know, embrace, and participate in this transpersonal Reality. Furthermore, this whole Reality is the electromagnetic field of love.

> The Beloved's water washes all illness away.
> The Beloved's rose garden of Union has no thorns.
> I've heard it said there's a window that opens
> between heart and heart,
> but if there are no walls,
> there's no need even for a window.
>
> —RŪMĪ, D 511

The reality of the moment can be summarized simply as: Being in becoming, a total field of Oneness unfolding, Love knowing itself. The reality of ourselves can be summarized as: we are integral to this reality, not just a part of it, but one with it. We are not a *part* of the whole, we *are* the whole. The human being is all of Being, the drop that contains the Ocean.

> Our pure hearts roam across the world.
> We get bewildered by all the idols we see,
> yet what we're trying to understand
> in everything is what we already are.
>
> —RŪMĪ, D 549

We human beings long to surrender ourselves to something great and be taken up into its greatness. A human being's measure is the measure of that which he or she surrenders to and serves. Some people surrender only to their own imagined self-interest. Some surrender to some social ideal, others to beauty, to love of family, to religious faith.

And yet so much that human beings surrendered to in the past has lost its relevance or been discredited. We live in a time when many people are trying to invent their own values and beliefs because those that exist are no longer convincing to their souls.

A few people sense that the purpose of life is to give one's life as a gift to Being itself.

> Secrets fall from the Sufi's hands,
> Whole kingdoms for the taking.
> Unlike someone who begs on the street for bread,
> a dervish begs to give his life away.
> —RŪMĪ, D 686

Only the strongest people are able to do this. The rest settle for the lesser satisfactions of conventional social ambitions and roles. Few human beings can both activate the passion for life that leads to creative self-expression and, at the same time, surrender their lives as a gift to the Creative Power of Being.

A SPIRITUALITY ADEQUATE TO OUR TIMES

We are searching for a spirituality adequate to the times we live in. We need a vision that will not only allow us to see the reality of our lives but will urge us on to a more complete expression of our complete humanness.

The spiritual challenge of our time is to realize our sacred humanness, that there need not be a conflict between the natural and the supernatural, between the finite and the infinite, between time and eternity, between practicality and mysticism, between social justice and contemplation, between sexuality and spirituality, between our human fulfillment and our spiritual realization, between what is most human and what is most sacred.

The human being is a threshold between two worlds, two realities: the reality of material existence, where the ego dwells, and the reality of spiritual Being, where the essential self is held and nurtured in an All-Compassionate embrace. It is in *the knowing heart* that these two dimensions meet and are integrated. Without an awakened and purified heart, the ego lives in the illusions of its own fears, opinions, separation. Without the knowing heart there is no connection between self and Being. The heart is the center of our being and our most comprehensive cognitive faculty. The eye of the heart sees more truly than our ego-based intellect and emotions. With such a heart, true surrender, and true happiness and well-being, become possible. It is one thing to propose that the highest human possibility lies in the surrender to Being; it is quite another to *know* in any moment whether surrender lies in the choice of one course of action over another, or perhaps in not choosing at all.

The lonely and isolated self in its anxiety knocks upon many doors. If we can bring it to the door of the heart, when it opens, the self will know that it has been inside all along. Inside and outside will be one. The heart itself will be seen as the door to infinite intelligence and life.

We cannot afford to live much longer in denial of the facts: that we are destructive to the planet and to ourselves. Nor can we afford to lose our awareness of the energy at the core of nature, the power of unconditional, spiritual unity, which is experienced by the knowing heart as love.

Love is the force that will heal us of our existential guilt and lift us to a new level of beauty and meaning. All human fulfillment is related to love and all human problems are signs of the denial of the centrality of love. In other words, love is the essential transforming and healing power.

We must know and apply the principles by which we can cooperate with this power of love. It is possible to open up to the experience of love through a practical education of the heart. The knowing heart is receptive to the intelligence of Being and is guided by Being. When the heart is awakened and purified, it establishes a connection to

Spirit; our finest and noblest capacities are unlocked, our sacred humanness is revealed. What it comes down to, the distillation of all wisdoms, is this: we can rejoin our isolated wills with Love's Will through the knowing of the heart.

> If the heart is restored to health
> and purged of sensuality,
> then *the Merciful God is seated upon the Throne.*[2]
> After this, the heart is guided directly
> since the heart is with God.
>
> —RŪMĪ, M, I, 3665–66

The Divine Being created human nature in beautiful proportions and breathed its Spirit into us. Because we have cut ourselves off from Being, we have swelled with false pride and thrown the world out of balance: our bodies and minds, our relationships, and our whole ecology is suffering the consequences of our denial of our own essential nature. Perhaps we needed to experience this separation in order to finally experience our intimate relationship with this Source. The human being has capacities that are unsuspected today; they can be known through a simultaneous surrender to Being and energetic activation of all our human faculties.

The Sufis have been the educators of hearts for at least fourteen centuries. Their teaching and methods are based upon neither dogma nor conjecture, but upon a divine and objective foundation that is the primordial "religion" of humanity. Sufism does not offer "salvation" in the sense of a guarantee of heaven in the afterlife. It offers a path to complete humanness, a state in which the spiritual and the human are unified, in which the world of spiritual qualities and material existence are seen as one. This education is a unified whole, but it touches on many areas of experience: individual psychology, relationships, marriage, family, community, livelihood, creativity, and worship. It is empirical, practical, and integrated with daily life. At the same time it is attuned to the most transcendent Truth. This is an education that

---

[2] Surah Ṭā-Hā (20):4.

restores the unity between substance and form, between the spiritual and human dimensions. The goal of this education is the living realization of an intimate connection between ourselves and the Divine.

> We are the mirror as well as the face in it.
> We are drunk on this life of God.
> We are both the pain and its cure. We are
> the fresh, cool water and the jar that pours.
>
> —RŪMĪ, D 1652

A Human Way of Life

I F YOU CAME TO A CROSSROADS AND THE SIGNS READ: "THIS way to Life," and "This way to God," which way would you choose?

How many generations of honest people have been bewildered by this apparent dilemma, believing that the way to God lies in the opposite direction from a human life? How many people's psychospiritual health has been undermined because they took the road away from life, away from their own humanity?

Can we imagine a spirituality that integrates the highest spiritual attainment with a fully lived human life? Is it possible that the realization of the Divine is the realization of complete humanness?

My own life has been a search, a quest not for religion but for reality, not for some "ism" but for truth. If I speak of Sufism, it is because I believe it has something to offer to our contemporary human situation. Yet, although I speak of Sufism as an example of a complete spirituality, I cannot point to many places in the Western world where this complete spirituality has been realized. In other words, it may not be a simple matter of finding your local Sufi group. What I am describing may need to be created from the ground up, on the soil of our own lands. What I am describing may be a vision more than an actuality, at least in the modern world we are faced with. And yet the hope of a pure and complete Sufism may be greater here at this time than anywhere else in the world.

Essential Sufism is neither an exotic cult nor a narrow specialization for a particular temperament; it is a process for recovering the human norm and reaching our full humanness. It describes a way of developing the subtle faculties of mind and increasing our capacity for love.

What makes Sufism, at its best, so important today is that it enables spiritual transformation in a natural way without denying our basic human nature. In Sufism, the moral and the material, the spiritual and the practical, have always been integrated into a pattern of life. Many of the spiritual problems that we encounter in our time and culture have already been explored if not solved in the Sufi tradition. Sufism has something to give to the modern world that, if received, can help to revive our ailing humanness.

Modern culture pays lip service to concern for the individual person, but the individual that our Western culture celebrates is a partial and fragmented caricature compared with the human being as understood in the great sacred traditions. This individual is a being whose real humanness is diminished, if not trashed, by a materialistic consumer machine. It is an increasingly toxic being cut off from its own essential source of healing. It is a being divorced from the sacred, a being that lives primarily to satisfy its own distorted desires.

INNER EXPERIENCE INFORMED BY REVELATION

This Path of Sufism has both an experiential and a theoretical dimension. Its experiential dimension involves a process of inner verification, or spiritual empiricism, that leads through particular experiences and states. Its theoretical dimension is founded upon the Qur'ān as it was understood by a broad lineage of enlightened or complete human beings. Muslims believe the Qur'ān is a revelation of the Compassionate Intelligence of the Universes as it was given to the Prophet Muhammad. Sufism is guided by an understanding of this revelation that is not only mystical but practical, offering a model for a mature human life. In the West this may be its least understood aspect—especially today, when liberal, secular culture offers no particular value system other than a tolerance based on the relativity of all value systems.

In the West, Sufism has sometimes been taken out of context and superficially understood in terms of methods and techniques, ideas, ceremonies, and states. Other sacred traditions have suffered a similar fate. Buddhism, for instance, has often been effectively reduced to a technique of meditation, while the Eightfold Noble Path (the ethical dimension of Buddhism) is left in the background. If Sufism is understood as a system of techniques for engendering ecstatic states, it is understood only very partially. We cannot steal the fire. We must enter it.

Sufism consists of both essence and form. Its essence is a state of loving mind. This enlightened and loving mind is supported by and integrated with a way of life, which is its form. Classical Sufism involves a pattern of living that includes regular disciplines such as ablution, prayer, and fasting, as well as the cultivation of qualities including affection, gentleness, patience, generosity, hospitality, sobriety, modesty, intelligence, and self-discipline. Practices removed from this pattern are at best incomplete; at worst, spiritual practices done outside the context of a whole way of life may contribute to the illness rather than to the cure, and may further the original addiction to self.

We need a spiritual recovery program for those addicted to the separate self. It is theoretically possible that one can overcome the addiction without any program, but the power of the addiction is easily underestimated, and often denied. Overcoming the addiction can be like trying to scale a high wall. One's best efforts can be frustrated unless one has a ladder of the right height with all its rungs in place.

In this tradition it is believed that the Reality we are seeking is also seeking us and has offered guidance in the form of revelation and inspired teachings. The sincere seeker will be guided step by step by his or her Sustainer (Arabic *Rabb*, which also means "educator").

> *Thus, step by step, We bestow from on high through this Qur'ān*
> *all that gives health and is a grace to those who have faith. . . .*
> —SURAH AL-ISRĀ' (17):83

SUFISM AS SYNTHESIS

Over some fourteen centuries of its continuous development, Sufism has been a vital spiritual and historical impulse that has guided and integrated the spiritual energies of hundreds of millions of people. It is a mistake to think of it as an Eastern or even a Middle Eastern tradition. Its spiritual claim to universality is based on an understanding of the Qur'ān as the inspired synthesis and reconciliation of earlier revelations. The Qur'ān proposes that countless prophets, or messengers, have come to the communities of this world over the millennia, bringing essentially the same message. The Qur'ān claims to be the confirmation of the authenticity of these earlier revelations, which were, however, more or less obscured or distorted, and a culminating statement of their essential truths.

Sufism's historical claim to universality consists in its power to assimilate into its own essence the spiritual attainments of cultures existing in the whole region from Spain through Africa, Greater Arabia, Turkey, Iran, Central Asia, India, China, and Southeast Asia.

Sufism integrates the Eastern and the Western, the impersonal and the personal dimensions of Spirit. Like the Eastern traditions, it recognizes the importance of deep contemplation and meditative awareness. And like them it looks beyond appearances to the essential oneness of Being. The highest truth of Sufism, the absolute indivisibility of Beneficent Being, is in harmony with such traditions as Mahayana Buddhism and Advaita Vedanta. Like the Western traditions, it recognizes the importance of a deeply personal relationship with the Divine and a relationship of love and practical service to our fellow human beings and the natural world.

Sufism is a path emphasizing self-awareness, human interdependence, creativity, practicality, social justice, and Divine Love. It is a spiritual way that is in harmony with human nature and does not oppose spiritual attainment to individual, social, familial, or conjugal life. In other words, the highest spiritual attainment is possible for someone living a fully human life. It teaches that seclusion, asceticism, celibacy, monasticism, and religious professionalism are not required, and may not be desirable for the attainment of the spiritual realization of the individual and the spiritual well-being of society. Sufism has fourteen centuries of experience with bringing people to their full spiritual maturity within the context of everyday life.

Sufism developed in many dimensions: social, cultural, aesthetic, scientific. The Sufi centers (known variously as *tekkes*, *dergāhs*, and *khāna-qāhs*) were typically places of a liberal spirit and lifelong learning. They offered not only the opportunity for spiritual training and service; they were cultural and intellectual centers as well, introducing into their respective societies the highest values and cultural achievements.

Celaleddin Chelebi, the late head of the Mevlevi Order and a descendant of Rūmī, was born and raised in a Mevlevi tekke in Aleppo, Syria. He recounted to me his precious memories of this place, how it was a community in which the sounds of music, discourse, and prayer were heard from every quarter. He described one older dervish who was a great violinist who could often be heard playing the classical compositions of the Mevlevi tradition, and often, too, the compositions of Bach and other Western composers, with tears streaming down his cheeks and beard. It was a place where spirituality flourished side by side with science, art, and agriculture. This Mevlevi community was progressive in its attitudes and often the first to introduce technological change into the wider community: the first tractor, the first radio, the first telephone.

More than a thousand years ago Sufism innovated the professional guilds in the Islamic world that spiritualized the arts and crafts and whose more secularized principles later spread to Europe. The principles of chivalry, or heroic generosity and honor, are also traceable to an Islamic mystical source, the Futuwwah orders that grew out of the teachings of generations of the Prophet Muhammad's family. Eventually these values were carried back to Europe by families of European nobility who had settled in the Middle East at the time of the Crusades. Sufi groups were responsible for the restoration of agriculture to Central Asia after the Mongol devastation. During the Ottoman centuries the Mevlevi Order contributed many of the finest examples of design and calligraphy, classical music, and literature. Mevlevi tekkes taught foreign languages including Arabic, Persian, and sometimes even Italian. Today Sufis are invisibly at work making profound contributions in the fields of human rights and conflict resolution, in the frontiers of consciousness and transpersonal psychology, in the arts and social services.

The model of enlightenment within the Sufi tradition is not usually the reclusive sage who has cut his ties with the world, nor the enlightened master elevated and served by a cult of followers. Spirituality is not a profession or specialization separate from life. The Sufi is someone who is likely to be married and have a family, and who is self-supporting through a socially useful occupation. He or she would not accumulate personal power or wealth through spiritual activities, but would exemplify the qualities of servanthood and modesty.

> A Sufi is a handful of dust, passed through a sieve, then moistened with a few drops of water. Stepped on, he neither bruises nor muddies the foot of the passerby.
>
> —KHWAJA 'ABDULLĀH ANSĀRI, *Rasā'el-e Ansāri*[1]

Sufism is one manifestation of the ineluctable pull of our Source. It is the awakening and development of our latent human faculties under the grace and protection of Divine Love. Its beginning is love and its end is love. What God wants from us is love, and the natural outcome of love is submission to Love.

The distillation of all spiritual traditions might be expressed in this way: we can rejoin our isolated wills with Love's will. The Sufi seeks to uncover and grasp the principles by which we can cooperate with this power of Love.

The effect of this cooperation will be that one's self is transformed through verifiable stages: from a compulsive and self-centered state to a state of balanced and conscious integration, and eventually to a state of *active surrender* in which the individual is guided directly by his or her own purified heart.

> Seven hundred Sufi masters have spoken of the Path, and the last said the same as the first. Their words were different, perhaps, but their intention was one. Sufism is the abandonment of affectation. And of all affectations, none is weightier than your "you-ness."
>
> —ABŪ SA'ĪD, *Asrār al-Tawhīd*[2]

---

[1] Quoted in Dr. Javad Nurbakhsh, *Sufism I: Meaning, Knowledge, Unity* (London: Khaniqa-Nimatullahi Publications, 1981).
[2] Ibid.

Completion

THE DROP THAT
CONTAINS THE OCEAN

I T HAS BECOME AN ACCEPTED SPIRITUAL IDEA THAT EACH PART
of the universe in some way reflects the whole. Contemporary spirituality has borrowed the holographic model from contemporary
science. This notion has always existed within Sufism and is expressed,
for instance, in the idea that the human being is not merely a drop
that can merge with the Ocean, but a drop that *contains* the Ocean.
Every divine attribute is latent within the human heart, and by the
cooperation of human will with divine grace, these attributes can be
awakened and manifested. We human beings contain within ourselves
the potential to experience completion, to know our intimate relationship to the whole of Being in such a way that we reflect this completion through ourselves. The highest spiritual attainment has been
expressed by the phrase *insān-i kāmil*, the Completed Human Being.

When I first entered on the Mevlevi Way, I was told that the aim
was "completion": "If you are a Jew, you will become a completed
Jew; if you are a Christian, you will become a completed Christian;
and if you are a Muslim, you will become a completed Muslim." I
was moved by the openness and generosity of this assertion, and I

came to understand that "completion" is the fulfillment of the message brought by the prophets of these great religions.

What brought my heart to its knees, however, was meeting a human being who exemplified this completion, who embodied the Divine Majesty and at the same time expressed the most perfect humility. This paradox put into perspective all the prior spiritual attainments I had witnessed. Life had introduced me to people who were highly developed in the areas of intelligence, will, consciousness, and even love. But no one, until that time, had seemed complete. I had glimpsed the awesome dignity and responsibility of being human: what is the point of will or consciousness without love? And, on the other hand, what value would humility have without the awakening and manifestation of the divine attributes latent within ourselves?

It has been said that we cannot know or judge a higher level of spirituality than what we ourselves have attained. The wise can understand the foolish because they have emerged from foolishness, but the foolish cannot understand the wise, because foolishness does not come out of wisdom. Some people buy into a mystique of enlightenment, believing that one who has a title and a retinue of disciples, wears robes and a turban, has written books, or is the descendant of a master has probably attained a level of spirituality that may even put him or her beyond the criteria of conventional morality. Too often we Westerners have abandoned our own inner knowing and common sense in offering our credulity to teachers who make claims of spiritual authority.

Yet real spirituality may be obvious to the heart of the simplest person. An illiterate villager may look at the face of a spiritual claimant and make an essence evaluation, while those who are more layered by personality may deceive themselves.

An authentic spirituality is characterized by a remarkable lack of self-consciousness or pretense. Effortlessness and spontaneity merge with modesty and self-effacement. And yet it is possible for this genuineness to occur in a teacher without a maturity appropriate to the needs of the student.

Imagine, for instance, that a psychiatrist from Zurich meets an authentic shaman from Mongolia. Because the psychiatrist has never encountered someone with such a degree of attainment in certain areas, she begins her apprenticeship with a high degree of trust and receptivity. What she will learn is a combination of objective and relative truths of shamanism. The objective truths are those capacities and principles which are universal and necessary to the process of being a shaman. The relative truths are those incidental and secondary aspects that originate from the sociological conditioning and personality of the teacher. She may begin to develop in her ability to contact invisible dimensions and at the same time acquire the personality characteristics and values of a Mongolian nomad. This may lead to a split within her, and she may weaken or fail to develop the kind of maturity that is necessary in her own culture, including, for instance, the analytical and social skills of her profession.

Sufism today needs teachers who have a maturity appropriate to the time and place and who can transmit what is objectively spiritual with a minimum of personal and sociological contamination.

THE COMPLETED HUMAN BEING

A spirituality adequate to the times we live in must first of all be centered in the reality of human completion itself. If it is based instead on any partial version of humanness, it will be insufficient. No matter what is sought to supplement this insufficiency, if the starting point is less than human wholeness, the result will only be a distorted version of humanness.

The attributes of the complete human being are the attributes of God appropriately reflected in human nature. God has innumerable qualities, ninety-nine of which are mentioned in the Qur'ān. Some of these are the everyday attributes of a human being: seeing, hearing, speech, will, life, awareness. The Sufi recognizes that these qualities are reflected through the human being from the Absolute Being. Becoming completely human is being able to reflect more and more of the divine qualities in everyday life.

This world is viewed as the mirror of divine qualities, the site of their manifestation. The human heart is even more so a site of their manifestation. Recognizing these qualities in the heart is at the same time recognizing them in life. There is no separation in the field of Oneness (*tawhīd*). There is, therefore, no antagonism between the human life and the spiritual life. Only when human life has become shaped by the demands and illusions of the isolated ego is it reduced to a caricature, a particularized distortion of its wholeness. Otherwise, to be fully human is to fulfill our spiritual destiny.

Sufism can be considered a path of completion in two important senses: First, it is a way that proceeds from and leads to the Completed Human Being. Second, it is a complete way that uses every possible effective means to orchestrate the transformation of a human being. It can thus multiply its effectiveness by using multiple channels of experience to achieve its purpose. Both of these facts—the completeness of the method and the completeness of the result—are of the highest significance.

The completeness of the Sufi method proceeds from the completeness of its apprehension of human nature. The means by which the human being will be transformed depend on our understanding of what a human being is and is designed to be.

Human completion is not glimpsed from the eye-level of the average human being; nor is it successfully theorized or described by science, sociology, philosophy, or psychology; it is a gift from the Creator of the human being. It is a proposal that comes from the Heart of Nature through its revelatory dialogue with humanity. When Nature bears its final fruit, it is the Completed Human, who speaks with the voice and intelligence of Nature itself, describing the attributes of Completion. Human completion is our innate destiny, which, however, requires our conscious cooperation with divine grace. What we can know about our essential humanness comes from those who have become completed human beings and who could listen within their own hearts to the guidance of the Creative Power.

The human being implies his or her own completion, as a plant implies the existence of the sun, as man implies the existence of woman. Sufism received the implicit knowledge of completion first from the Qur'ān, which describes itself as "a mercy and a guidance for humanity," a "reminder" confirming and clarifying previous revelations to humanity, revealed to the Prophet Muhammad. Sufism also draws upon the ever more explicit understanding of this completion as witnessed in the lives and teachings of its many saints and masters, beginning with Muhammad.

THE METHODOLOGY OF COMPLETION

The Sufi process exists essentially on the basis of the *shaikh-murīd*, mentor-student relationship, and typically this relationship is supported and enhanced within a "spiritual family" of seekers. There have been many metaphors offered to describe the role of a shaikh (or shaikha): as a shepherd of a flock, as the father (or mother) of a family, as a spiritual monarch. None of these, however, seems appropriate to the times we live in. First of all, spiritual seekers who are awakening and developing their latent human capacities should not be considered sheep. Even the metaphor of a parent is fraught with danger, because it may encourage seekers to become dependents. Nor is a shaikh fundamentally a king, because spiritual love cannot coexist with the exercise of power or privilege.

I would rather liken a shaikh to the conductor of an orchestra. A conductor is responsible for harmonizing the various members with each other. He is also responsible for maintaining the classical repertoire as well as introducing new elements into the orchestra's repertoire. He is thus both the guardian of tradition and the continuing creator of it. The shaikh is even more than a conductor, because the Sufi way uses every aspect of human existence to accomplish its purpose.

Within the Sufi way, these are some of the principles and methods that are used in the orchestration of human transformation:

> *The remembrance of God under all circumstances.*
> Remembrance implies two dimensions: the state of presence in which a person is whole and self-aware, and the state of being in continual relationship with God: known, held, guided, and loved.
> *Worship, understood as the integration of all one's faculties in the act of expressing love and respect to the Absolute.*
> In its most specific sense, worship is a complete human action,

including but not limited to ritual and ceremony, intended to harmonize ourselves with Divine Being. In its general sense, it is the purpose of life on earth. One of our teachers, Hasan Shushud, said, "Our human egoism can create a world that is a mirage and a poison; the antidote is acts of worship."

Submission, which is allowing the Divine to be the Center of our reality.

The effective result of this submission is both self-transcendence and a capacity for sacrifice. Submission proceeds from the conditioned to the Unconditioned, the compulsive self to the essential Self, the finite to the Infinite.

Ethics, especially those straightforward and self-explanatory moral principles revealed in the Qur'ān and other authentic revelations.

Ethics, apprehended by a loving heart, contribute to a sense of harmony and trust through right relationships and sensitivity to appropriate boundaries.

Brotherhood, the Sufi code of chivalry centered on love, interdependence, and heroic sacrifice.

We lack an adequate word in the English language to convey the profound alliance of seekers, the bond consciously accepted by those who have undertaken a life's journey together.

The art of spiritual conversation.

When minds join together and communicate for a spiritual purpose, an active receptivity is sustained, energy is exchanged, and realization of meanings is deepened.

Reasoning and conscious reflection.

Reason allows the intelligent ordering of ideas around the master truth of existence: the Oneness of All Being. It is evaluating or discriminating among ideas based on the degree to which they reflect the truth of Oneness. Reason, in this context, is the working of the conscious intellect to decondition, recondition, and finally uncondition the whole of the mind, including the subconscious or unconscious.

Reading sacred texts.

Reflecting upon the Word of God and the inspired language of

God's friends, the masters and saints, awakens the soul and purifies the heart.

Refining the subtle faculties of Mind.

As the human nervous system is refined through spiritual practice, subtle faculties of perception develop that open us to the imaginal world, a dimension in which meanings are embodied as images. Our dreams become more lucid and objective, our intuitions more accurate.

Fasting.

Just as the mind needs to be purified and refined to be able to make contact with the Infinite, the body needs purification and refinement so that the veils of desire and compulsion may be lifted.

Movement and bodywork.

The ritual prayer of Islam, done five times a day, is a complete "yoga" that maintains the health and equilibrium of the body. In addition, from the sublime whirling of the Mevlevis to the *zikr* gatherings of other orders, which involve chanting and a vigorous bodily worship, Sufism has typically included the exercise of the body in its ceremonies. The ritual prayer provides a grounded and dignified sobriety, and the zikr allows a degree of self-transcendence through the ecstasy of expansion.

WHAT ESSENTIAL SUFISM IS NOT

The idea of completion is so important, because without it we may settle for less than human maturity. Without it we might mistake some part for the whole. Just as egoism can reduce our humanity, various distortions of spirituality can produce impressive human attainments that are incomplete, restrictive, imbalanced, or even pathological.

Essential Sufism is not a specialization apart from life that requires the renunciation of human interests and desires. In other words, it does not aim at the absolute transcendence of the human condition.

Sufism does not focus primarily on a single-pointed inner concentration on the Divine through which all the created world falls away.

It is not concerned with developing a micro-attention to the minutiae of consciousness in order to deconstruct the ego.

Nor is it concerned especially with altered states of consciousness, soul travel, or shamanic ecstasies. Although a mature human being may incidentally have the facility to enter other realms of consciousness and states of being, one's submission to and trust in the Absolute Compassion significantly reduces the need for and preoccupation with such explorations.

Nor is Sufism necessarily characterized by bewilderment and intoxication, although one may pass through such states before attaining the sobriety that embraces and transcends all intoxication.

Sufism is not a way of making the ordinary seem miraculous, but of integrating the truly miraculous into ordinary human life.

ENLIGHTENMENT AND MATURITY

Many of us have experienced various disappointments and disillusionments in our search for a spirituality adequate to our times. Aside from those false teachers who are not really worthy of discussion, there are spiritual guides who clearly have some kind of enlightenment and yet fall short of what we would expect of even an ordinary decent human being. Such people may have charisma, the ability to read thoughts, the power to alter others' states of consciousness, and so on; yet they are immature in certain essential respects.

It may be possible to create what could be called a "hothouse enlightenment," a kind of theoretical or induced enlightenment that is nonetheless unripe and incomplete. If, for instance, it were possible to give a monkey in a laboratory an experience of monkey enlightenment, that monkey would not necessarily have the wisdom of a monkey who had matured in the jungle. Some people are granted the experience of very high states of consciousness, and yet if these states are not accompanied by a development of character through a prior education that involves every department of human experience, you might have an enlightened being whom you would not trust even to be a baby-sitter.

Worse still is the kind of teacher whose enlightenment has been used for egoistic ends, who manipulates others, who is incapable of having a mature sexual relationship with an equal partner, or who has addictions he or she cannot control.

Our mistake was in assuming that people who have some attributes of enlightenment are perfected human beings.

In Sufism the phenomenon of immature enlightenment is well known. It is a biological and energetic transformation that directly affects the nervous system and energy centers, the result of which is that the veils between the conscious mind and the unconscious mind have been removed, yet the person has not necessarily acquired the qualities, experience, and virtues that I have termed maturity.

In Sufism, the point is not to enlighten everyone as quickly as possible, but to go step by step, developing the attributes of maturity without which enlightenment would be a curse. A certain prior education must be passed through before one has the privilege of receiving the kind of help that would increase the chances for biological enlightenment.

What is a Spiritually Complete Human Being? Even the words with which we ask this question contain assumptions about what is attainable for us and how it is attained. Some of these assumptions are: that some kind of attainment or perfection is possible, and that we become complete through spirituality. Other ways we could ask this question: What is human perfection, enlightenment, or spiritual attainment? What are the ultimate criteria for human development? What is a full-spectrum development for the human being?

I do not claim that the following list is the ultimate answer to these questions—only that it represents my own present level of understanding.

QUALITIES OF A SPIRITUALLY
COMPLETE HUMAN BEING

Self-knowledge. The degree to which we know ourselves—our weaknesses, limitations, characteristics, motivations.

Self-control. The ability to guide and transcend the promptings of the self.

Objective Knowledge. A knowledge that is in accord both with the practical needs of life and an objective Reality that can be known through an awakened and purified heart.

Inner Wisdom. The ability to access guidance and meaning from within oneself.

Being. The capacity to remain in a state of presence, to consciously witness experience.

Selfless Love. A love for God and His creations without selfish motives.

Sustaining the Divine Perspective. The ability to always see events and people from the highest perspective of Love and Unity and not to slip into egoistic judgment and opinion.

Divine Intimacy. Awareness of one's connection to the Divine Source.

So many people have been engaged in a search for a spirituality adequate to the times we live in. This means, first of all, that it should be able to offer some orientation to the psyche after the doors of perception have been opened through the awakening of consciousness and spiritual emergence that many people have experienced in recent decades. Furthermore, a spirituality adequate to the times would have to offer a way of living in harmony with human nature itself, in a partnership of man and woman, and within the ecological balance of this planet.

Sufism is the reconciliation of all opposites: the outer and the inner, the material and the spiritual, the finite and the infinite, the here and the hereafter, servanthood and liberation, the human and the divine. Enlightenment in this tradition does not prevent us from functioning in a practical and humble way in life, does not entitle us to special treatment, does not exclude us from the inevitable joys and griefs of life. The Sufi's union with God does not cancel servanthood.

What I found through Sufism far exceeded my hopes. As an example, one poet said to me: "All of my reading, study, and creative writing could not have prepared me for the poetry of Rūmī." And yet all Rūmī's poetry is just the wave on the surface of the ocean of Sufi spirituality. Perhaps it is consistent with the idea of Divine generosity that it should exceed in actuality the gift we had foreseen in our imagination. The Source is not only infinitely generous, it is infinitely creative, and its gifts surpass human imagination.

The Idea of Spiritual Training

THE ROLE OF A SUFI TEACHER IN MODERN CULTURE IS analogous to an athletic coach who would like to train people to develop their abilities to an Olympic level. He would have been educated for this and have the appropriate degree. Without necessarily being the greatest athlete himself, he would be in a position to train others who have particular talents that he may not have. He would have the general knowledge and the principles, and he would have some decades of experience in training others, as well as himself.

What if, however, we lived in a society that was ignorant of Olympic-level training and performance? What if most people had a lack of interest in or resistance toward any notion of training, their attitudes having been formed by a fast-food culture? What little they have experienced of athletics might have come from elementary school gym teachers and the coarse and sweaty environments of locker rooms. What if, in addition, their physical health were weak and their emotional health characterized by a legacy of shame and abuse? They would have no love of their body since it had been associated with pain and defilement rather than freedom and joy. Such people would need to learn to work out, to learn about their bodies and what they are capable of. Our culture's preparation for and receptivity to spiritual training may be no better.

It would be foolish if a horse trainer were to receive a half-wild,

30

starving and crippled horse and insist that it put on a saddle and prepare itself for the rigors of dressage. It would be equally foolish if a medical doctor were to receive patients in critical condition from starvation and lecture them about the benefits of organic versus processed food. We live in a culture that is starved for spiritual reality. The immediate need is to save people from starvation. Anyone who insists that starving people pledge loyalty to the brand name of the food that saves them from starvation is not in service but is self-serving. There are distinctions to be made among both earthly and spiritual foods—whether these are synthetic, natural, or organic, for instance—and under the best circumstances, in the normative human condition, these are important distinctions.

The immediate need, however, is to help people in a state of starvation. Later we may consider what is a suitable diet, what are appropriate calisthenics, and which specific skills to concentrate on.

FOLLOWING THE PATH THAT IS GIVEN

When I look at where I find myself, intellectually and spiritually, it certainly seems strange—given where I started from—and yet it makes perfect sense that I have followed the particular path I am on. At first we wander over the broad plains of life where it is relatively easy to change direction, to go this way or that. But at a certain point we are attracted to some hills that we see in the distance. As our journey takes us to those hills we find that certain trails make sense—they have been traveled already and a way has been worn by other travelers, or perhaps we find some other hikers going our way. Eventually those hills become mountains and it is no longer a matter of where do I want to go, but how to be strong enough and skillful enough to stay on the trail.

The choice becomes whether to go forward or to go backward. For your own safety and well-being you depend on a few committed, courageous, and experienced people. More and more you become grateful for where you are and for the journey itself. The freedom of the plains to go this way or that is only a nominal, relative freedom within the horizontal dimension. The real freedom may be in whether to ascend or stay at a certain level. To ascend you may need to acquire some specific information and skills, as well as overcome some of your own fears and weaknesses. Where you find yourself cannot easily be described to someone who hasn't experienced the journey. You don't feel superior to anyone, but within yourself you know that you have chosen what was possible and necessary for you.

THE PREMISES OF SUFI EDUCATION

Sufism is based on certain premises that are unfamiliar, if not foreign, to our contemporary environment, in which transcendent realities have been relegated so far to the background of life that they are effectively ignored.

The first of these is the idea that the soul itself needs to be educated and trained. The soul needs knowledge and practice in areas such as self-awareness, attention, will, relationship, service, and worship. In the modern world we don't reflect much on the soul, let alone on its development. We may be willing to spend years and tens of thousands of dollars to receive professional training and yet resist the idea of taking time for a weeklong retreat.

The second important principle of Sufism is that this education and training is best conducted together with others—not just for the sake of convenience, but because of the opportunities to know ourselves through relationship and because of the quality of energy that is generated and shared in a group. We may read the occasional book on spirituality and form our own inner convictions but rarely commit to the ongoing process of spiritual education and transformation.

The third principle is that there are people who have experience and knowledge in this area and who may be empowered through a spiritual lineage to provide wisdom, guidance, and inspiration. We resist the idea of such a relationship because relationships demand something of us: honesty, commitment, change. Even if we consider ourselves on a spiritual path, we would rather commit to a technique, such as meditation, which preserves our imagined autonomy and freedom, than to a relationship and a spiritual family.

Of course, there are many good reasons why we should be skeptical about people who set themselves up as spiritual teachers and groups that proselytize or seek to enlist members. The real spiritual paths may seek to offer knowledge to the societies in which they exist, yet, because they trust in a greater guidance, they never seek members merely to increase their numbers. In fact it has been a conscious principle that the path exists to serve those who choose it, although this was in societies with enough general education to know the purpose of the *tarīqa*, or path.

Because spiritual transformation is not a form of conditioning, it cannot be accomplished only through the sharing of information and techniques. The spiritual dimension of it is more mysterious, more creative, more unpredictable. No matter what kind of training program is devised, it can never guarantee that its graduates will have attained freedom from the self, love of other human beings, and sincere love of God. And yet this is what Sufi education aims at.

Finally, there is the question of Sufism's relation to religion in general and Islam in particular. The Sufi who has attained some maturity belongs to all of humanity. His or her wish is to see other individuals attain the highest level of human completion that is possible for them, and the Sufi realizes that the question of belief and religious affiliation is between each person and God.

The Sufi teacher looks to the spiritual realization of human beings, not to any nominal adherence to belief. If the Sufi loves the classical heritage of Sufism, it is because of the richness the tradition offers, because of the inspiration, purity, and practicality of its message. Those who are uneasy about the relationship of Sufism to Islam are usually people who are relatively uninformed about what traditional Islam represents. We need to look beyond the distorted image of Islam that is common in the West to the real Islam, the Islam of Muhammad and the Qur'ān, and the Islam of classical Sufism. The more one looks to this essential Islam, the more clear it will become how close are the qualities that we admire in Sufism to the essence of the Qur'ān and the character of Muhammad. The humanness of Sufism, its wholeness, its integration with ordinary life, its nobility, liberality, and humility are almost inconceivable without the revelation of the Qur'ān and the personality of Muhammad. In fact, to the extent that various modern adaptations of Sufism distance themselves from the classical Islamic tradition, the more they seem to become fragments of a wholeness. In some cases Sufism is reduced to the search for ecstasy; in others it is reduced to a dry epistemology. In still other cases it becomes religious fanaticism; and in others a kind of free-spirited mystical sensuality. But Sufism, at its best, is a path of completion. It proceeds from the living example of human completion and leads toward that completion.

THE KNOWLEDGE OF LOVE

Love's Universe

I DO NOT REALLY KNOW IF TODAY'S WORLD IS FURTHER FROM the truth than many civilizations that have preceded it. Yet so much of what occupies our attention is a fiction, and through these fictions we live a life of delusion, of separation, of selfishness, of loneliness. Behind our sadness and anxiety is a simple lack of love, which translates into a lack of meaning and purpose.

Unless we look with the eyes of love, we cannot see things as they are. We have searched for love in all the wrong places: in building ourselves up, in making ourselves more special, more perfect, more powerful. Love's substitutes are driving the world. We strive after anything but love, because love is so close that we overlook it.

One of the most painful experiences for any person is recognizing that most human beings take themselves as the exclusive goal and center of their thoughts, feelings, and activities. It can be utterly terrifying for a sensitive soul to live in a world where everyone is so busy achieving his or her own goals and interests that real human needs are pushed aside or trampled in the process.

For most people, even "love" is primarily a form of desire, preference, or obsession; love, in other words, has been confused with self-gratification. And for most people, "spirituality" is reduced to a way of feeling good about themselves. The diseases of self, once at least partially mitigated by the vaccinations of faith, are becoming more rampant. This self-centered way of living and being is exactly the "sin" that all authentic traditions of spirituality would save us from. Even the notion of spiritual "health"—as a self-giving and an awareness of a suprapersonal Center beyond one's ego—is becoming suspect.

It doesn't matter what we have accomplished, what recognition we have received, what we own; there is nothing as sweet as loving—not necessarily being loved, but just loving. The more we love—the more people, the more manifestations of life we love—the richer we are. Nothing is more beautiful or more sacred than the impulse of love we feel for a friend, a child, a parent, a partner. Nothing would be sweeter than to be able to love everywhere and always.

Rūmī has written, "Whatever I have said about love, when love comes, I am ashamed to speak." At the same time, if Love is the essential power within and behind this universe and our inner life, no subject has greater precedence. C. G. Jung said as much in his last book:

> I might, as many before me have attempted to do, venture an approach to this daimon, whose range of activity extends from the endless spaces of the heavens to the dark abysses of hell; but I falter before the task of finding language which might adequately express the incalculable paradoxes of love. Eros is a kosmogonos, a creator and father-mother of all higher consciousness. . . . Whatever the learned interpretation may be of the sentence "God is love," the words affirm the complexio oppositorum of the Godhead. In my medical experience as well as in my own life I have again and again been faced with the mystery of love, and have never been able to explain what it is. . . . No language is adequate to this paradox. Whatever one can say, no words express the whole. To speak of partial aspects is always to say too much or too little, for only the whole is meaningful. Love "bears all things" and "endures all things" (1 Corinthians 13:7). These words say all there is to be said; nothing can be added to them for we are in the deepest sense the victims and the instruments of cosmogonic "love." . . . Man can try to name

love, showering upon it all the names at his command, and still he will involve himself in endless self-deceptions. If he possesses a grain of wisdom, he will lay down his arms and name the unknown by the more unknown . . . that is, by the name of God.[1]

Although a mind as great as Jung's can assert that love is a complete, unknowable mystery, I am convinced that there is a knowledge of love, that it desperately needs to be shared, and that in fact no knowledge is more valuable and essential.

It may be that failure in any field is essentially a failure of love. In the nineteenth century, for instance, when progressive psychiatry consisted of the surgical removal of sexual organs or lobes of the brain, organs that were believed to contribute to the moral illness of human beings, this was not only a failure of intelligence but a failure of love. And in the twentieth century, when mental health was sought through shock therapy, behavior modification, or prescribed chemicals, it was once again a fixation on the outer, material being and the overlooking of the requirements of the inner being—again a failure of love.

Likewise, economic systems based purely on outer values, including communism and capitalism, are destined to fail if they do not incorporate at their heart the values of love.

Art, too, must be inspired by love. It degenerates into technique and decoration when it comes into the service of ego or economics.

THE SCHOOL OF LOVE

We are all students in the school of love, although it may take us a long time and much suffering to admit this fact. Something obstinately refuses to see the obvious. It is amazing how stubborn and slow we are, and how often we still forget. We forget whenever we think ourselves more important than others, whenever we see our own desires and goals as more important than the feelings and well-being of those we love. We forget whenever we blame others for what we our-

---

[1] C. G. Jung, *Memories, Dreams, Reflections* (New York: Vintage Books, 1965).

selves have been guilty of. We forget whenever we lose sight of the fact that in this school of love it is love that we all are trying to learn.

Yunus Emre, the first and greatest Turkish Sufi poet, says, "Let us master this science and read this book of love. God instructs; Love is His school."

We have all been failures in love. This is our conscious starting point. Only a saint is an expert and complete lover, because only a saint has been freed by God from what stands in the way of love.

We can practice meditation and seek spiritual knowledge for years and still overlook the central importance of love. One of the subtlest forms of egoism is when we engage ourselves in a practice to be more spiritual than others, when we turn spirituality into an arena for our ambition. But Love eventually forgives even that.

We are not merely Love's passive instruments; we are its servants. In order to know how to serve, our love needs to be grounded in knowledge.

Love without knowledge is dangerous. With love alone we could burn ourselves and others. With love alone we could become lunatics. In ancient tradition they warn us of the person who is unconsciously "in love." Such people, it is said in Central Asia, should wear bells on their ankles to warn others of their state.

Love is such an extraordinary and complex power, and the human being has such a great capacity for love, that to dismiss it as an unknowable mystery is like standing in awe before a fire and saying we don't know what this is, how it started, or what to do with it.

Love is both mystery and knowledge. Furthermore, it is a mystery that has spoken to us about itself in the form of those revelations that have profoundly altered the course and quality of human history. The lives and teachings of Buddha, Jesus, and Muhammad have influenced and transformed so many billions of people because they are essentially teachings of love.

The universe is an expression of Love

Many believe that this is an impersonal material universe, a universe that is more darkness than light, more cold than warmth, more vacuum than substance. Furthermore, many people feel that the random, isolated consciousness at the heart of each human life is endangered by vast forces that do not recognize its fragile existence.

For those with spiritual vision, however, we are living *within* an infinite heart. This whole universe is a manifestation of cosmic love. This whole universe was created from just a spark of love. In the Sufi tradition these words are attributed to the Creator, the Source of our being:

> I was a hidden treasure and I longed to be known,
> so I created both worlds, the visible and the invisible,
> in order that My hidden treasure
> of generosity and lovingkindness would be known.
>
> —HADĪTH QUDSĪ

This universe is an expression of love. We live in an ocean of Love, but because it is so near to us, we sometimes need to be shocked or hurt, or experience some loss, in order to be aware of the nearness and importance of love. A little fish was told that without water it could not live, and it became very afraid. It swam to its mother and, trembling, told her about the need for water. The mother said, "Water, my darling, is what we're swimming in."

I have known people to go through exactly this experience through their contact with the Way of Love. One person expressed it to me this way: "I used to believe that compassion was something within myself and other human beings, but I was not convinced that this compassion existed outside of ourselves. Our work together has made it clear that compassion is outside of ourselves and that is why we also find it within. We are living in it!"

Every being and thing is set in motion by Love

The planets revolve around the sun, and the sun radiates its energy to the planets. Atoms are held in a delicate but immensely powerful balance by love. Every species has its own form of love or desire that motivates it. Every human being has its own unique form of love through which it approaches life. Everything is seeking union with the object of its desire. And all of these desires are the derivatives of one Love.

Perhaps this morning you wanted some Ceylon tea and fresh bread. Later you had a hunger for some soup and salad. In the evening you had stir-fried vegetables over rice, with blueberries and cream for dessert. The motivation behind all of these was the hunger of the body. In the same way, Love is the motivation behind every yearning.

We believe that we love this or that, but the fundamental Love is the pure experience of Being. This Being, this *isness*, is the fundamental energy and substance of the universe. When we are in a state of presence, fully awake and alive, we are open to this *isness*, to Being, and since the essence of this Being is the Love that created existence, our experience of Being is Love.

In all of life Love is seeking to discover itself. We come into this world, and we experience a profound forgetfulness; we are asleep. Everything that happens from then on is the process of waking up to the fact that Love brought us here, that we are loved by a Beneficent Unseen Reality, and that the core of our being is Love. The whole purpose and meaning of creation is to discover the secret of Love.

The experience of love is the most fulfilling and important experience we can have, the highest of all values. We can't compare love to anything. It is its own meaning and its own criteria. Since everything is explained by something subtler than what is being explained, nothing can explain love because love itself is the subtlest of all things we can experience.

Love is seeking us. Love brought us here, whether we know it or not. Love nudges us to make plans, to seek relationship, to create the possibility of a meeting of hearts. It puts the pen to paper; it puts a word on the tongue. Love is not the goal of anything; it is the cause of everything.

> See how the hand is invisible while the pen is writing;
> the horse careening, yet the rider is unseen;
> the arrow flying, but the bow out of sight;
> individual souls existing,
> while the Soul of souls is hidden.
>
> —RŪMĪ, M, II, 1303–04

The Sufis know that Love is the most active, the most powerful force in the universe. Love is always acting on us. We think we are the creators and directors of our lives, but our actions may be just the slightest visible signs of a process that is vast and invisible. We know only a fragment of what can be seen; of the unseen we know very little. Like children we are unconscious of all the forces and factors that sustain us, care for us, guide our life and our world.

The spiritual life requires a reversal of our usual egoistic thinking and wanting. We believe that we are seeking, but what if it is Love itself that is the seeker? Rūmī says:

> Abundance is seeking the beggars and the poor,
> just as beauty seeks a mirror. . . .
> Beggars, then, are the mirrors of God's abundance,
> and they who are with God
> are united with absolute abundance.

> —RŪMĪ, M, I, 2745, 2750

The idea that we live in Love's Universe may seem a sentimental and naive proposition to some people. Why then do we live in a world of such injustices and horrors?

Life brings us very real suffering, and this suffering can be the cause of some doubt about the beneficence of life. Often, when we are in the midst of our suffering, we cannot see a purpose in it. We may lose our trust in the meaning of life. The soul faces a critical choice at this point: whether to be embittered by reality or to allow the pain of life to reorient us to a deeper truth, to help us form a connection to a reality beyond space, time, and even beyond our individual selves.

The idea that we live in a universe created by love is anything but sentimental and naive, because it does not deny the pain of life but embraces this complex reality with all its contradictions. We see that we are turned from one feeling to another and taught by means of opposites and contrasts.

> He alone has the right to break,
> for he alone has the power to mend.

He that knows how to sew together
knows how to tear apart:
whatever He sells,
He buys something better in exchange.
He lays the house in ruins;
then in a moment He makes it more livable than before.

—RŪMĪ, M, I, 3882

Sometimes we need to be shocked out of our complacency and indifference to know the reality of love. We need to find a way to restore the proper perspective. We need to be reminded of the centrality of love.

Without becoming passive, we can stop resisting and submit to Love. We begin to see the infinite power of Love as the greatest cause in the universe, and little by little we begin to serve it. Eventually, we begin to see that even a bitter drink is sweet when it is from the Beloved.

Knowing that Love is the master of the universe helps us to accept and learn from every experience. Knowing that there is an eternal dimension residing here in intimate association with material existence will begin to free us from fears. When we are less governed by negative thoughts about God's creation, we will be freed from many fears.

The human being is God's beloved

The human being is the macrocosm, not just the microcosm, of the universe. While in outward form a human being is the microcosm, a miniature universe, in truth, according to the masters and prophets, humanity is the macrocosm, the cause of the existing universe.

This subject is being debated today in cosmological physics. It appears to those who have done the necessary calculations on the formation of the universe that if you were to change any one of the physical laws one iota, there would not be a universe that could support the human being—nor would there be a universe at all. It appears to those who have looked carefully that the universe was virtually designed to create the human being.

Maybe this is what Mevlānā Rūmī means when he says that the fruit is the cause of the tree, not the other way around. In the simplest terms, the gardener planted the tree in order for it to bear fruit. How many fruits are on a tree? How many trees are within the fruit?

God says: "I created the whole universe for you and you for Myself" (Hadīth Qudsī).

Every human being is the creation of love and a beloved child of the universe. And every human being is free to turn his or her back on love.

> Water says to the dirty, "Come here."
> The dirty one says, "But I am so ashamed."
> Water says, "How will you be made clean without me?"
>
> —RŪMĪ, M, II, 1366–67

The more we live in our individual sense of isolation, loneliness, alienation, in our envy, resentment, pride, and shame, the more we allow this love to be obscured.

If we attempt to go this way alone, we will only find our own ego. God loves us to be together. God is us-with-us and doesn't like loneliness. Trying to attain truth through books alone is like trying to fall in love with a picture. We cannot at first fall in love with something we don't see. But if we meet the divine love in others who have melted in that love, if we stay close to those who have understood this love, then we begin to sense the Love behind all the forms of love. We enter spiritual work and spiritual community so that love might be more revealed and known, less obscure.

Something has brought us together, established the relationships of our lives, and there is a reason for this and a reason behind the reason. Among other things it is our purpose to discover the reason and to explore what connects us. An infinite Intelligence has arranged our situation, and that infinite intelligence is certainly not you or I, although it operates *through* you and me. We are here to be in communication with one another and to explore the mystery of Love. It is Love that has arranged all this. It is Love that brought us here. We are here to open a space that Love can enter and be more known, more apparent, more understood. If we can keep this intention in mind—opening a space for Love—it will help us to stay aligned with its power.

The Spectrum of Love

PEOPLE MEAN SO MANY DIFFERENT THINGS WHEN THEY refer to love. For some it means desire or lust, for others compassion, for some need, for others generosity, for some an impersonal ideal, for others devotion or yearning. Love is one power that is reflected on many levels of our being: physical, emotional, mental, social, spiritual, and cosmic.

Love is not primarily an emotion. Sometimes the greatest enemy of love is sentimentality, the cheapening or trivializing of the greatest power in the universe. Once a certain shaikh, someone who had given a lifetime to the path, was visiting us. He spoke about the efforts and sacrifices that are needed if we truly want to know the Truth. There was a guest in our circle that day, someone who was filled with a sentimental enthusiasm. "But what about *Love?*" she asked with her dreamy eyes.

"Love? I'm afraid I don't know what you're talking about," our foxy mentor replied.

"Well, love is wonderful, love is incredible, love is what spirituality is all about. You mean you don't know about love?" An excruciatingly long pause followed.

"My dear," he said to her, "should one use such a word unless in the moment that one uses it, one *is* that love?" There are dangers in talking about love without *being* love. The dangers of not talking

46

about love are also great. Worst of all may be convincing ourselves that love is far removed from ourselves.

The most elementary and limited form of love is desire, or *eros*, to use a more suggestive term. We all have desire, or passion. At the most basic level it is animal desire—desire of the desirable, love of the lovable. Eros is attracted to what it finds desirable or beautiful. Its power is valuable as long as we are not enslaved by it, but often eros knows no limits in its desire.

The domain of eros is attraction and pleasure. Eros is the power of the universe as it is reflected at the level of our natural, animal self. From the spiritual point of view, eros is a derivative, metaphoric love. It searches without satisfaction through many objects of desire but never reaches full satisfaction. Sufis refer to it as "donkey love," because the donkey brays—not a very pleasant sound—when it is aroused.

Philos is a form of love characterized by sharing or participation. It is a more comprehensive form of love, wider, less self-centered than desire. It brings people into relationships. Philos engenders all forms of sharing: family life, social clubs and political organizations, brotherhoods, sisterhoods, cultural bonds.

The highest, most comprehensive level of love is *agape*—a spiritual, objective, unconditional love. Immature love needs to be loved; mature love simply loves. Agape, or unconditional love, can dissolve the false self. By removing the obstacles we put in the way of agape, by grounding ourselves in the principles and knowledge of love, and by being with those who love Spirit, we may come to live within the reality of agape. Eventually agape will refine and expand our sense of who we are to infinite dimensions. It will dissolve our separate existence. Then, instead of seeking the security and consolation of the ego, instead of seeking to be loved, we will *be* love itself.

I once asked someone whose spiritual maturity I trusted, "Is there ever a time when you no longer need others' love?"

"Yes, *when you love*." When you *are* love. When there is no difference between you and what you love.

Once a certain man knocked at a friend's door. His friend asked him, "Who's there?"

"It's me," he answered.

"Go away. This is not the time. There's no room for two at this table."

Only the fire of separation can cook the raw. Only loneliness can heal hypocrisy. The poor man went away and for a whole year burned with longing to be with his friend. Eventually his rawness was cooked, and he returned to the door of his friend, but no longer as he had been. He walked back and forth, in humility and respect, cautious lest the wrong word should fall from his mouth. Finally, he knocked.

"Who is there?" the friend called.

"It's only you here at this door."

"At last, since you are I, come right in, O myself, since there isn't room for two I's in this house. The double end of the thread is not for the needle. If you are single, come through the eye of the needle."[1]

Intimate conversation is one of the most important practices of the way of Love. Without a spiritual friend/teacher/guide our possibilities of advancement are very limited. The spiritual friend should be a humble human being who has melted in God. The implicit call of such a person is: "Fall in love with me, just as I fall in love with you; then in our mutual nonexistence we will be complete." The phrase "to fall in love" is not to be confused with romance or any form of possessiveness, but it strongly suggests a kind of intimacy and mutual devotion that is necessary in this spiritual relationship. A Sufi of the twentieth century, Ishmael Emre, has said: "The compassionate and perfect human beings kill the seekers of Truth with humility and the sword of love."

Yet despite these high-minded thoughts on love, we must acknowledge that we have all failed in love. This is our starting point. We have all been broken and disappointed in love because our love has been identified with our egoism, when it was meant to dissolve that egoism. We can love when we expect to get something. We can love when we have the perfect person to love. But there is no such perfect person, and even if there were, we would not know it unless we too were perfect, because we would inevitably project our own imperfection onto the other, as the masses have always done to the prophets. God's

---

[1] This is a retelling of the story that can be found in Rūmī's *Mathnawī*, I, 3056–64.

messengers were not loved; they were more often hated. Hatred is frustrated love, the shadow of love. It implies the presence of love corrupted by egoism. Egoism can turn beauty into ugliness, generosity into selfishness, love into hatred.

RELATIONSHIP, HUMILITY, AND INTERDEPENDENCE

We do not reach love completely on our own. If we are loveless in and of ourselves, it is because we are living with our center of gravity in the false self. The false self is created from the desires and compulsions of our own separateness. This false self believes strongly in its own existence as separate from the rest of life, and it recruits the intellect to help defend this illusion at the expense of the whole of the mind.

There is nothing more difficult than to make two minds one; that is, to help them to love each other. If two or more people are in love, there is harmony, a unity of purpose without the loss of individuality. When we are thinking only of our own desires and needs, there is disharmony with others and we feel at cross-purposes. We live in a culture that emphasizes the individual at the expense of relationship. More and more people are alone and lonely.

Can the ego overcome its own separation? Most probably not, because it will still be playing the ego's games, trying to become better than others or to attain its own desires and security at the expense of others. Only Love can tame the ego and bring it into the service of Love. It is the nature of Love to create relationships. You might say it is Unity expressing itself. The lover, the beloved, and love itself are all one in reality.

In order to really love, our ego structure has to dissolve and re-form on a new basis. Our hearts may have to be broken, our false pride humbled. Love then re-creates the self.

Sometimes we feel that we want to love others but we cannot; we just don't have the capacity for it. Just as the cause can produce the effect, the effect can also produce the cause. The tree produces the fruit; and the fruit can produce the tree. Love has many fruits: kindness, patience, generosity, courage, self-sacrifice. Love will produce these fruits; and these fruits will engender love. This is a two-way street. The effect can produce the cause. An apple contains the seed of a tree.

One of the greatest Sufis I have known, a man whose love was so tangible it was barely possible for us to be in his presence without tears, used to say: May my imitation become real. By practicing the fruits of love, by showing kindness, patience, and generosity to others, especially when it doesn't come easily, we may summon the cause of these fruits, namely, real love. The tree bears fruit, and the fruit can also produce the tree.

Love is conscious relationship in presence. With presence we are in conscious relationship; our essences are present to each other. If we love without presence, we are merely projecting our neediness, lack of fulfillment, or desire onto another person. The higher Love is the welcoming of otherness into ourselves as ourselves, recognizing the stranger as a friend.

Love is the absence of defenses; it is emotional nakedness. "Only one whose garment has been stripped by love is free of desire and defect."[2] In the presence of love we find acceptance. Our self-disclosure, our emotional nakedness, helps to open the space for love. With presence we hold no image of ourselves that separates us from others. Love accepts imperfection; it loves the actuality and recognizes the potentiality.

Sometimes it is not until we know our helplessness and our failure at love that we can come under the grace of love. This is the great value of the humiliation of sin and failure, because our ego, the shell that keeps love out, has broken open. Love is not the attribute of the self-righteous and the perfect. It is the attribute of the humble, those who have realized their own nothingness, those who have failed in love.

RELATIONSHIP BEYOND TIME AND SPACE

Just as we recognize our interdependence with our fellow human beings with whom we are in relationship here on this earth, we can also

---

[2] Rūmī, *Love Is a Stranger* (Putney, Vt.: Threshold Books, 1993), p. 69.

recognize our interdependence with a source of grace and guidance that is outside of time. We need to find some connection with a spiritual source or tradition that can wean us from this false self's illusions and fears. If we search without true guidance, we will only find this false self, and we may lead ourselves in circles back again and again to our own ego.

We need to make a call to some source of love. The Sufi tradition not only has its living exemplars, it also has many great beings who live on in the world of meaning: including all the important figures of the Prophetic tradtion: Abraham, Moses, David, Solomon, Jesus, Mary, Muhammad, Imam 'Alī; as well as the saints and masters of the Sufi tradition: Rābi'a, Ibn 'Arabī, Shams of Tabrīz, Mevlānā Jalāluddīn Rūmī, Yunus Emre, Abdul Qādir Jīlānī, Ahmed Rifai, Moinuddin Chishti, Bahāuddin Naqshband, may God be pleased with them all.

With a spirit of humility we call upon these great beings who attained unity with the Source. It is possible to establish a connection, *rabita*, so that the effectual grace, *baraka*, of that particular enlightened being can flow to us. Such a connection can be attained through love and intention, through cultivating an inner dialogue and resonance with that being. As a member of a particular lineage it would be considered essential to establish this connection with the Pir, or founder, of one's particular order, and at the same time, since Sufism is a tradition that is completely unified on the foundation of the Qur'ān, all the Sufi saints are in harmony with each other.

If we can open to the saints through our own devotion and humility, we may receive a protective grace that can safeguard us from our own egos. In the end, the only thing we need to be protected from is our own ego. The ego is the enemy of our true existence. Fortunately the ego can be tamed by love, not devalued or annihilated, but tamed and put into the service of our essential self. If we can learn to make a clear call to the Source of love, how could that Source not respond to our call? The importance of this principle should never be underestimated. This is the most important relationship for us to cultivate.

The Inborn Power
of Love and Presence

W E HUMAN BEINGS HAVE A POTENTIAL INSIDE OF OUR-selves that is the source of all our motivations. When this potential is applied to the material world, it can be productive. Without this power, humankind could not have produced its greatest achievements. When this power turns toward that aspect of the material world known as sexuality, it is procreative. So this inborn power serves to maintain our physical existence, bringing an appetite for life and a kind of happiness; but if we restrict it to material existence alone, we are caught in a vicious cycle of attempting to satisfy endless and often contradictory desires.

If we disperse our love in the things of this world, its power will be dissipated. If we choose to love a human being, at least we are choosing to love the most valuable thing in this world. A human being is a treasure of qualities and has the capacity to respond to our love more completely than anything else on this earth.

We also know that when we give our love to a human being, it is possible that this person will not be able to respond to our love. We may find our love ignored, rejected, or betrayed. This kind of love may result in unfulfilled desire, and if the frustration is great enough, it may even turn to hatred. Love of anything finite involves the risk of failure and loss.

In Greek myth, Eros is attracted to a beautiful young girl named Psyche. There is alchemy in this attraction. Eros is attracted to the lovable things of this world; Psyche is more spiritual. The beauty of Psyche, who is Spirit in disguise, will transform Eros through her own spiritual nature. Through this relationship with Psyche Eros is uplifted and transformed and brought closer to his Source. This myth is the model or archetype of how our desire nature can be transformed through spiritual relationship.

The potential we have stored within ourselves is like an ore that needs to be extracted and refined. If we do not put this power to its highest and best use it will disturb us. Through our ignorance of this potential for love, through our desperate turning away from it, through our misuse of it, through our addictions, it may even destroy us. This is the awesome power of cosmic love frustrated and denied.

We have a certain amount of love to invest. We can invest it in things, in people, or in God. Whatever we give our love to will respond to our love to the extent that it is able. A well-made automobile may return our love in one way; a beloved pet may return our love in another way. Of all things that we can love, a human being has the capacity to respond to our love most completely; but directing our love to God will make us the beloved of God.

LOVE OF OUR SOURCE

Any temporal love is based on attraction and can turn to its opposite. If the beloved is deficient, the love returned will share its deficiency. If the beloved is perfect, the love returned will be perfect. We have the possibility of loving Love itself, of loving the Source of all loves. We metaphorically call the Divine Being "Friend" and "Beloved." This love has the possibility of developing infinitely. The highest purpose of a human being is to know and worship that alone which is worthy of worship. We can learn to call that which can answer our call. The response of this Beloved has no limits. This Love is never one-sided. It is seeking us even more than we are seeking it. Sometimes you are the lover and God is the Beloved; sometimes God is the Lover and you are the beloved.

It could be said that the souls of the lovers of God came into earthly life to rediscover the love of their Source, to express that love, and to serve it with all their faculties. Everything that consciously responds to the love of the universe becomes a gift to the universe, a mercy to all of creation. To enter into the Divine Love is to both be drawn to and respond to that which is drawing us. We serve love when we feel and know that we are loved. It is natural to want to return this love.

Spiritual love, however, is not abstract love. We cannot love God and remain insensitive to all the manifestations of life around us. Love of God is also love of His creation. This is done with the wholeness of mind, including its conscious and supraconscious faculties: presence, reason, heart, and will. The more we love, the more we are present. The more we are present, the more we love.

Presence is the state of transcendent awareness, which embraces and comprehends all our other functions, including thought, feeling, action, and intuition. Unless we develop in presence, we are not wholly here. We exist in our thoughts, in our desires, but not in our Being, and therefore we cannot really love because we are not fully here. Without presence our dialogue is primarily mental or emotional but not fully spiritual. Without presence we cannot develop in love. Continual presence eventually opens and allows a continual dialogue with our Source.

Presence can offer us a continual relationship with Being. This continual presence merges into God's presence; it is the same presence. Awareness of the presence of God inclines us to submission and love. We can pray for our spiritual needs from a position of contentment and acceptance. We can always include the saving clause, "God willing," that submits to the Divine Wisdom in either granting our prayer or not. We can begin to be in continual relationship with God. *Truly, it is only in the remembrance of God that hearts find their rest.*

Many gifts are bestowed upon those who learn to be in continual remembrance. The loveliness of this world may increase. Taste, sight, fragrance, and sound intensify and are experienced as gifts from infinite Being. Even the senses are brought to spiritual ecstasy. Simple pleasures become infinitely rewarding; at the same time the pleasures that most people wildly chase after begin to look foolish and insignificant.

Worries and fears diminish because we have turned all our cares over to the Beloved, who we know loves us and sustains us.

> Someone who worries only about You
> is saved from many fears.
> The heart that falls into Your love burns and burns.
> The one who gives himself to You
> gives up everything else.
> Worldliness looks like a poison.
> Someone who lives with a vision of the End passes up poisons.[1]

Whatever we do for the love of God benefits our souls and our lives in a way that ego-motivated actions never can. Whatever we do for the love of God is done with sincerity because it is not motivated by self-interest. We leave our concern for gain and loss, success and failure, in the hands of God. We stop considering ourselves the sole cause of our actions and their results. Consequently, we become the instruments of a deep wisdom and love.

The lover of God undergoes some of the same difficulties as those who are ignorant and unaware of God, but these difficulties do not disturb the heart in the same way; therefore she is protected from much pain. If you love God, creation will love you. Yunus Emre says: "A soul in love is free of worries. With love all problems left me. With love I became happy."[2]

The food of the heart is love. The heart needs continual nourishment if it is to be healthy. If we limit ourselves to worldly, materialistic satisfactions, we will deprive ourselves of real nourishment, satisfaction, and peace. One only needs to spend some time with those whose yearning is limited to worldly success to know how unsatisfactory such success is. On the other hand, to spend some time with the lovers of God is to find out what it means to be really happy and free.

---

[1] Yunus Emre, *The Drop That Became the Sea* (Putney, Vt.: Threshold Books, 1987), p. 20.
[2] Ibid., p. 39.

Some people enter into the Divine Love so deeply that they become a source of love. They are like an abundant spring in a dry land. They become an oasis of gardens, fruit trees, and palms. They belong to all people, and their love is not confined by sects or religions. Some people enter the fire of love and become one with the fire. Because they have entered into this love and been received by it, they also radiate it. They glow like the red-hot iron that has plunged into the fire. Like a fine Damascus sword, they have acquired the qualities of the fire without losing their iron-ness, their strength. Having been through this fire their substance has changed forever.

THE RELIGION OF LOVE

Mevlānā Rūmī said, "The religion of love is like no other." He did not wish to start a new religion but to reveal the essence of all religion, which is submission to God in love. All love leads toward God. All love is a metaphor, a symbol of real love. It is not necessary to replace one religion or no religion with another, but to purify our religion and ourselves with love.

In the religion of love we are not seeking love, because we know that love is not the goal or end, but the origin and cause of everything. We are within this field of love. We only need to open up to it. Love created us. Love guides us. And we will all return to love, either willingly or unwillingly. We can go willingly and consciously, by realizing that love brought us here in the first place. Let us trust this truth. Let this be our starting point.

All religions exist because Love is trying to establish itself in human life. Since the object of all religions is One, all religions are related to each other. Sometimes it looks as though the enterprise of religion has been an utter failure on this earth, but who really knows. Appearances can be deceptive. Sometime failure is the seed of greatest success.

> They said: "You are crazy in love!"
> I said: "May God increase my Love."
> They said: "But your being has vanished."
> I said: "It's not in me, God knows."

They said: "You are filled!"
I said: "I wish I were empty."
They said: "You are burned out!"
I said: "I wish I were ash!"
They said: "You are fading."
I said: "I wish I had died."
They said: "But you are dead."
I said: "God willing."
"The cup," they said.
"Let me be quenched," I said.
"Drink!" they said.
"Let me turn," I said.
"The moth," they said.
"Let me burn," I said.
"Fool!" they said.
"So be it! It comes from God," I said.
They said, "O Zeynep, you will be heartbroken,
drunk on love for the rose, like the nightingale.
In the end you will go mad in the way of truth."
I said, "What can I do? It's up to God."

—ZEYNEP HATUN[3]

---

[3] Translated by Murat Yagan.

THE MAP AND THE
PSYCHOLOGY

Inner Struggle

THE STRUCTURE OF THE SELF
WITHIN SUFI PSYCHOLOGY

T HE INHERENT PSYCHOLOGY OF TRADITIONAL SUFISM IS A
vocabulary of Being, derived from the Qur'ān, with which the
Sufi begins to know and understand himself and his relationship to the Divine Being, Allāh. This sacred psychology and its spiritual vocabulary offer an implicit model of humanness as well as a map
of a spiritual landscape. No one who has studied the circumstances of
the Qur'ān's revelation would deny that it proceeded from a deep level
of inspiration. Whether one views the source of this inspiration as the
Divine Intelligence speaking through its prophet or as an upflowing
of meaning from the purest depths of the unconscious, one cannot
deny that it is all of a piece. This is part of its miracle: that the closer
one looks, the more precision and order seem to reveal themselves. Its
terms—which on the surface may be read as mythic or metaphoric—
are increasingly appreciated for their objective quality. Gather together
all the references to "heart" within the Qur'ān, for instance, and you
will see how they inform each other and suggest an objective and
practical knowledge. The psychology of Sufism, therefore, is not something formulated by the theorizing intellect; rather it is a unified body

of knowledge whose source is this inspired text as it has been apprehended by generations of completed human beings.

The outcome of this knowledge and practice is humanizing and
life-enhancing. Even if there were no God as an external, independent
agency, and no "heaven" for the eternal perpetuation of one's individuality, the principles of Sufi self-development would still stand as remarkable tools in purely humanistic terms. For the Sufi, however,
there is the faith that one's actions and intentions *here* will resonate
forever in an eternal dimension and that our choices here have consequences far beyond our immediate earthly life.

Psychology means "knowledge of the soul (psyche)." Our best contemporary psychologies are mostly a collection of subjective and cul-
ture-driven conjectures. There are dozens of theories of personality,
theories of learning, and so on, but a true science still proves to be
elusive. Insofar as they claim to be scientific, these theories are rudi-
mentary experiments that hardly begin to fathom the most important
issues of meaning and purpose in life. Here we must face the central
question that separates those who defend and maintain a purely secular reality from those who believe in the revelatory power of Being.
The former essentially "believe" that human beings can construct an
effective and satisfactory knowledge of the human psyche from the
ground up, so to speak. Freud and Marx are the outstanding examples
of this mentality for the twentieth century. The failure of Marxism
(which does not imply the success of Western-style finance capitalism)
is hardly a matter of debate. The failure of Freudianism, though qui-
eter, is no less noteworthy. These systems were not without their elements of powerful insight and truth, nor were their discoveries and
critiques entirely irrelevant. However, their failure was that they could
not offer a satisfactory model of the highest purpose of human life.
What we are witnessing at the turn of the millennium is a cultural
collapse of modernism.

Those who believe in the revelatory power of Being, who acknowledge the possibility of one Great Tradition being revealed within all
traditional human communities, are essentially in accord with the Sufi
understanding. Postmodernism, though inadequately defined in reac-
tion to a failed modernism, implicitly recognizes the mistake of the

dominant paradigm, which was ethnocentric and materialistic, and yet it fails to offer a unified worldview or objective understanding of humanness.

The structure of the human individuality within Sufi psychology can be understood through three primary elements: *nafs*, or ego-self; *qalb*, or heart; and *rūh*, or Spirit. Together these form the person.

In attempting to bring some clarity to these terms, we are faced with the problem that our English language uses them in vague, if not contradictory, ways. So we are compelled to create a spiritual glossary of our own. I will begin with the Sufi term, and its simplest English equivalent, followed by a parenthetical list of synonyms.

Nafs, or self (the ego-self, natural self, carnal self), can be considered a complex of psychological manifestations arising from the body and related to its pleasure and survival. The ego has an intimate relationship not only with the body but with the socialized personality as well. The ego has no limit to its desires, whether these are appetites of the body or of the personality, and it needs the spiritual self (rūh) to guide and moderate it.

On the other hand, the spiritual self needs the energy of the natural self (nafs) to aspire toward completion, or perfection. The self has its servants as well: ambition, self-importance, rationalization, delusion, fantasy, selfishness, and desire. The most disruptive and evil manifestation of the self is known as the commanding self (*nafs al-ammāra*). When the self has, however, become pure, reasonable, and in order, it may be called the inspired self (*nafs al-mulhama*).

Qalb: heart (the core of our being, the soul,[1] our deepest and most comprehensive knowing, including our psychic functions), is like a container made of the substance of presence. It is the midpoint of the psyche, halfway between self and Spirit. It includes the subconscious and supraconscious faculties of perception, memories, and complexes.

---

[1] *Soul* is one of the most confusing terms in English. It can mean simply the "self," as in "What a poor soul." It can refer to the heart aspect of the human being, as in "She has a lot of soul" or "He put his heart and soul into it." Here it is used as that core of our being which can be developed and spiritualized and which forms a connection between ego and God/Spirit.

The heart can be under the influence of either the ego or the spiritual self. When we speak about involving ourselves "heart and soul," we are speaking about this aspect of the self. Living from the heart or having a pure heart refers to a deep condition of spiritualized desire, spiritual passion. Losing one's soul refers to a condition of having the soul dominated by material, sensual, and egoistic concerns. Such a "heart and soul" is veiled, dim, unconscious.

Rūh, Spirit (spiritual self, essence), as an attribute of the human being is described as an impulse or command from God. Spirit is the essence of life itself. It is like a nondimensional point that is linked to the realm of Unity and has access to the realm of Attributes, the Divine Names. Spirit can send its messages to the heart. It has several important servants, including reason, reflection, and conscience.

The individuality, the totality of the person, is the result of the relationship of these three. The individuality is generally described by seven stages of development, which will be covered in the chapter called "The Knowing Heart." The stage of self-development depends on whether one is dominated by the commanding self, at one extreme, or the spiritualized heart.

On the Sufi path we work in three realms at once: transforming the ego, purifying the heart, and activating spirit. Yet, in a certain sense, it is most effective to begin with the heart, which is the midpoint between the other two, and the place where they meet.

The heart work begins with the development of presence and remembrance of God (zikr). Remembrance draws the light of Spirit into the heart, from where it is distributed to the psyche as a whole. With light and presence in the heart, the compulsions of the commanding self can be witnessed and transformed. With presence and the subsequent opening of the heart, the egocentric aspects of the self (nafs) can be transformed into more evolved human qualities.

In the classical texts we find such a strong emphasis on the commanding self (*nafs al-ammāra*), the compulsive ego, that we may wonder whether this is because the people being addressed by those texts were significantly more under the command of the nafs, or are we in the same situation today? How much should this "war" with the nafs be emphasized? Must its every impulse be opposed, as some suggest?

This is certainly not the example of Muhammad and the Qur'ān, which suggest that the self has its rights, so long as these are within lawful, moral limits. The lawful pleasures of the earthly life are not considered a detriment to our spiritual life as long as we are not en-slaved to them. What we see, however, in the lives of those who have been transformed by the grace of God is a growing independence from the world of the senses; and yet this is not the result of a deliberate asceticism. Muhammad once said, "This world is for me like a tree under which a traveler takes shade for a short while."

One fact that we must take into account, however, is that both the spirit and the self, as two opposing elements within human nature, want for themselves alone complete control over the heart. Ibn ʿArabī writes:

> The conflict between reason and the evil-commanding self is caused by their very nature, which induces each of them to try to dominate the whole of the human being and to be the ruler of it. Even when one of them is able to conquer the whole realm, the other still strives to regain what it has lost and to repair what has been destroyed.[2]

The manipulativeness of the ego need not take a grossly carnal or emotionally negative form; it may exhibit itself as a need for attention or praise, or a quite subtle insistence on having its own way. It can even take the form of doing spiritual practices from a self-serving mo-tive, or it can permeate our whole being as the inability to step outside of our own egocentric viewpoint. The classical advice is that we can give to the nafs its due and no more. If we start to compromise on small points, we are in danger of being overcome by the egocentric self and losing touch with the guidance of the heart and spirit. What begins as a small garden snake, however, can become a dragon. Within our own culture, the egocentric nafs faces very little opposition except, perhaps, the opposition of other egos. The nafs is always in conflict—especially with other egos and with other parts of itself—but the

---

[2] Ibn ʿArabī, "Divine Governance of the Human Kingdom," translated by Tosun Bayrak (Louisville, Ky.: Fons Vitae, 1997), p. 57.

struggle of nafs with nafs does not usually lead to any positive transformation.

We in our society pride ourselves on the freedom and rights of the individual, while relatively little emphasis is placed on responsibility to the community and human family, and practically no emphasis on our relationship and responsibilities to the Divine Reality. Sufism proposes that the attainment of our humanness depends not on our following every impulse of the self but on our making a connection between ego and Spirit. Ibn 'Arabī continues:

> What can save the human realm from danger is its obedience to a beneficent influence that comes from outside. That influence from outside of the human being is the divine principles. It is only when a person is open and ready to accept the divine principles that the spirit in him recognizes that its influence has the same nature, the same characteristics, as itself. Only then may it distance itself from the evil-commanding ego. When this happens, reason imagines that it has found an ally against the ego, and rises against it—and the war between them starts.
>
> The two forces fighting to dominate the human being become aware of their differences only in their relation to the divine principles. Yet viewed from the outside, it is evident that one of these forces is aimed at bringing the human being to destruction, and the other, to felicity.[3]

It is not until we begin to oppose the nafs that we see how much influence it has and how powerful this influence is. If the nafs is denied expression in one way, it can easily change its strategy and satisfy itself in another way. For example, we may curb its lust but find that its anger increases. Since this battle between the spirit and the self is virtually a battle between equals, the struggle sometimes seems hopeless.

> Although God has created His deputy [the human being] with the most perfect attributes, He saw that, on his own, he

---

[3] Ibid., p. 57.

was nonetheless weak, powerless and in need. God wanted His deputy to realize that he would only find strength in the help and support of his Sustainer (*Rabb*). He created a strong opposition for him to provoke this realization. That is the secret of the two opposing possibilities for human selfhood.[4]

In other words this struggle between the two principles of one's nature will only be concluded when a higher power comes into play. For this it is necessary to make a call for divine assistance, to realize in humility our dependence on God, and, without abandoning the struggle with our egocentric compulsions, to pray that these compulsions be dissolved. The nafs, however, will typically resist such a call.

As a pure wind blows fire into flames, the fire of the ego suffers from the pure divine light. And as the ego feels pain from the light, it thinks that the human realm that it governs will also be pained by the divine light generated by the spirit. Therefore it tries to protect its realm from pain by covering it with many veils of unconsciousness, imagination, and desires. The spirit, which generates divine light, tries to do the same, to protect the human being from the pain of the fire. The two adversaries vie to convince the human realm of their convictions and impress upon it their beliefs, hoping that it will join them and assume either the attributes of fire or the attributes of light. Thus the realm would adhere to either one or the other, and be subject to it.

This is the sedition, the trouble between the two, the cause of these inner wars. If only one of them, instead of just looking at itself, would heed the voice always coming from outside! It would then indeed see who is truly the cause of all this, who is really making each of them do what it does. Then it would have found the truth. Then truth and justice would be established. Then neither the spirit nor the ego would be able to say about the other that there is danger in "this" or salvation in "that."

---

[4] Ibid, pp. 58–59.

If they were even able to view each other, there would have been a chance of peace within the realm of the human being. Do you think that the opposition to inner peace is only from the evil-commanding ego? If it would just disappear, all that is being discussed here would not have existed. Indeed it is the source of all conflict. If it would have disappeared, all would disappear.

This is the secret which the Sustainer opens to some and hides from others. The Creator does not have to explain His actions, while the created being is created responsible for its actions. The proof is in the Sustainer's words: *If the Sustainer had so willed, He could have made mankind one people, but they will not cease to dispute except those on whom the Sustainer has bestowed His mercy* [SURAH HŪD (11):18–19].[5]

"Those on whom the *Sustainer* has bestowed His mercy" are those who have surrendered their selves and been qualified with His own beautiful names and attributes. Such a person has seen the egocentric qualities transformed with the help of the uplifting agency of the divine principles and ways of life. Such a person will have realized in herself or himself those qualities that are truly human.

---

[5] Ibid.

The Knowing Heart

THRESHOLD BETWEEN
TWO WORLDS

ANYONE WHO HAS PROBED THE INNER LIFE, WHO HAS SAT in silence long enough to experience the stillness of the mind behind its apparent noise, is faced with a mystery. Apart from all the outer attractions of life in the world, there exists at the center of human consciousness something quite satisfying and beautiful in itself, a beauty without features. The mystery is not so much that these two dimensions exist—an outer world and the mystery of the inner world—but that we are suspended between them, as a space in which both worlds meet. It is as if the human being is the meeting point, the threshold between two worlds. Anyone who has explored this inwardness to a certain degree will know that it holds a great beauty and power. In fact, to be unaware of this mystery of inwardness is to be incomplete.

According to the great formulator of Sufi psychology, al-Ghazālī:

There is nothing closer to you than yourself. If you don't know yourself, how will you know others? You might say, "I know myself," but you are mistaken. . . . The only thing you know about yourself is your physical appearance. The only thing you know about your inside [*bātin*, your unconscious] is that when you are hungry you eat, when you are angry, you fight, and when you are consumed by passion, you make love. In this regard you are equal to any animal. You have to seek the reality within yourself. . . . What are you? Where have you come from and where are you going? What is your role in the world? Why have you been created? Where does your happiness lie? If you would like to know yourself, you should know that you are created by two things. One is your body and your outer appearance (zāhir), which you can see with your eyes. The other is your inner forces (bātin). This is the part you cannot see, but you can know with your insight. The reality of your existence is in your inwardness (bātin, unconscious). Everything is a servant of your inward heart.[1]

In Sufism, "knowing" can be arranged in seven stages. These stages offer a comprehensive view of the various faculties of knowledge, within which the heart makes up the sixth level of knowing:

1. Hearing about something, knowing what it is called. "Someone who has learned to play music on a musical instrument is a musician."
2. Knowing through the perception of the senses. "I have seen a musician and heard music."
3. Knowing "about" something. "I have read some books about music and musicians."
4. Knowing through doing or being something. "I studied an instrument and became a musician."
5. Knowing through understanding and being able to apply that understanding. "I have mastered my instrument and taught others to be musicians."
6. Knowing through the subconscious faculties of the heart. "I play more than the notes on the page; I play from my heart."

---

[1] Al-Ghazālī, *The Alchemy of Happiness,* translated by Claude Field (Armonk, N.Y.: M. E. Sharpe, 1991), pp. 5–6.

7. Knowing through Spirit alone. This is much more difficult to describe, but in the moment when all separation dissolves, there is nothing that cannot be known. In such a state one has a kind of omniscience at least to the extent that if there is a need and one is triggered by the right inquirer, one can access any knowledge because one is unified with the Whole.

The outer world of physical existence is perceived through the physical senses, through a nervous system that has been developed by nature over millions of years. We can only stand in awe of this body's perceptive ability.

On the other hand, the mystery of the inner world is perceived through other, even subtler senses. It is these "senses" that allow us to experience qualities like yearning, hope, and intimacy, or to perceive meaning and beauty, and to know our situation in the universe. When our awareness is turned away from the physical senses and the field of conventional thoughts and emotions, we may find that we can sense an inner world of spiritual qualities, independent of the outer world.

Our modern languages lack precision when it comes to naming or describing that perceptive capacity which can grasp the qualities of this inner world. Perhaps the best word we have for that which can grasp the unseen world of qualities is *heart*. Although this word *heart* is used rather loosely, a look at a dictionary yields these definitions, among others: the seat of the emotions and will, the inmost conscience, the vital or most essential part, secret meaning.

In the vocabulary of Sufism, which derives chiefly from the Qur'ān and the sayings of Muhammad, the heart is not a vague or accidental term, but a precise term, rich with meaning. Some hearts are described as diseased or hardened, while some are "humble before the unseen." One of the axioms of the tradition is expressed in this saying of God: "The heavens and the earth cannot contain Me; only the heart of My faithful servant can contain Me" (Hadīth Qudsī).

The Sufi is someone who approaches the Divine Reality through the heart. The heart is an intelligence beyond intellect, a knowing that operates at a subconscious level, and the only human faculty expansive enough to embrace the infinite qualities of the universe. Intellect can take us only so far; it can *think* about faith, hope, and love, for instance, but it cannot entirely *experience* these qualities. This is the function of the heart. The heart is the faculty of knowing that can apprehend a qualitative universe.

A UNIVERSE OF QUALITIES

The heart is the perceiver of qualities. If we say, for instance, that a certain book has a particular number of pages on a certain subject by a particular author, we have described its distinguishing outer characteristics. If we say, however, that the book is inspiring, depressing, boring, fascinating, profound, trivial, or humorous, we are describing qualities. Although qualities seem to be subjective and have their reality in an invisible world, they are more essential, more valuable, because they determine our relationship to a thing. Qualities modify things. But where are qualities experienced if not within ourselves? The significant question is this: Is this inner world of ours completely subjective, that is to say, contained within the individual brain? Or are qualities, somehow, the objective features of another "world," another state of being?

According to the understanding of Sufism, Reality possesses qualities, or attributes. All of material existence manifests these qualities, but the qualities exist *prior* to their manifestation in material forms. Forms manifest the qualities of an invisible dimension, an "inner world." A cosmic creativity is overflowing with qualities, and these qualities eventually manifest as the world of material forms.

The human being, living both in an outer and an inner world, is an instrument of that cosmic creativity. The human heart is a kind of mirror in which divine qualities and meanings may appear. Those qualities are as much within the heart as within the thing that awakens those qualities in the heart. The situation is like two mirrors facing each other, the heart and the world, while the original reflection comes from a third source, the divine source. But choice appears to reside in one of these mirrors, the human heart.

We human beings have a capacity to project qualities onto things. A cheap, mass-produced teddy bear becomes an object of love because it has been lent qualities by the affection of a child's heart. Things lose or gain importance for us as they are qualified by qualities whose immediate source is the human heart but whose ultimate source are the divine qualities themselves.

This subject may seem abstract and elusive because we are so conditioned to attributing qualities to the things and events of the world. In so doing, we overlook the fact that everything of true significance is happening *within* us. When a parent loves a child, for instance, the parent's capacity for love is projected upon the child. The love itself is a quality that preexists in a greater reality upon which both parent and child depend.

Another way of saying it is that we live in a universe of love, and we know this through the relationship between our own capacity for feeling and the objects of our love.

So far we have proposed that:

1. We live in a universe that is not only material and quantitative but qualitative as well, and that the heart is the organ of perception for this qualitative universe. Furthermore,
2. Every quality that the human being recognizes in the world of outer appearances is derived first of all from the inner knowing of its own heart, which contains a complete sampling of the universe of qualities. The divine qualities are primary; the heart is the interior mirror, and the world is the outer mirror that reflects the heart's projections of these divine qualities.

The significant conclusion we can draw from this is that while the mirror of the world can reveal to us what the heart itself contains, the qualities themselves are contained entirely within the heart. All of outer existence is merely a pretext for revealing to us what the heart itself encompasses.

PURITY OF HEART

The subtle faculties of the heart are our deepest knowing. That knowing is frequently veiled, or confused by more superficial levels of the mind: by opinions, by desires, by social conditioning, and especially by our fears. The mirror of the heart may be obscured by the veils of conditioned thought, by the soot of emotions, by the corrosion of negative attitudes. In fact we easily confuse the ego's emotions with the feelings of the heart. Typically, in the name of following our hearts, we actually follow the desires and fears of the ego. It may also be that certain people glorify and celebrate their personal emotions and mistake these for the heart, but a highly emotional person— reacting from the limited perspective of the small self—is not necessarily a person of heart. One can be quite emotional and yet be out of touch with one's own heart.

The heart may be sensitive or numb, awake or asleep, healthy or sick, whole or broken, open or closed. In other words, its perceptive ability will depend on its capacity and condition.

Purity of the heart refers to the heart's overall soundness and health. The heart, if it is truly a heart, is in contact with Spirit. Only then can it reliably respond to the spiritual qualities that are reflected within itself. Traditional teachers agree that one of the consequences of preoccupation with "the world and the worldly" is the death of the heart. If the heart assumes the qualities of whatever attracts it, its attraction to the dense matter of the world results at best in a limited reflection of the Divine Reality. At worst, the heart's involvement with the purely physical aspects of existence results in the familiar compulsions of ego: sex, wealth, and power.

Sufi wisdom offers cures for an ailing heart.

The first and most important of these is the zikr, the remembrance of God. Zikr is a state of conscious presence and invocation of God. The purpose of this remembrance is to bring "light" into the heart in order that the heart may function as a perceptive organ.

Another is contemplating the meanings of the revealed books of the sacred traditions, and the words of the saints, since these perform an action upon the heart, removing its illusions, healing its ills, restoring its strength.

Another cure for the heart is keeping one's stomach empty. An excess of food hardens the heart. Fasting is the opposite of the subtle and not so subtle addictions with which we numb ourselves to the experience of heart. When through fasting we expose the heart's pain to ourselves, we become more emotionally vulnerable and honest. Only then can the heart be healed.

Keeping a night vigil and prayer before sunrise have been mainstays of the Sufis. In these early-morning hours the activity of the world has been reduced to its minimum, the psychic atmosphere has become still, and we are more able to reach the depths of concentration upon our own unconscious.

Finally, keeping company with conscious people can restore faith and health to the heart. "The best among you are those who when seen remind you of God" (Ḥadīth). It is only a matter of degree to move from the ailing heart to the purified heart. This eventual purification could be understood to proceed through four primary activities or stages:

1. Liberating oneself from psychological distortions and complexes that prevent forming a healthy, integrated individuality.
2. Freeing oneself from the slavery to the attractions of the world, all of which are secondary reflections of the qualities within the heart itself.
3. Transcending the subtlest veil, or illusion, which is the self and its selfishness.
4. Centering oneself and all one's attention in the reality of divine Love, which has the power to unify our fragmented being and reconnect us with the unified field of all levels of existence.

The first three stages—minimizing our psychological distortions, overcoming the slavery of our attractions, and seeing beyond the veil of selfishness—prepare us for making our contact with the divine reality of Love. Without the power of Love, we can only follow our egos and the desires of the world. Without the centering power of Love recognized by the heart, we suffer fragmentation, dispersion in the multiplicity. To work on transforming the ego from within the ego is a tedious and discouraging process. But if we can bring the ego, the intellect, the emotions into the boundlessness of the heart, this places them in a truer context. To view them apart from the heart is to view them in a partial or distorted context. Much of our human foolishness is the result of our mind and feelings being divorced from our hearts, divorced from our love.

When we can center ourselves and our attention in the presence of the Divine Reality, we not only become unified within ourselves, we recognize our unity with all of Life. This is the unifying function of the heart.

OUTER AND INNER

As we begin to sense with the heart that there is a meaningful order behind appearances, we may begin to wonder if there is a reason for our being embodied in this world. Were we brought into the world only in order to escape it? The perspective of Sufism is always one of unifying all levels of existence, from the material to the spiritual. If the human heart is a space in which the world of the senses and the world of inner spiritual qualities meet, in which a spectrum of senses operate, then it is possible to function on many levels simultaneously.

In this life, no pleasure is entirely physical or spiritual, outer or inner. The most outer, material pleasures would mean nothing if there were not some qualities of personal relationship, anticipation, and other associations. Likewise, for a living human being, the most spiritual pleasure is nevertheless experienced through the mediation of the human nervous system. We experience the spiritual qualities as states of relaxation, of heart expansion, of coming alive.

The word for heart in Arabic is *qalb*, which literally means "that which fluctuates"; the heart expands and contracts and even in its purified condition passes through many states.

Ibn 'Arabī says:

> God made the heart the locus of longing to bring actualization of His reality near to the human being, since there is fluctuation in the heart. If this longing were in the rational faculty, the person might seem to be in a constant state. But since it is in the heart, fluctuation comes upon him always.

For the heart is between the two fingers of the Compassionate, so its situation is not to remain in a single state.[2]

The heart experiences constant expansion and contraction, but if
the heart is awake, it begins to grasp the Divine through the intoxication of expansion and the aridity of contraction. The heart is always
occupied with some object of longing through which it is coming to
know the qualities of the spiritual life.

LIVING FROM THE HEART

I have proposed that the heart includes a spectrum of subconscious
faculties for knowing reality immediately and qualitatively. In other
words, the heart is intuitive. The heart, however, is obscured, or
"veiled" from its intuitive knowing by much of our habitual thoughts
and emotions, and particularly insofar as these are derived from the
distortions of the false self.

How can we know whether we are following the concealed desire
of the false self or the guidance of the heart? The ego desires multiplicity and suffers the fragmentation caused by the conflicting attractions
of the world. In the condition we find ourselves, life continually pre-
sents us with ambiguous situations.

Reason, which is the wise and skillful use of the conscious mind,
can be used to clear the mirror of the heart from the distortions of
compulsion, defensiveness, and illusion. To some extent this is the
work of a true psychotherapy. But while the effects of past wounds
can be mitigated by making psychological patterns more conscious, an
authentic spirituality can awaken the healing qualities contained
within the heart: humbleness, gratitude, and love.

However, for these qualities to be authentic and spontaneous, and
not merely the outcome of a moral obligation, it is necessary to establish a rapport with Spirit, the Divine Reality that is the source of these
qualities, deep within the heart. Spirit, here, can be imagined as a
nondimensional point contained within the heart.

---

[2] *Futuhat al-Makkiya,* II 532.30.

THE MIDPOINT BETWEEN EGO AND SPIRIT

Now we must make a further clarification in our practical understanding of the heart. For most people, the ego-self is constructed from and identified with the outer world. The ego is our attempt to attain control and security as a separate entity. An extreme example of this is the materialistic person who believes only in material existence and seeks satisfaction through acquisition of things and security through power over the material world. If ego is the part of ourselves most identified with outer existence, and if in our most inner point we are one with Spirit, then the heart with all its subtle faculties is the midpoint between the two. The heart occupies a midpoint between the ego-self and God. Like a transformer, the heart receives the energy of the Spirit and conveys it to the ego-self, which is transformed through this relationship.

But if the heart is dominated by the demands of the ego-self, the heart is, in a sense, dead; it is not a heart at all.

If, on the other hand, the heart orients itself toward Spirit, which exists like a nondimensional point within the heart, it discovers within itself objective and essential qualities such as faith, hope, patience, generosity, humility, and love. To the extent that it is receptive to Spirit within, it can receive the qualities of Spirit and distribute these according to the capacity of every part of the human being, from where these qualities can radiate to the rest of creation.

A person of heart is someone who is primarily concerned with the cultivation of qualities and meaning. Such a person can trust in the qualitative universe, the beneficent and meaningful order that lies behind outer appearances. Such a person, therefore, lives in a different reality than the materialist.

The Sufi aspires to live consciously within this boundless heart-space. Another way of saying it is that one lives within a Compassionate Universe. Everything that happens, happens within this boundless Affection. Even the self's preoccupations, our petty thoughts and emotions, are seen within this context.

The heart is the center of the individual psyche. It is suspended in a dynamic tension between the two poles of ego and Spirit. It is through the mediation of the heart that the completion of the human psyche is attained.

The heart always has an object of love; it is always attracted to some sign of beauty. Whatever the heart holds its attention on, it will acquire its qualities. Rūmī said, "If your thought is a rose, you are the rose garden. If your thought is a thorn, you are kindling for the bath stove."[3] Being between the attractions of the physical world and the ego, on the one hand, and spirit and its qualities on the other, the heart is pulled from different sides. But ultimately behind all these various attractions lies one great Attractor. Rūmī addressed this issue in a conversation recorded and presented in *Fīhi mā fīhi* (Herein Is What Is Herein):

> All desires, affections, loves, and fondnesses people have for all sorts of things, such as fathers, mothers, friends, the heavens and the earth, gardens, pavilions, works, knowledge, food, and drink—one should realize that every desire is a desire for food, and such things are all "veils." When one passes beyond this world and sees that King without these "veils," then one will realize that all those things were "veils" and "coverings" and that what they were seeking was in reality one thing. All problems will then be solved. All the heart's questions and difficulties will be answered, and everything will become clear. God's reply is not such that He must answer each and every problem individually. With one answer all problems are solved.[4]

There are countless attractions in the world of multiplicity. Whatever we give our attention to, whatever we hold in this space of our presence, its qualities will become our qualities. If we give the heart to multiplicity, the heart will be fragmented and dispersed. If we give the

---

[3] Rūmī, M, II, 278.
[4] Rūmī, *Signs of the Unseen (Fīhi mā fīhi)*, translated by Wheeler Thackston, Jr. (Putney, Vt.: Threshold Books, 1994), p. 34.

heart to spiritual unity, the heart will be unified. Ultimately what the heart desires is unity, in which it finds peace.

> *Truly, in the remembrance of God hearts find rest.*
> —SURAH AL-MU'MINŪN (23):28

THE SUBTLE ORGANS OF KNOWLEDGE

The Sufi schools have sometimes delineated the subconscious intelligence of the heart into various modes of knowing. What are known in some schools as the *latīfas* (literally, the subtleties, plural: *al-lataif*) are subtle, subconscious faculties that allow us to know spiritual realities beyond what the senses or intellect can offer. This knowing is described as subconscious because the aperture of consciousness is necessarily selective and partial. Our spiritual development, however, consists in our becoming able to both focus our attention and widen it to include these subtle perceptions.

These latīfas are developed by carrying the light-energy of the spiritual practices of zikr to precise locations in the chest and head in order to energize and activate these faculties. It is, of course, impossible to exactly define these faculties, although they can be experienced in a more or less objective way. The first five are really refinements of one another: Qalb contains rūh, rūh has the inner dimension of *sirr* (see below), and so on. When enough spiritual refinement is realized, it is used to transform the self (nafs). Whether we understand these to be a literal anatomy of the subtle nervous system or metaphors for our spiritual capacities, the seven latīfas and their functions are as follows:

1. *Qalb* (heart).[5] Through this faculty we begin opening to an inner spaciousness. At this stage we purify our emotional life, and we come in touch with a sense of essential, objective hope.
2. *Rūh* (Spirit). With the awakening to rūh, we discover that the heart contains a point of contact with the infinite dimension of

---

[5] While the qalb is identified as a latīfa with its particular location, it also in some sense contains the totality of all the following organs of knowledge.

Spirit, the source of all qualities. If we can allow Spirit instead of ego to rule our hearts, a new life flows in. At this stage we begin to purify ourselves of mental distractions and projections. We dissolve self-images, our narcissistic fictions. We learn to keep our thought processes in alignment with the Divine Reality.

3. *Sirr* (secret). With the awakening of sirr we begin to discern the Real from the illusory. We strengthen our faith and trust in the Divine Reality through a more conscious relationship with it. We begin to see the Divine Reality more clearly in the multiplicity of forms.

4. *Khafī* (hidden). With the discovery of *khafī* we recognize that everything we long for is infinitely close. Infinite possibilities are contained within a dimensionless point accessible to us within our own heart.

5. *Sirr al-asrār* (Secret of secrets). With the attainment of the Secret of secrets we know ourselves as a reflection of the Divine. We are elevated to Unity. The Sufi never claims identity with God; rather he or she understands his or her servanthood to be subsumed in God.

6. *Nafs* (soul/self). At this stage we bring all of the above qualities and capacities "down" into our individuality. We embody Spirit more fully and begin to radiate the divine qualities.

7. *Haqq* (Truth). At this stage we are further expanded, realizing our identity with all levels of Being, knowing the truth of the Qur'ānic statement: *Wheresoever you look is the Face of God* [Surah al-Baqarah (2):115]. This latīfa could be understood as the final perceptual organ of unity and wholeness, the unitive "sense."

The heart can be understood as the totality of qualitative, subconscious faculties, which function in a unified way. Once activated, these faculties support and illuminate each other, much as eye-hand coordination is superior to either touch or sight alone. Although these functions seem to be separate, they serve a unifying purpose, which is to know the unity beyond multiplicity. They are the subtle nervous system's means of realizing unity.

The fathoming of the human heart and the disclosure of spiritual qualities it contains is the work of all life, art, spirituality. Our purpose in life is to know the heart without the veils of our fears, preoccupations, desires, and strategies. A human heart is the hologram of the seen and unseen universes, the part that reflects the whole.

The purification of the heart is a comprehensive education that has physical, intellectual, psychological, and moral dimensions. And yet all this work is more effective if it can proceed within the boundless context of the heart.

An essential practice is to bring the thinking mind down into the heart, to submerge it in the heart space, and thus to bring reason and heart into unity; then, in that state, to allow a deep receptivity to infinite spiritual Presence. Through this we establish a relationship with the All-Sustaining Presence, which is our ultimate Nature and Source.

The heart is that organ of perception which is capable of knowing all levels of reality, and of knowing the Whole as well as the parts. It may be that what the heart can know is the most a human being can know, and that is infinite.

> If a wealthy person brings a hundred sacks of gold,
> God will only say,
> "Bring the Heart, you who are bent double.
> If the Heart is pleased with you, I am pleased;
> and if the Heart is opposed to you, I am opposed.
> I don't pay attention to "you"; I look to the heart:
> bring it, poor soul, as a gift to My door!
> Its relation to you is also mine:
> 'Paradise is at the feet of mothers.' "[6]
> The heart is the mother and father and origin of all creatures:
> the one who knows the heart from the skin is blessed.
> You will say, "Look, I have brought a heart to You":
> God will respond, "The world is full of these hearts.
> Bring the heart that is the axis of the world
> and the soul of the soul of the soul of Adam."

---

[6] Hadīth.

The Ruler of all hearts is waiting
for a heart filled with light and goodness.

—RŪMĪ, M, V, 881–88

To keep "God" present in our hearts means that "God" will become our reality. This Essence will become our essence. This Power will become our power. This Wholeness is our wholeness.

The heart can be understood as the *center of the unconscious*, the potential integrative power at our core. In *The Alchemy of Happiness*, al-Ghazālī describes the human being in the following metaphor:

> The body is like a country. The hands, feet, and various parts of the body are like the artisans. Passion is like the tax collector. Anger or rage is like the sheriff. The heart is the king. Intellect is the prime minister. Passion, like a tax collector using any means, tries to extract everything. Rage and anger are severe, harsh and punishing like the police and want to destroy or kill. The ruler needs to control not only passion and rage, but also the intellect and must keep a balance among all these forces. If the intellect becomes dominated by passion or anger, the country will be in ruin and the ruler will be destroyed.[7]

The heart is the point at which the individual human being is closest to the Divine Reality. Sufi tradition expresses it this way: The heart is the throne of the All-Merciful Spirit; when the heart is pure, it is guided directly by God. The heart is the center of our motivation and our knowing, possessing a depth and strength of will that the personality lacks. The heart may even know what the conscious mind denies. When we say that the heart has an integrative power, we are not talking in abstract, metaphorical, or merely intellectual terms. The realization and purification of the heart both open a doorway to the Infinite and also result in a restructuring of neural pathways, a refinement and reorganization of our entire nervous system, without which we are not completely human.

---

[7] Al-Ghazālī, *The Alchemy of Happiness*, translated by Claude Field (Armonk, N.Y., M. E. Sharpe, 1991), pp. 7–8.

Themes for Contemplation
from Rūmī

There are true promises that make the heart grateful;
there are false promises, fraught with disquiet.
The promise of the noble is Sterling;
the promise of the unworthy breeds anguish of the soul.

[M, 1, 180–81]

Anger and lust make a man squint;
they cloud the spirit so it strays from truth.
When self-interest appears, virtue hides:
a hundred veils rise between the heart and the eye.

[M, 1, 333–34]

Companionship with the holy makes you one of them.
Though you are rock or marble, you will become a jewel
when you reach the man of heart.

[M, 1, 721–22]

Feed your heart in conversation
with someone harmonious with it;
seek spiritual advancement from one who is advanced.

[M, 1, 726]

Your praise of God is a breath
from your body of water and clay.
Make it a bird of Paradise
by breathing into it your heart's sincerity.

[M, I, 866–67]

Water in the boat is the ruin of the boat,
but water under the boat is its support.
Since Solomon cast the desire for wealth out of his heart,
he didn't call himself by any name but "poor."
But the stoppered jar, though in rough water,
floated because of its empty heart.
When the wind of poverty is in anyone,
she floats in peace on the waters of the world.

[M, I, 985–88]

The light that shines in the eye
is really the light of the heart.
The light that fills the heart
is the light of God, which is pure
and separate from the light of intellect and sense.

[M, I, 1126–27]

Although your desire tastes sweet,
doesn't the Beloved desire you
to be desireless?
The life of lovers is in death:
you'll not win the Beloved's heart
unless you lose your own.

[M, I, 1749–51]

The Prophet said that God said,
I am not contained in the container of high and low.
I'm not contained in the earth nor in all the heavens.
But I am contained in the heart of my faithful servant.
How wonderful! If you seek Me, seek Me there.

[M, I, 2653–55]

Fast from thoughts, fast:
thoughts are like the lion and the wild beasts;
people's hearts are the thickets they haunt.

[M, I, 2909]

Someone with a clear and empty heart
mirrors images of the Invisible.
He becomes intuitive and certain
of our innermost thought,
because the faithful are a mirror for the faithful.

[M, I, 3146–47]

In the presence of His Glory,
closely watch your heart
so your thoughts won't chain you.
He sees guilt, opinion, and desire
as plainly as a hair in pure milk.

[M, I, 3144–45]

People do works of devotion
and set their hearts on approval, expecting rewards.
It is really a hidden sin.
That which the pious thinks pure
is really foul.

[M, I, 3384–85]

Everyone is so afraid of death,
but the real Sufis just laugh:
nothing tyrannizes their hearts.
What strikes the oyster shell doesn't damage the pearl.

[M, I, 3495–96]

Surely the heart is the seal of Solomon
and holds the reins of the senses.
Five external senses are easy for it to manage;
five internal senses are also under its control.

[M, I, 3575–76]

If the heart is restored to health
and purged of sensuality,
then *the Merciful God is seated on the throne.*
After this, He guides the heart directly,
since the heart is with Him.

[M, I, 3665–66]

The Sufi's book is not of ink and letters;
it is nothing but a heart white as snow.

[M, II, 159]

Don't put musk on your body,
rub it on your heart.
What is musk?
The holy name of the glorious God.

[M, II, 267]

On the back of the donkey
are the goods and the money;
but the pearl of your heart
is the investment that supports
a hundred donkeys.

[M, II, 726]

The heart eats a particular food from every companion;
the heart receives a particular nourishment
from every single piece of knowledge.

[M, II, 1089]

The unsuspecting child first wipes the tablet
and then writes the letters on it.
God turns the heart into blood and desperate tears;
then He writes the spiritual mysteries on it.

[M, II, 1826–27]

Through the window between heart and heart
flashes the light that tells truth from lie.

[M, II, 2462]

The troubled heart finds no comfort in lies:
water and oil kindle no light.
Only truthful speech brings comfort:
truths are the bait that attract the heart.

[M, II, 2735–36]

When the heart becomes whole,
it will know the flavors of falsehood and truth.
When Adam's greed for the forbidden fruit increased,
it robbed his heart of health.
Discernment flies from one who is drunken with desire.
He who puts down that cup,
light enters his inner eye,
and the secret is revealed.

[M, II, 2738–43]

Fools honor the mosque
yet seek to destroy those in whose heart God lives.
That mosque is of the world of things;
this heart is real.
The true mosque is nothing but the heart of spiritual kings.
The real mosque that is the inner awareness of the saints
is the place of worship for all: God is there.

[M, II, 3108–11]

The Prophet said, "My eyes sleep,
but my heart is not asleep to the Lord of creating beings.
Your eyes are awake, and your heart is sunk in sleep;
my eyes are asleep,
but my heart is contemplating the opening
of the door of divine grace.
My heart has five other senses than the physical:
both worlds are the theater
for the senses of the heart."

[M, II, 3549–51]

Everyone can distinguish mercy from wrath,
whether he is wise or ignorant or corrupt,
but a mercy hidden in wrath,
or wrath hidden in the heart of mercy,
can only be recognized by one whose heart
contains a spiritual touchstone.

[M, III, 1506–08]

O heart, you will be regarded with favor by God
at the moment when, like a part, you move toward your Whole.

[M, III, 2243]

Come, seek, for search is the foundation of fortune:
every success depends upon focusing the heart.
Unconcerned with the business of the world,
keep saying with all your soul, "Coo, Coo,"[1] like the dove.
Consider this well, O you whom worldliness veils:
God has linked our invocation to the promise,
"I will answer."
When weakness is cleared from your heart,
your prayer will reach the glorious Lord.

[M, III, 2302–05]

The intelligent person sees with the heart
the result from the beginning;
the one lacking in knowledge
only discovers it at the end.

[M, III, 3372]

That which God said to the rose,
and caused it to laugh in full-blown beauty,
He said to my heart,
and made it a hundred times more beautiful.

[M, III, 4129]

---

[1] *Ku, Ku* means "Where, where" in Persian.

Surely there is a window from heart to heart:
they are not separate and far from each other.
Though two earthenware lamps are not joined,
their light mingles.
No lover seeks union without the beloved's seeking;
but the love of lovers makes the body thin as a bowstring,
while the love of loved ones makes them shapely and pleasing.
When the lightning of love for the Beloved
has shot into this heart, know that there is love in that heart.
When love for God has been doubled in your heart,
there is no doubt that God has love for you.

[M, III, 4391–96]

Your resolutions and purposes now and then are fulfilled
so that through hope your heart might form another intention
that He might once again destroy.
For if He were to keep you completely from success,
you would despair: how would the seed of expectation be sown?
If your heart did not sow that seed,
and then encounter barrenness,
how would it recognize its submission to Divine Will?
By their failures lovers are made aware of their Lord.
Lack of success is the guide to Paradise:
Pay attention to the tradition
"Paradise is encompassed with pain."

[M, III, 4462–67]

The bird tempted by the bait may still be on the roof,
but with wings outspread,
it is already imprisoned in the trap.
If with all its soul it has given its heart to the bait,
consider it caught, even though it may still
appear to be free.
Consider the looks it gives to the bait to be
the knots it is tying on its own legs.

The bait says, "You may be stealing looks away from me,
but know that I am stealing patience and constancy away from you."

[M, IV, 620–23]

God has given you the polishing instrument, Reason,
so that by means of it the surface of the heart
may be made resplendent.

[M, IV, 2475]

Listen, my heart,
don't be deceived by every intoxication:
Jesus is intoxicated with God,
the ass is intoxicated with barley.

[M, IV, 2691]

The greed of hunting makes one oblivious to being a prey:
the hunter tries to win hearts, though he has lost his own.
Don't be inferior to a bird in your seeking:
for even a sparrow sees what is *before and behind.*

When the bird approaches the bait,
at that moment it turns its head several times to the rear and the front,
as if to say, "Is there a hunter somewhere near,
Should I be careful? Should I touch this food?"

[M, V, 752–55]

The Prophet said,
"God doesn't pay attention to your outer form:
so in your improvising, seek the owner of the Heart."
God says, "I regard you through the owner of the Heart,
not because of prostrations in prayer
or the giving of wealth in charity"[2]
. . . The owner of the Heart becomes a six-faced mirror:
through which God looks out upon all the six directions.

[M, V, 869–70; 874]

---

[2] Hadīth Qudsī.

Strip the raiment of pride from your body:
in learning, put on the garment of humility.
Soul receives from soul the knowledge of humility,
not from books or speech.
Though mysteries of spiritual poverty are
within the seeker's heart,
she doesn't yet possess knowledge of those mysteries.
Let her wait until her heart expands and fills with Light:
God said, *"Did We not expand your breast . . . ?*[3]
For We have put illumination there,
We have put the expansion into your heart."
When you are a source of milk, why are you milking another?
An endless fountain of milk is within you:
why are you seeking milk with a pail?
You are a lake with a channel to the Sea:
be ashamed to seek water from a pool;
For *did We not expand . . . ?* Again, don't you possess the expansion?
Why are you going about like a beggar?
Contemplate the expansion of the heart within you.

[M, V, 1061; 1064–71]

To follow one's own desires is to flee from God
and to spill the blood of spirituality
in the presence of His justice.

This world is a trap, and desire is its bait:
escape the traps and quickly
turn your face toward God.

When you have followed this Way,
you have enjoyed a hundred blessings.
When you have gone the opposite way, you have fared ill.

So the Prophet said, "Consult your own hearts,
even though the religious judge
advises you about worldly affairs."

---

[3] Surah ash-Sharh (94):1.

Abandon desire, and so reveal His Mercy:
you've learned by experience
the sacrifice He requires.

Since you can't escape, be His servant,
and go from His prison into His rose garden.
When you continually keep watch over
your thoughts and actions,
you are always seeing the Justice and the Judge,
though heedlessness may shut your eyes,
still, that doesn't stop the sun from shining.

[M, VI, 377–84]

Should Love's heart rejoice unless I burn?
For my heart is Love's dwelling.
If You will burn Your house, burn it, Love!
Who will say, "It's not allowed"?
Burn this house thoroughly!
The lover's house improves with fire.
From now on I will make burning my aim,
for I am like the candle: burning only makes me brighter.
Abandon sleep tonight; traverse for one night
the region of the sleepless.
Look upon these lovers who have become distraught
and, like moths, have died in union with the One Beloved.
Look upon this ship of God's creatures
and see how it is sunk in Love.

[M, VI, 617–23]

Though you read a hundred volumes without a pause,
you won't remember a single point
without the Divine decree;
but if you serve God and read not a single book,
you'll learn rare sciences within your own heart.

[M, VI, 1931–32]

Abandon eminence and worldly energy and skill:
what matters is service to God
and a good heart.

[M, VI, 2500]

The Seal of the Prophets, Muhammad, has related the saying
of the everlasting and eternal Lord:
"I am not contained in the heavens or in the void
or in the exalted intelligences and souls;
but I am contained, as a guest,
in the true believer's heart,[4]
without qualification or definition or description,
so that by the mediation of that heart
everything above and below may win from Me
abilities and gifts.
Without such a mirror neither earth nor time
could bear the vision of My beauty.
I caused the steed of My mercy to gallop
over the two worlds.
I fashioned a spacious mirror."
From this mirror appear at every moment
fifty spiritual wedding-feasts:
pay attention to the mirror,
but don't ask me to describe it.

[M, VI, 3071–77]

Listen, open a window to God
and begin to delight yourself
by gazing upon Him through the opening.
The business of love is to make that window in the heart,
for the breast is illumined by the beauty of the Beloved.
Gaze incessantly on the face of the Beloved!
Listen, this is in your power, my friend!

[M, VI, 3095–97]

---

[4] Hadīth Qudsī.

O sea of bliss, O You who have stored
transcendental forms of consciousness in the heedless,
You have stored a wakefulness in sleep;
You have fastened dominion over the heart
to the state of one who has lost his heart.
You conceal riches in the lowliness of poverty;
You fasten the necklace of wealth to poverty's iron collar.

[M, VI, 3567–68]

Radical Remembrance

FOR THE SUFI, THE REMEMBRANCE OF GOD ALWAYS AND everywhere is the aim of existence. But Who or What is God, and what is "remembering"?

Is human language capable of expressing, or at least pointing toward, the reality of this word *God*? Some people—especially those who prefer a purely existential or scientific worldview—become disturbed when this word is used. Others become complacent and self-righteous. Perhaps it is better to be somewhat disturbed by the idea of God, especially if the disturbance causes us to crack the shell of our fixed concepts. Whatever God is, God is not one of our fixed concepts.

One cannot be a human being and not wonder about the real significance of being an individual, a person with self-awareness. Each of us has a flame of consciousness at our core. What is the nature of this flame, and what kindled it within us? This consciousness is the most startling fact of our existence, and at the same time it is most often taken for granted.

It is said in our tradition: "You are God's secret. And God is your secret." To the gnostic, God is to be known through the flame of consciousness. To remember God is to be aware of that flame of consciousness. But we can only be aware of that flame *through* that flame. This is the paradox in which duality dissolves.

The flame of consciousness exists in us because consciousness permeates the universe. But the word *consciousness* implies something mental, abstract, almost impersonal. What if that flame is not only a flame of consciousness but also a flame of infinite qualities? What if fire not only contained heat and light, but love, creative power, and infinite intelligence?

What then if the human being could become aware of this inner flame as a spark of infinite creativity and love? What if the activation of our essential human qualities depended on our awareness of a spiritual connection to the Source of Life? This is the central premise of our work. Is this religion? Is this psychology? Is this art? Is this just common sense? Is it called becoming a complete human being? It doesn't matter.

> *Remember Allāh, as He has guided you.*
> —SURAH AL-BAQARAH (2):198

This deceptively simple statement enjoins us to remember and suggests that we have been "guided" to this remembrance by God. *Remembrance* is a translation of the Arabic word *zikr*, which has a number of meanings, including "mentioning" and "remembering." *Remember* can be traced back to Middle English and Old French and comes from the Latin *rememorari*. To remember, however, is not simply the calling up of something from the past, but a calling to mind, a state of retaining something in one's awareness. We are reminded to remember by the One who instilled remembrance in us. This Qur'ānic verse, this *ayat*, is a thin veil over the oneness of Being: our remembering is His remembering.

For the Sufi this remembrance has an essential nature beyond forms, which can be practiced anywhere and anytime.

> *And remembrance is the greatest.*
> *And God knows all that you do.*
> —SURAH AL-'ANKABŪT (29):45

REMEMBRANCE THROUGH THE NAMES OF GOD

Zikr has its specific forms, or exercises, which lead to experiences on different levels within our own being. Al-Ghazālī, one of the greatest formulators and interpreters of Sufism, gave these instructions regarding the practice of remembrance:

> Let your heart be in such a state that the existence or nonexistence of anything is the same—that is, let there be no dichotomy of positive and negative. Then sit alone in a quiet place, free of any task or preoccupation, be it the reciting of the Qur'ān, thinking about its meaning, concern over the dictates of religion, or what you have read in books—let nothing besides God enter the mind. Once you are seated in this manner, start to pronounce with your tongue, "Allāh, Allāh," keeping your thought on it.
>
> Practice this continuously and without interruption; you will reach a point when the motion of the tongue will cease, and it will appear as if the word just flows from it spontaneously. You go on in this way until every trace of the tongue movement disappears while the heart registers the thought or idea of the word.
>
> As you continue with the invocation, there will come a time when the word will leave the heart completely. Only the palpable essence or reality of the name will remain, binding itself ineluctably to the heart.
>
> Up to this point everything will have been dependent on your own conscious will; the divine bliss and enlightenment that may follow have nothing to do with your conscious will or choice. What you have done so far is to open the window, as it were. You have laid yourself exposed to what God may breathe upon you, as He has done upon His prophets and saints.
>
> If you follow what is said above, you can be sure that the light of Truth will dawn upon your heart. At first intermit-

tently, like flashes of lightning, it will come and go. Sometimes when it comes back, it may stay longer than other
times. Sometimes it may stay only briefly.[1]

The method of attaining the "Truth" begins with this simple and
beautiful practice of repeating "Allāh," the essential name of God. Just
by moving the tongue with a certain intention and presence of mind,
we are taken into the reality of the Name until "only the palpable
essence or reality of the name will remain, binding itself ineluctably to
the heart." Through this simple process, the remembrance is trans-
ferred from the tongue to the mind, from the mind to the feelings and
the deeper levels of the personality, until its reality is established in the
core of the human being.

More and more, remembrance begins to fill one's life. Instead of
the usual inner dialogues, commentaries, judgments, and opinions
that make up the majority of people's inner life, we may begin to
experience the breath and rhythm of remembrance. The divine names
are seen to be alive, animate, spiritually prolific—much more real than
the repetitive scripts of our superficial personality.

This path requires no exceptional leap of faith, no abandonment of
reason, no complex theology or intellectual attainment. The simple,
mindful invocation of God's essential name will take us to the reality
of what is being remembered.

REMEMBRANCE OF THE HEART

The remembrance that begins with the tongue can guide us to the
remembrance of the heart. Perhaps it is evidence of the divine generosity that what begins with the simple repetition of a word could lead to
the Secret of secrets, the innermost core of the heart. The repetition
of the word *Allāh* focuses our thought on God. The rhythm of remembrance inevitably affects brainwaves, and the superficial layers of the
mind are calmed. In this transparent stillness of the superficial mind,
a deeper level of mind becomes revealed. It is that deeper level of

---

[1] Al-Ghazālī, *The Alchemy of Happiness.*

mind, called heart, which is capable of perceiving "something" that is apparent neither to the intellect nor to the senses. It seems as if becoming aware of this "something" has the effect of clarifying the mind, harmonizing the emotions, enhancing the senses, and bringing peace to the heart.

> *Truly, in the remembrance of God hearts find rest.*
> —SURAH AL-MU'MINŪN (23):28

> *And contain yourself patiently at the side of all who invoke their Sustainer, mornings and evenings, seeking His face, nor allow your eyes to go beyond them in search of the attractions of this world's life, and pay no attention to any whose heart We have made unaware of all remembrance of Us because he had always followed his own desires, abandoning all that is just and true.*
> [Surah al-Kahf (18):28]

Westerners who are familiar with various spiritual paths may ask, "What is the difference between zikr and meditation?" If by meditation is meant that refined "listening within," the activation of a presence capable of witnessing inner and outer events without becoming absorbed in them, then there is much in common. We can, however, distinguish zikr from the more superficial techniques of concentration. Remembrance is more than an exercise performed for individual purposes such as attaining calmness, clarity, or relaxation. While zikr must include that state of concentration, it is more than that. Remembrance of God is establishing a relationship with infinite Being, which is both nearer to us than ourselves and, at the same time, greater than anything we can conceive. It is also experienced as loving and being loved by Love.

I once received a letter from a person who was in the midst of years of intensive practice within what he described as a "nontheistic tradition." During a three-year solitary retreat he began to practice a Sufi zikr using the name Allāh. He described how in all his years of spiritual practice, and despite the many benefits of his practice, his heart had not found rest. "Perhaps there is something in approaching a God who can be named. My heart, for the first time, has found rest." Little did he know that he was quoting the Qur'ān almost verbatim. Is his experience valid, or is it merely settling for some lesser satisfaction? Our understanding of remembrance is that the Divine has the qualities of indefinable transcendence, as the nontheistic approaches emphasize, and at the same time the Divine has a personal, intimate aspect, which is experienced as profound relationship.

While the invocation of the names or attributes of God is a primary practice, this remembrance can and should permeate the entire range of human capacities and activities. The Qur'ān commends those who *remember God standing, sitting, and lying on their sides* [Surah al-'Imrān (3):191], meaning under every possible circumstance. Every cell of the body longs to be in this state of remembrance. Sufism has many practices that allow remembrance to be incorporated at the bodily level: the standing, bowing, and prostration of the ritual prayer, *salah*; the whirling ceremony of the Mevlevi dervishes; the movements of the group zikrs of various Sufi orders.

REMEMBRANCE THROUGH REFLECTING UPON ONENESS

Remembrance also consists of the mental and emotional recognition that everything is a manifestation of a single Source. Allāh is the Oneness, and all of manifest existence reflects the qualities and will of Allāh, the life and being of Allāh. As we see the budding of flowers in spring, we recognize al-Khāliq, the Creator, or al-Latīf, the Subtle, and al-Musawwir, the Bestower of Form. When we see the power of a great storm or an earthquake, we recognize and remember al-'Azīz, the Mighty, and al-Jabbār, the Compeller. When we view the incredible balance within the ecology of nature, we may recognize ar-Razzāq, the Provider, and al-Wahhāb, the Bestower, and al-Muhyī, the Giver of Life, and as-Sabūr, the Patient.

REMEMBRANCE THROUGH PRAISE

As we deepen in recognizing the attributes, we may be led more and more to a sense of awe and to spontaneous appreciation and thankfulness for the invisible order that manifests existence. As it is said in the Qur'ān, *Wheresoever you look is the Face of God* [Surah al-Baqarah (2):115]. The one who remembers God acquires a sensitivity to the manifest world as well as a sense of the numinous dimensions of existence. More and more the traditional religious terminology of "praise" and "glorification" may correspond to the reality we are experiencing. We may be led to experiences of such power and beauty that our everyday remembrance may be colored by the memory of these events as well. We may wish to remember the intensity of those experiences in which the veils between the earthly and the Divine became very thin.

REMEMBRANCE THROUGH MORAL SENSITIVITY

Another aspect of remembrance that must be included is the need for an ethical/moral sensitivity. The Sufi—and that is to say Islamic—conception of Allāh also includes a sense of the laws of cause and effect. Since we as individuals are integral to the wholeness of this reality, everything we do has its effect within the whole. This realization demands more self-awareness, more sensitivity regarding the effects and consequences of one's own actions, feelings, and thoughts. With this new sensitivity, conscience awakens, and one's personality and relationships are refined. One may begin to walk more gently on the earth. What began as a mental repetition deepened into a more continuous awareness of the whole field of existence permeated by moral and spiritual presence.

REMEMBRANCE THROUGH SURRENDER AND UNION

Who can say where this remembrance ends? There are states of pure contemplative presence in which Spirit itself becomes the most satisfying experience imaginable and one is freed of all other concerns. Through this experience Love increases, and the surrender of the isolated individual will becomes possible. God says in the Qur'ān:

Remember Me and I will remember you.

—SURAH AL-BAQARAH (2):152

The Sufi comes to know that this statement is not a statement in linear time, not an if-then proposition. Intention, effort, and perseverance are essential, and at the same time, when the human being remembers God, it is really the action of God.

Ultimately one merges into the Divine Presence just as individual stars disappear in the light of the sun.

And remembrance is the greatest.

—SURAH AL-ʿANKABŪT (29):45

The Transparent Self

IN LIGHT OF THE MODEL OF INDIVIDUALITY DESCRIBED EAR-
lier, we might reflect on what kind of being comes into existence
when the "self" has come into relationship with "Spirit" through
the mediation of the heart. Without the mediation of the heart, the
individuality is dominated by a socially constructed and conditioned
persona, the false self. The preoccupation with the false self is a fundamental characteristic of our modern Western culture. It is so pervasive
that it requires a long reconditioning and reeducation to overcome our
enslavement to this persona.

There are two very different approaches to happiness, fulfillment,
and well-being: self-absorption and self-transcendence. The one that
dominates in our materialistic, consumer society is, of course, self-
absorption. The security, pleasure, and status of the self are the primary intentions behind all activities. This attitude is not limited only
to the desires and ambitions of the world; it may also affect, and even
infect, one's assumptions about "spiritual development."

We might even ask ourselves: "To what extent is my approach to
the spiritual path a preoccupation with myself, and to what extent is it
a self-transcending openness to Being?" To visualize this more clearly,
imagine yourself represented by a colored silhouette against a background. How much of your energy and attention is focused on the
silhouette, how much on the relationship between the silhouette and
the background, and how much on the background?

For many people the silhouette itself is all-important. "You" are Number One in "your" universe. Your states of consciousness and your self-development are the primary focus; meanwhile, the background may represent anything that is not the self: the outer world, which can oppose you, distract you, or offer you fulfillment. This is quite a common approach to spirituality in our society.

There is another approach, which suggests that only the background, the Divine Being, is real, and everything the silhouette represents is unreal. The ego silhouette must die or be "annihilated." This understanding is characteristic of certain extreme forms of spirituality.

The approach of Sufism is that the background is infinitely compassionate, meaningful, conscious, and loving, and that the "ego silhouette" needs to find its proper relationship to this "background." The self can open to a new relationship with Being; it can fall in love with the background, the Ground of Being, and a kind of dance begins between the foreground of self and the background of compassionate Being. Without this relationship to the ground of Being, the self is living a painful, loveless existence, cut off from the Wisdom-love that can guide and inform its earthly journey.

Gradually, in the humility of presence, in the transparency of self, the colors of the background and the foreground become One. Moreover, it often happens that the background and the foreground seem to shift in playful ways. The lover disappears in the Beloved, and the Beloved disappears in the lover. The self gives up its illusion of control; it begins to recognize the synchronicities and meaningful patterns that occur; it begins to sense that our lives are an expression of hidden yet meaningful and benevolent forces, that there is a transpersonal aspect to reality, an intelligent and compassionate field of activity of which we are a part. The self begins to understand the importance and reality of worship: a loving and respectful relationship to the Divine Being. It begins to understand prayer as a dialogue with Being. It begins to remember this Being as the most significant attribute of existence. It begins to fall in love with God. The discipline of building up the self is not the same as the discipline of making the self transparent. Both require the methodical pursuit of a goal, but one may lead to various forms of imprisonment and the other may lead to freedom. True humility develops out of a presence that is in relationship with the ground of Being. *Presence is our capacity to be whole in the moment, in alignment with our deepest wisdom, with Being itself.* Presence is a transcendent awareness and a capacity for wholeness that can grow to include more and more. It could also be described as a magnetic power that gathers and harmonizes all our parts and functions—including thought, feeling, intuition, and behavior. With presence all of these functions work together in a balanced and harmonious way. Without presence we feel one thing, think another, and perhaps say neither. We live a fragmented existence in which actions, thoughts, and feelings often conflict and in which there is no human *being* present. I would suggest that at least 99 percent of us know this state, and yet our capacity for presence is quite limited; it may be that we do not value it enough for it to really establish itself in our lives.

Humility is a condition of the transparent self. Humility is not necessarily considering ourselves less important or valuable than other people. It is not a lack of self-esteem; nor is it a form of modest behavior, and it is not the result of humiliation.

Humility is the right attitude of the finite to the Infinite, the conditioned to the Unconditioned, the part to the Whole. Humility is our awareness of our dependence on something greater than ourselves, and our interdependence with our fellow human beings and all of life. Establishing the right relationship between the individual human personality and the infinite, unconditioned Whole may be the central question of both spirituality and transpersonal psychology. What is the *trans* in transpersonal?

The dominant themes of transpersonal psychology—work on self-esteem, creative visualization, affirmation, intuition, and awareness of archetypes—may be useful, but is this work necessarily or essentially transpersonal if it all proceeds from that self which exists in separation? Is the transpersonal another ingredient in the recipe for self-esteem and success, or is it something that we surrender to and serve, to which we totally belong?

We have taken the individual human personality as the primary unit of reality, and this leads to profound failure and disillusionment. This is the central problem of our existence. Our American culture on the whole, and the so-called New Age movement in particular, shows many signs of being still immature and naive in relation to this central question. If we look at the offerings of any New Age center, we will see that most of them are aimed at helping us to receive consolation and relief from stress through mystical pacifiers; or to be more empowered and effective in attaining our goals, or to be more attractive and interesting people, or to attain greater control through a magical knowledge. Many of these offerings can be divided into three categories: Band-Aids for the wounded (self-esteem seminars, meditation for stress-relief); tools for do-it-yourself reality builders (affirmations, creative visualizations); narcotics for the spiritually addicted (ecstatic techniques, recreational tantra, pampering the body).

In recent decades we have used the word *holistic,* thinking that it merely means eating whole foods, or integrating stress reduction techniques and bodywork into psychotherapy. Or we may think of *holistic* as not separating the bran from the kernel of the grain; or not separating the mind from the body, or the individual from nature. But there is a much more comprehensive wholeness, which is seeing the individual as integral to the wholeness of Being. What if we could recognize that there is a continuity between the core of individual consciousness and all levels of Being? This is such an immense idea and yet so basic that it is hard to grasp with the mind; but let us try to bring it to earth.

What are the means to overcome this separation, this false reality in which we view the individual as a separate unit of reality, somehow alone and yet conscious within a vast, material existence? The central question could be put in various ways: What do we do with individual human consciousness? Should we develop the ego or annihilate it? What is the right relation of the individual self with the wider reality? What are the proper and real boundaries of the self? A spiritual psychology is, above all, a psychology concerned with qualities and values. How can we bring spiritual qualities and values into action? How could we reframe this theme in a truly holistic, transpersonal context?

Webster's defines *value* first as the price or worth in a monetary sense. Only after we get to definitions number six and seven in the list do we begin to get to the meanings we are looking for: "that quality of a thing by which it is thought of as being more or less desirable, useful, estimable, important; its degree of worth; that which is worthy for its own sake." Values are the important, desirable, and estimable qualities, worthy for their own sake. In short, values are qualities that are essentially good.

If we were existentialists we might say that the universe is absurd, and yet we human beings might, nevertheless, choose certain values to live by. From the transpersonal Sufi perspective, however, I think most of us would agree that these values are not just fabricated by individual brains as a desperate attempt to establish some meaning and order. Rather they are essential attributes of reality. Reality is fundamentally beneficent. Even if there is pain and suffering, the beneficence has precedence and is revealed all the more clearly through the hazards of this unpredictable existence.

The qualities of compassion, generosity, wisdom, justice, beauty, and glory are inherent in our universe. We find them reflected in our own beings, and we also find that if we work on ourselves, if we polish our own hearts, we become more capable of reflecting these qualities.

It is important to consider that we do not originate or create these qualities; we reflect them. In and of ourselves we do not have the intelligence or creativity to invent wisdom or love. We can only discover them as they are revealed to us; then we can reflect them in this existence. From one perspective all these qualities exist in the invisible, transpersonal treasury of Being. It is we who bring them into existence and manifestation by removing the obstacles presented by the false self.

One of the first principles of this model of *the self as reflector* is that we attribute nothing to ourselves except the limitations we impose on expression. We take responsibility for our limited capacity to reflect the qualities of Being, and we allow this recognition to motivate us toward polishing our hearts, developing our nervous system, awakening all our faculties to reflect more. The greatest limitation on our ability to reflect is the false self, the superficial identity, which is, after all, the result of conditioning. The false self is a role, an artificial self-image, a package of received ideas, opinions, illusions, desires, whims, self-justifications, insecurities. We have an unreal personality that is living our life for us. Too often we have been living as mere self-representations in a representational world. We have lived as a fictional self in a fictional world, oblivious to the Beneficent Reality.

Here we begin to see practically how we ourselves are resistant to the expression of those qualities. Our own habits of relationship, our fears, our lack of trust in the beneficence of Life cause restriction and contraction.

There is no higher purpose other than the recognition of our own relative nonexistence in relation to the Whole. At this level the Oneness becomes our only wish. We learn to approach a state of positive, functional nonexistence. What would this state of positive nonexistence look like? The state of positive, functional nonexistence is the state of living from our essential Self, manifesting through an individual personality but not dominated by the role it plays, by its personal likes and dislikes, by the conditioning and customs of its culture. In contrast, the false self lives in fear and lies, hating to have these exposed, desperately defending its artificial self-image.

The essential Self is fundamentally invulnerable and at ease, because it is anchored in Being. This anchoring at the core of oneself allows the personality to be much more vulnerable, open, honest. If the essential Self adopts a provisional or social identity—which may be necessary for certain reasons—it does not take it too seriously, does not become completely identified with it. The essential Self does not become inflated with its identity; it lives in the humility of presence and can keep a sense of humor about itself.

Once Rābi‘a, a tenth-century Sufi saint, had nothing to eat in her house, and she was standing at her door with an empty pot. For a moment she wished she had an onion. Just then a bird flew over and dropped an onion from its mouth into Rābi‘a's pot. Rābi‘a looked at the onion and looked again at the sky, smiled, and said, "But don't expect me to believe the Almighty is a mere onion vendor." The humility of presence opens us to our own essential Self and its essence qualities. Humility is our connection with our own fundamental Being, which has certain qualities:

Acceptance of what is, rather than complaints of "poor me" or "Why me?"

Openness, rather than preoccupation with "me."

Gratefulness, rather than resentment for what has happened to "me."

Generosity, rather than possessiveness.

Modesty, rather than the self-importance of "me."

Forgiveness, rather than blame of others or ourselves.

Trust, rather than insecurity and doubt.

One way this process of transformation can be described is in terms of the changes of state from solid to liquid to gas. The compulsive-obsessive self is like ice—hard, separate, and alone. The balanced self is more like water, fluid, able to merge with others and flow, able to dissolve and even purify the negativity of life. The higher stages are more like the molecular state of a fragrance—very subtle, penetrating, not nearly as limited in space or time. We can visualize the self as something that can become ever more subtle, refined, spacious, pene-trating. The more we spiritualize our animal qualities and bring them into service, the more we tame "the beast" with love, the more we attain wholeness, and the more that natural self can be the instrument of real values, which are transpersonal or spiritual in nature.

THE SEVEN LEVELS OF THE SELF (NAFS)

The Sufi tradition has generally understood the transformation of the human being in seven stages. Previously we described a model of the self consisting of an interplay of three aspects of individuality: self, heart, and Spirit. In the healthy, spiritual state the self is in relation-ship to the heart, which is in deep spontaneous communication with Spirit. Our individuality is the synthesis of two aspects of our being: self and Spirit. We could also call these the natural (or animal) self, on the one hand, and the transpersonal (or spiritual) Self, on the other. The animal self is not necessarily evil, but it lacks self-awareness and self-control. It is motivated primarily by instinct and desire. The spiri-tual self, on the other hand, can supply consciousness, higher reason, wisdom, and guidance. The synthesis of these two forces, as I said, is the individuality.

Now, the individuality can be described on a scale of seven stages, which in English could be named as follows.

1. The compulsive-obsessive self, *nafs al-ammāra*, is totally dominated by its desires and instincts. There is almost no separation between desire and action. One is under the command (*ammāra*) of one's compulsions. The nafs al-ammāra may convince us that it is acting in our interest, but the evidence is otherwise. Through its chaotic desires it leads further from Reality even while it exercises a tyranny over the heart. The quality that must be awakened at this stage is repentance, or remorse of conscience.

2. The blaming self, *nafs al-lawwāma*, is aware of the need to control its compulsions and desires. Here begins a state of inner turmoil, because one may not be able to do very much about one's desires other than to observe how much one is enslaved to them. The quality that must be awakened is abstinence, or temperance.

3. The balanced or inspired self, *nafs al-mulhama*, is the state in which the good has begun to predominate in this struggle. The tyranny of egoism has been overcome, and a more or less integrated self is attained. The quality awakened here is the renunciation (*zuhd*) of worldly longings and ambitions, a freedom from the conditionings of desire. This state is the aim of most religion and psychology. It is the boundary of conventional ego development. Although it is only the third level of human development in the Sufi system, it is no minor accomplishment. For some it requires a great deal of personal, psychological work.

4. The tranquil self, *nafs al-mutma'inna*, has begun to live from higher consciousness in the remembrance (zikr) of God. This is the stage at which a human being steps upon the Path of conscious development. The awakening of individual presence and the remembrance of God become the focus of life activity. One may still have issues to deal with from all the prior levels, but it is possible to deal with them from a wider context of experience.

In the Qur'ān it is said, *"Indeed, in the remembrance of God hearts find tranquillity."* This describes the stage of the tranquil self. The quality to be awakened here is spiritual poverty (*faqr*), by which is meant detachment from worldly concerns, freedom from worries, and peace of mind. It is the beginning of seeing through appearances and recognizing the Being of God behind all appearances. At this stage one's separation from God is just a veil of light.

5. The fulfilled self, *nafs al-radiyya*, has become happy with God. He realizes the truth of these words of Sufi saint, 'Abdul Qādir Jīlānī: "Good and evil are relative to the created. But for the Creator all are equal. A human being advances as much as he abandons personal opinions and thoughts such as 'for me,' 'in my opinion,' or 'as far as I am concerned' and fuses his orientations and himself with his Sustainer's opinion. It is for this reason that the one who has matured in his perception of reality does not see faults or flaws in creation."[1] Whatever happens is greeted with patience and acceptance. This is the stage of the first melting (*fanā*) or union with God. Remembrance has matured to a state of acceptance, forgiveness, and gratitude. The individuality has been fundamentally transformed, some would say "enlightened." The self enters a phase of spontaneous altruism. From this point on in its progress, its ascent to God will continue eternally; not even death can end it.

6. The self of total submission, *nafs al-mardiyya*, is the self that is not only pleased but has become pleasing to God. It is the beginning of a descent from the bliss of union to embodiment as an individual human being; it is a descent that can be characterized by phases of shattering bewilderment. This is the stage in which both crucifixion and resurrection are experienced. After the blissful melting in God that is the fifth stage, the self must face great tests in order to recognize that it lives for nothing but God, that it wants nothing else but Truth. The individuality is returned to the one who comes to this station, but this individuality no longer thinks it owns itself. True awe of God is only possible after one has returned from unity to individuality. At the same time, it is a deeper stage of friendship and communion with God in which the self exists side by side with the Being of God, in which every test, every loss, every state is experienced in total submission. The self reaches a state of utter humility, purification of heart,

---

[1] 'Abdul Qādir Jīlānī, "The Divine Bestowal," translated by M. Bayman, unpublished manuscript.

the annihilation of everything that resists, complains, resents, or distrusts Reality.

This humility is like the state of being in love—in love with God and feeling loved in return. Just as two lovers can sit together in contentment, happiness, and peace, two become one in purpose without losing their distinctive individualities. When we are deeply in love, the wills of the lover and the beloved are one, without argument or disagreement. And so the self is pleased with Reality, and Reality is pleased with the self. This station is the realization of the truth of the words attributed to God in a discourse by 'Abdul Qādir Jīlānī: "Sinners are veiled by their sin, while the pious are veiled by their piety. But, beyond them, I have a community who neither intend sin, nor trust their piety. For I am as close to My rebellious servants when they forsake their sins as I am close to My faithful servants when they forsake their piety. For no one is far from Me in his sins, and no one is near to Me with his promises."[2] The quality that awakens at this stage is complete trust, the turning over of one's affairs to God as the ultimate Trustee. Such a person is a true friend (*walī*) of God and emanates a vibration that is beneficial to humanity and the creation.

7. The complete or perfected self, *nafs al-kamila,* has attained the full palette of attributes *and* completed the return to the state of exceptional ordinariness. The spiritual poverty that began to develop in the fourth stage is completed here. An important quality attributed to this stage is contentment (*ridā*). Ibn 'Arabī described this attainment when he said, "My journey was entirely within myself, and pointed to myself. And I saw that I was nothing but servanthood, without a trace of Lordship."[3]

All qualities and actions belong solely to the Transpersonal Reality. There is no existence separate from that Oneness. At this level the individual self, though fully functional, exists in and through the Oneness. He or she has become a universal human being, belonging to all of humanity. Finally that Oneness reflects itself through such an individual in a way that cannot be described or predicted.

---

[2] Ibid.

[3] *Futūhāt al-Makkiyah*, chap. 367.

*   *   *

We began by considering the quick fixes of the present age, and we progressed to the state of positive nonexistence, the humility of presence in which one lives without any self-image in a state of modesty, openness, gratefulness, forgiveness, acceptance, and trust. There is nothing impractical about the process or the goal, because it is our human destiny. The end result is the unrestricted manifestation of Life and Wisdom.

RELATIONSHIPS
AND COMMUNITY

Grapes Ripen Smiling at One Another

LEADERSHIP AND
THE GROUP PROCESS

> The tart and hearty grapes, destined to ripen,
> will at last become one in heart
> by the breath of the masters of heart.
> They will grow steadily to grapehood,
> shedding duality and malice and strife.
> till in maturity, they rend their skins,
> and become the mellow wine of union.
>
> —RŪMĪ, M, II, 3723–25

I T IS EIGHT O'CLOCK ON A THURSDAY NIGHT, AND A CIRCLE of about a dozen people are kneeling on a large carpet. "In the name of the Infinitely Compassionate and Merciful, the Source of Life." The stillness is deep; a tangible presence fills this room. "Let us bring our finest attention to the breath." Outside the wind is blowing strong on this Vermont hilltop. Inside an experiment is continuing—as it has for more than twenty years—a journey into the future and back to the Source.

For a Sufi it is difficult to imagine the spiritual process apart from the Sufi circle, or group—that is, apart from a brother/sisterhood that gathers primarily for the purpose of awakening the Divine Essence in each person. A saying has it that one log will not burn by itself, but with a little kindling a number of logs leaning against each other will make a good fire. A group, any group, generates energy; but the kind and quality of energy and what it is used for determines whether that group becomes a mob, a cult, or a circle of lovers. The Sufis have at least fourteen hundred years' experience in group dynamics, and their record is excellent, being relatively free of the deviations and abuse that have characterized so many groups, especially in recent decades here in the Western world.

The Sufi path, or *tariqa,* is an ideal that can be clearly distinguished from cults and other forms of social conditioning. Cult behavior has been thoroughly studied and analyzed. It typically involves unquestioning devotion to a charismatic leader, coercion of the will, thought control, behavior modification, beliefs that are usually outside the ethical matrix of a sanctioned and revealed tradition, and a distrust of other groups and the outside world.

AN ESSENTIAL INGREDIENT

We live in a "do-it-yourself" culture; we basically believe that we can accomplish anything if we try, but sometimes we may not realize that, left to ourselves, we lack essential ingredients and capacities. Especially in the field of spirituality, we may assume that all we need are good intentions and some instructions we can follow. In the Sufi tradition, maturing a soul is something like culturing yogurt. It is not so difficult if you have the milk, the yogurt culture, the right environment, and the necessary time. Each of us has the milk already, but whether this milk sours or becomes a fine yogurt depends on certain influences, not the least of which is the presence of a little yogurt culture.

Any authentic tradition of enlightenment is based on the fact that someone at some time had a breakthrough and was able to pass that breakthrough along. Without the reality of this state of mind, any group will remain sterile. No Sufi group exists except in relationship with and under the direction of someone who has matured within the teaching. The Sufi concept of maturity describes someone who has melted his or her own existence in Being, who has removed the veils between the conscious mind and the heart. The spiritually mature person has outgrown the neediness of the personality, the ambitions and satisfactions of "worldliness," and the subtle coercions of self-importance.

An authentic spiritual process is essentially independent of forms, practices, rituals, beyond even the visible world, and receives its kindling energy from someone who can transmit the transforming energies needed to catalyze the potential within a group. There must be burning; and this requires a living human being who has made a conscious connection with the source of Being. Every human being has this possibility, but most human beings are burdened with the weight of conditioning and live in a state of unconscious slavery to their desires, fears, and self-image. It is entirely possible, in fact likely, that a group gathering without the help and guidance of someone sufficiently advanced on the journey will become only a fertile environment for the breeding of confusion, misunderstanding, and resentment. The group may at least be protected if it has information from an authentic teaching tradition, but for the process to be *transformative,* the group needs the presence of someone who can be an opening to the unconditioned energies of grace.

THE NEED FOR A TEACHER

Our cultural situation does not favor the kind of respect and commitment that is expected between a guide and a seeker in the traditional ways of enlightenment. On the one hand, some people will always be willing to turn over responsibility for their lives to an authority figure in order to escape the burden of free will. The real teacher, however, will use his or her influence to activate real will in the student by helping students to face their slavery in every form, especially the slavery to the compulsive ego.

On the other hand, the vast majority of Westerners are skeptical of the possibility of there being teachers of wisdom (especially from within their own culture), people who can reliably guide others to new levels of being. We prefer to think that these are very private and personal matters, that truth is "a trackless land," that one attains wisdom primarily through one's own experience, independent of guidance. But the Sufi point of view is expressed in the adage "Whoever has no guide has Satan for a guide." Satan is a symbol of the untransformed ego. It is also said, "If you follow the path alone, you will only arrive at your own ego."

We are not accustomed to distinguishing, for instance, whether impulses that arise within us are impulses of desire or inspiration, of compulsion or love. We are inclined to see feelings, knowledge, and actions that are qualitatively different as if they were all on the same level. Because we are not really awake, we ignore the hierarchy of being that exists within our own selves.

Hierarchy is a concept disdained by our culture, which imagines itself to be egalitarian and democratic. *Webster's* defines a hierarch as "a steward or keeper of sacred things." The Western notion of hierarchy has been identified with a power structure in which a class of religious professionals performs sacraments that ordinary people could not do for themselves. The hierarchy would typically be supported by the society as a whole and sometimes possess excessive economic power besides. Hierarchy is also evidenced in cults, which are typically organized around a charismatic leader who holds power over every aspect of the followers' lives. This kind of hierarchy rightfully has a bad name.

Sufism developed within a more egalitarian matrix, one that was supposed to have no priesthood—that is, no professional religious class with sacramental or economic privileges. In Islam every human being has a direct relationship with the Divine. In Sufism, however, this individual's relationship with the Divine is assisted by a sharing of mind with someone who has broken through the barrier that separates the alienated self from the wholeness of mind, which is transpersonal. Someone who can live and be in this unity with Spirit becomes a more accessible point of contact with that Spirit. The student, the teacher, the founder of the tradition or order, and the Prophet are connected in a line that carries a purified state of mind. One participates in this state of mind through a relationship of friendship and respect while gradually strengthening one's inner contact with that state. This is not a hierarchy of personal achievement, power, or sacramental privilege. Hierarchy exists in the degree to which individual hearts can embrace Spirit, but it is a hierarchy that makes one humble rather than proud. This is a hierarchy of service and responsibility. The role of a nurturing guide is not a job that a selfish person would want, because it involves a continual giving of oneself. For the sensitive person it involves an emotional price as well. The guide must experience the suffering of others and must bear the projections and demands of people who have not been fully transformed. Rūmī said, "A trainer of horses should expect to get kicked."

The guide, ideally, represents the purified state of mind. Becoming of one mind with the guide is a way of experiencing one's own essential Self. The transformed human being can be likened to a harbor that allows one to enter the ocean. Ultimately, the harbor is also the Ocean.

The Sufi guide does not proselytize or promote himself. The teacher waits to be found by those who feel a strong need for what the path offers. More than anything else, the guide is the servant of the student's yearning and can only give as much as the seeker's yearning allows.

QUALIFICATIONS OF LEADERSHIP

But how can one find someone who deserves our trust? I once asked a certain shaikh what it meant to him to be "licensed" within the tradition. He said this signifies that you have the means to pass on the teaching and that you are trusted to do it without gaining any material benefit for yourself. Sufi teachers have usually been householders with a livelihood apart from spiritual teaching. Even if sometimes they received some part of their support because they lived at a Sufi *dergāh* supported through some religious endowment and the service contributed by their dervishes, they did not allow themselves to become economically dependent on those whom they were serving. Among Sufis it is said, "The one who knows is the servant of the one who doesn't know." There can be no profit motive in sharing the knowledge of illumination. A professional class of spiritual advisors does not fit with the Truth and eventually corrupts it.

In Sufism, spiritual teaching is not a profession. On the other hand, the student should not expect that the teacher is his or her slave and that there is no reciprocal obligation. It would be presumptuous to expect this service from another human being without some form of reciprocity. Might some form of voluntary support or service be appropriate in the support of the Work itself?

In Western culture, where there is at present very little supporting this teaching, some structure for support needs to be found. If a minimal degree of organization is required to allow communication, to organize the space and time for essential activities, a certain amount of expense for management and overhead may need to be accepted. It may be necessary to cover certain expenses and to create a means by which people could *voluntarily* support the tradition, while not commercializing the teaching by charging for weekly meetings or for being accepted as an initiate of the Order.

In Islamic cultures those who wish to study spiritual subjects are supported by society as a whole. Their education is essentially free, but this does not mean that the teachers receive no compensation. They too are supported by the society at large. People recognize the need to voluntarily contribute to the founding and maintenance of spiritual institutions.

Once, when I offered to compensate a Palestinian friend for some time he would be giving to a group of us studying the Qur'ān in Arabic, he merely said, "Don't you know that in Islam knowledge isn't for sale?" We probably couldn't afford it anyway.

The modern world, however, is a commercial world. We have put a price on almost everything. In America we pay a high price to have someone listen to us. For those who have left the traditional churches and sought guidance from therapists, workshops, and seminars, the cost is not insignificant. As soon as people think they have some understanding (usually of how we can more efficiently attain our desires), they trademark a training program. People who are eager to live off God are sadly missing the point. The Divine Reality is our sustainer; it invites us to trust and surrender. The attempt to market and make a profit out of Spirit is fraught with hazards. In a lyric poem of Rūmī's that was quoted to me, this story was told: Once someone was walking through a beautiful rose garden, and the thought entered his mind, "What if I were to pick one of these roses? Would I be caught? What would the gardener do?" Just then he heard a voice say: "Why steal one rose, when I am offering you the whole garden!"

The greatest teachers I have known have invited us, their students, to their tables. They have given the best that they had to us—more, in fact, than we could have given or knew how to give in return. They have been willing to talk with us until dawn if necessary, as long as we were willing to listen. The Sufi teachers I have known were the kind of people who found joy in going hours out of their way to serve someone. Jesus washed the feet of his students; he taught them that if their Master would treat them thus, then how kindly and respectfully should they treat each other?

I once heard an American complain about her teacher because he expected to be met at the airport when he returned from long lecture tours. She questioned his sense of specialness, his right to be treated with this consideration. Some Westerners, in my experience, suffer from a sense of entitlement and do not recognize the sacrifices that are being made to bring the teaching to them.

One mature shaikh whom I know refused to allow himself to take the role of shaikh, saying, "If I am your shaikh, there will be no one to show you how to treat a teacher. Choose someone from among yourselves, and then see the kind of support and respect that I give to him or her. That will be best for you."

God manifests most clearly through a humble person, and at the same time, to play a part in the transformation of other human beings requires confidence and inner strength. In my own experience there has been a lot to learn about accepting the responsibility of power while remaining aware of my own nothingness. Strong leadership is not necessarily a denial of humility but the manifestation of this humility in energetic service. The spiritual leader is not someone who puts himself above those who are served. If one person has gone through the door before others and invites others in, this is not from superiority but from friendship. It is entirely possible that a shaikh will help to raise up individuals who will far surpass him in spiritual attainment. More than anything else, this is a special kind of friendship—one that calls forth new qualities and attainments. A shaikh is someone who is willing to become empty of himself in order to serve, and this service is more than service to individual people; it is service to the humanness in everyone. At the same time that a shaikh sees many individuals, each one equally special, he also sees *One Being* to be served.

In Sufism it is understood that there is no point to having a shaikh or shaikha unless you love and respect him or her in a spiritual way. It is this love which opens the channel to the spiritual state. Only this love and respect will enable one to accept the leader's inevitable human idiosyncrasies and limitations and allow these to appear as insignificant and even loveable frailties rather than as intolerable defects. This is not to say that a student should condone immorality in the leader, but rather that personality conflicts are easily transcended or dissolved by a mutual affection.

STUDENTS MAKE THE TEACHER

I know from my own experience that good teachers or leaders do not usually arrive ready-made. The leader needs those who are served, and the seekers have a very active role to play in the process of maturing the leader. A leader is someone we elevate in order to serve us. We give loyalty and love because this person serves us. We give to this person what is needed to get the job done. Good students make good teachers. Of course, the necessary ore needs to be there in the leader for it to be refined and put into service, but the students are also responsible for the kind of leadership they receive. In a very real sense it is they who create the guide with their own sincerity and yearning.

When a group can achieve solidarity and loyalty, which are some of the fruits of love, a respect develops among the individuals. One of the ways this solidarity is manifested is through respect for the leader. Respect paid to the leader is respect paid to the group. The leader becomes a focal point for the group because he or she *is* the group. The leader receives energy from the group and functions at his best when he is serving the needs of the group. When you see the leader, you see the group, and what you see is the focal point of this dynamic, harmonious entity that is the group. When he speaks, he doesn't speak as a personal individual as much as a point of contact of all the interrelationships within the group and within the tradition itself. Ideally, the leader represents a timeless, spaceless higher influence that is working within the group. As the maturity and refinement within the group develops, and as the individuals realize their active role in the possibility of creating this model of service, then they can help to lift this leader up to be more of service. They will get back all that they give and much more.

The leader cannot demand this respect; authentic respect must be freely given. Submission is different from subservience. Moral authority is different from the authority of raw power. The shaikh may have considerable power without necessarily wielding it. Love itself will overcome most obstacles and solve most problems.

CULTIVATING THE RELATIONSHIP WITH A GUIDE

Not only must the student accept the shaikh but, just as important, the shaikh must accept and find affection for the student. This is something that is sometimes overlooked. Many people feel they have a right to judge the teacher, that their teacher should be a Jesus or a Muhammad, without considering what kind of student they themselves are willing to be. The power of a mature human being to transmit the state of love and presence, to untie the knots within another's heart, to incinerate the subconscious impurities and complexes—this power can be blocked by the inconsiderateness, presumption, or arrogance of those who think they are on the path but who are instead in a state of narcissism, selfish independence, or unconscious resentment. Sincere submission is necessary for any benefit to be received.

The great dervish Yunus Emre said that the student places himself in the hands of the shaikh in the same way that a dead body is washed and wrapped in a clean cloth before burial! Rūmī said, "Die in love in order to be truly alive."

In my experience the relationship between student and teacher has never meant that one turns one's life over to another for a complete overhaul; rather, the student needs to cultivate a mature receptivity to the often subtle help of the teacher. Most Americans, for instance, are in great need of learning some basic manners and will not go very far on the spiritual path without developing respect and thoughtfulness.

I once heard it said that to fall out of favor with your shaikh is worse than a fall from a high building. Only those who have experienced this can know the darkness of being cut off from the spiritual protection and support that this living relationship offers.

I know of one case that was played out in a rather dramatic way; it is a story that makes the point quite well. When a man I know first became the student of a certain shaikh, he owned a small shop. In a little while it prospered, and he was able to buy the building in which it was located. Later his increasing profits enabled him to buy a neighboring building, and so on, until he owned practically the whole block. But one day this man arrived late for an important meeting with his shaikh. "Why are you late?" the shaikh asked.

"Oh, I was very busy with my shop and some phone calls, and you know how these things are."

"You were very busy, you say?" the shaikh asked softly. Well, from that time on, one business failed and then another. One building had to be sold, and then another one, until finally the man was left with the single shop he had owned when he first met his shaikh. What is the real cause of prosperity, and what is the cause of failure? Was this a punishment, a gift, or a coincidence? Was the rise and fall of this man's fortunes from his shaikh or from himself?

THE PATH OF INTENSIFIED SPIRITUAL RELATIONSHIP

Sufism, like any authentic spiritual path, has its inexpressible joy, which makes material benefits seem inconsequential. Not only is there the joy and love between the guide and the student, but there is also the joy of being in a circle of spiritual lovers. That state of being is not confined exclusively to the leader but reflects throughout the brother/sisterhood. Where many lamps are together, although each is separate, yet their light is one. Therefore the spiritual light that is ignited from the shaikh and his spiritual line is reflected from one to another, and that shared state also teaches everyone.

It is curious to me when I hear people say that they are interested in spiritual development but do not want to be involved in a group. They are willing to receive the teaching, but they are not willing to learn to love others, especially if those others do not share their own preferences, tastes, interests, and so forth. This is usually a clear sign of being stuck in one's own separateness, the very separateness that must be melted in order to know one's essential self. We cannot do the work alone; we need to learn from the experience of others; we need others to show us ourselves and to help us become complete.

This melting into affection is not the dissolving of one's boundaries but the expansion of one's boundaries. In other words, boundaries, whether subtle or obvious, are to be respected. The ethics of the path are very clear: one must never interfere with another's will, not through any kind of conditioning, not even through subtle suggestion. The subtle change that begins to take place in a group is that one's sense of self begins to change and expand. One begins to feel responsible for others as if their well-being were one's own. Muhammad said, "The faithful are like a single body. If one part hurts, the whole body feels the pain."

One of the critical points in our group's development came about because I was not recognizing the need for others to express their pain, to share more of the everyday pain of life as well as the pain of being reared in our culture, and to look at factors such as low self-esteem and self-doubt. A lot of this pain found expression during a period when I was away. What could not come out while I was leading the meetings came out when the group was on its own. It had been my tendency to focus our attention on spiritual work, on developing remembrance and inspiration, but I had not fully recognized that some people were not able to sustain that kind of work because their fundamental wounds had not been recognized. I had been trained in an environment in which it was taught that "a dervish is all courage," that one is very careful not to speak from the concerns of one's ego, but from one's essence.

The Sufi system developed in a culture and times that were much less wounding to a person's soul. People in our time typically begin from a different point than the seekers of the past. We cannot assume that people are beginning with a healthy, integrated ego. Much more often, we have to begin with a wounded ego that has not known that it is loved. In our times and in our culture, the needs of psychological healing and spiritual development are interdependent. Until people know that their pain is heard and recognized, until they know that they are loved, it is much harder to let go of contraction and separation and to come into who they really are.

Work within a group is a path of intensified relationship through which our own personal and unconscious obstacles will be shown to us, both in relation to the leader and to one's brothers and sisters on the path. Everything that comes up needs to be recognized and washed clean by love.

The Prophet Muhammad said, "The best of my people will enter paradise not because of their achievements, but because of the Mercy of God and their being satisfied with little for themselves and their extreme generosity toward others." Muhammad not only enjoined the faithful to love each other but also taught this love by example. His actions and words were faithfully recorded and have become a model for human kindness and solidarity.

The Sufi saints, such as Abū Yazid Bistāmī, continued this line of teaching through countless stories like the following:

A man asked Abū Yazid, "Show me the shortest way to reach Allāh Most High."

Abū Yazid replied, "Love those who are loved by God and make yourself lovable to them so that they love you, because Allāh looks into the hearts of those whom He loves seventy times a day. Perhaps He will find your name in the heart of the one He loves and He will love you, too, and forgive your mistakes."

The subtle, nondualistic teaching behind this saying may be that God's love is not other than nor separate from the love that is reflected between two hearts—two or more mirrors reflecting one light among themselves.

THE HEALTHY SPIRITUAL FAMILY

It has seemed to me as if one can become impregnated through contact with an authentic tradition, and that something wants to be born in us through the spiritual process—a child of the heart. An immaculate conception—that is, without the aid of an authentic tradition of enlightenment—is theoretically possible but extremely rare. If we do conceive this child of the heart and carry it full term, there is still the rearing and education of this child. Here, a "family" is vital. The group becomes the milieu in which the soul experiences its fulfillment and grows into maturity.

A family can be very close, but it should not be cut off from the wider society. Even one's participation in a Sufi group should not be carried too far. While it should be among the highest priorities in one's life, it is not meant to displace the relationships with one's own family, community, and livelihood. This is a way of spiritual attainment within everyday life, not apart from it.

Continuing this metaphor, we might ask whether there are any safeguards that would prevent dysfunction within such a spiritual family. Most of the problems that have arisen recently among groups where abuses of power have been recognized can be traced to the disregard of the ethical matrix that got left behind (as in the authentic Eastern traditions) or never existed (as in some New Age experiments). The conception and maturing of the child of the heart take place within the structure of a revealed, sacred law, an ethical matrix that is the outer protection of the inner truth. The purpose of such a law is both to safeguard the harmony within society and to preserve the best conditions for one's own spiritual advancement. This is not to say that the "Law" is rigid, absolute, black and white. There is a saying of Muhammad that is quoted by Rūmī: "Follow your heart, even if the religious judge offers a different opinion." But we should do our best to measure our behavior against certain objective principles.

In addition, some Sufi orders have specific rituals that support the moral integrity of the group. The Bektashi tradition of Turkey, for example, while having a reputation for a disregard of some social conventions, nevertheless has some of the highest ethical standards of any Sufi order. For instance, it is incumbent on every member to pass before an annual peer review. Members of the group are encouraged to bring up any moral inadequacies or issues that need attention before this public review. This annual review is the last chance to bring something up or hold their tongues until Judgment Day. Even the shaikh is not exempted. This review process has the effect of airing grievances and minimizing negative undercurrents within the brother/sisterhood.

Another practice found in certain Sufi orders is the asking of three questions before beginning the collective worship, zikr. These questions go something like this:

Is there anyone in this group who has been wronged by another and wishes to bring this before us?

Is there any married person here who is experiencing difficulties that they would like to put before this group for counsel and support?

Is there anyone who has any need, material or otherwise, that they would like us to be aware of?

For worship to reach its higher levels of refinement, emotional and egoistic obstacles, whether real or imagined, need to be removed. The whole process is maintained by openness and freedom from any ill-feeling within the group. The solution is to bring the pain or the difficulty forward within this atmosphere of trust and affection. When this is done, it is amazing how these things can be dissolved or transformed, allowing the energy to flow freely once again. The openness of everyone in the circle is important in creating a beautifully resonating system. Everyone must be working on him- or herself to be a better reflector or conductor of the energies of transformation.

THE REAL SUBMISSION

The group is the environment where the often rebellious ego can begin to have a taste of authentic servanthood and submission. In actuality, all submission is to one's higher Self. The only reason to submit to a teacher is because that teacher is in submission to what you wish to submit to, but haven't yet learned how. The other members of the group are also working toward that deeper submission.

When one respects a teacher, a certain receptivity and cooperation develops. I have been taught that this submission and trust are exhibited by the students' having only one response to the shaikh whether they are praised or damned, and that response is, "Thank you." No arguments, no rationalizations, no defenses, no justifications, just "Thank you." We need to maintain this quality of gratitude. In Sufism, there is a phrase, "Eyvallāh," which means something like "Yes, God," "So be it," "Amen," or "All good is from God." It is a typical response when one is offered something, when one loses something, when one is praised, when one is criticized. Transformation is learning what lies behind this *Eyvallāh*. If, for instance, someone's feelings are hurt by the leader, there may be a reason for this. Whatever is done by the guide is theoretically done for the benefit and well-being of the students. This leader is certainly a thoughtful and aware person who knows very well that he has said something that might sting. Maybe he is teaching something; for instance, he could be highlighting the student's narcissism or vanity. But even if what was said or done came out of some weakness of the leader in the moment, if this person, who is undoubtedly well known to the leader, complies readily with, "Eyvallāh, thank you," the leader will know that the student's egoism is diminishing and that he is capable of learning. If the leader made a mistake, he himself will be touched by this as well. In either case, the student will gain, because the false self is being diminished. Sometimes the leader may appear to be indifferent or even rude to a student. If this person cannot say, "Eyvallāh," it means that he or she is not cut out for this training.

Perhaps this sounds dangerous in light of the abuse of submission at the hands of certain cult-entrepreneurs and self-proclaimed enlightened beings, but the dangers of being in the hands of your own ego are also great. The path of transformation is the path of submission, but this submission is done not out of self-abnegation but out of love. Unless one is willing to comply with this discipline, one might as well find something else to do, because one is not ready for this process, and nothing will be gained without this submission and love.

I was once in a situation where I felt the need to leave a teaching after an investment of some years. At the time, I struggled over my reasons for leaving, and this struggle postponed for two years the choice I inevitably made. It seems that I made the right decision—perhaps I could have made it sooner. So I would never suggest that others ignore their conscience, to endure too much enigmatic and morally questionable behavior because "it must be a test," or to tolerate a situation that feels like imprisonment or dependency.

There will, of course, be times when we have to do what our ego does not enjoy, or when the ego needs to be stripped of its satisfactions and face its own will to rebel or be in control. Any real teacher will help to create these situations, too. But the criterion of transformation is love. If this process is going on within a milieu of love, it can be trusted.

This does not mean that one is there because one desperately needs love, or needs a surrogate parent or family. It means that love has created the situation. It means that love is not the goal, but the cause of the situation.

I once asked a dervish, "Do we ever reach a point when we no longer need to be loved?"

"Yes, when we love," he said.

The submission learned in the context of Sufi training is ultimately to one's own essential Self, to the core of one's own being, which is love and which is naturally and spontaneously in submission to God. According to a Sufi saying, "The moon is a dervish before the sun, and yet among the stars of the night it stands as the greatest light." Submission to that sun confers a great power, because it frees one from the slavery to many other things.

The cultural obstacles to realizing the ideal situation of Sufi education are formidable in the West. American spiritual seekers are especially recalcitrant when it comes to supporting and respecting their leaders. The axiom that "All people are created equal" has come to mean something more like "We are all the same, each of us has his or her own truth, and no one is superior to anyone else." And yet, generally, the more accomplished a person is, the more he or she is willing to acknowledge the need to submit to a learning situation without feeling devalued in the process.

On the other hand, the West with its traditions of openness, freedom, and liberal humanism can and must contribute to the revitalization of a stagnant Sufism that has lost touch with its own spirit of emancipation. The sheer abrasiveness of the West can polish the rust from the mirror of Sufism.

Neverthless, despite the many obstacles, I have seen many North Americans mature in this process and discover new qualities within themselves that surpassed anything they could have imagined. The power of Love is waiting to do its work, and if we stubbornly independent and isolated people would humble ourselves enough to overcome our separateness, our suspicion, and our pride, the miracle of unity and affection would still be possible. According to a Sufi saying, "Grapes ripen in the sun smiling at one another."

The Way of the Dervish

A DERVISH IS AN APPRENTICE, ONE WHO IS LEARNING THE profession that will provide eternal livelihood. This profession is still taught in certain "schools of higher learning." While there are many skills that can be self-taught or learned alone, the skills of dervishhood are learned by being in relationship to a shaikh, or guide, and within a spiritual family, a Sufi circle. There will always be much to learn on one's own, through one's own efforts, and within one's own understanding. The final responsibility, of course, lies with ourselves, and in reality there is no intermediary between us and our God. And yet one can no more become a dervish alone than one can become a lover alone.

People will dedicate the whole of their lives to becoming an accomplished musician or a professional athlete. In doing so they will have to organize the whole of their lives around this one master desire. A dervish is one who has made Truth his or her master desire and is willing to bring all other desires and aims into alignment with this aim. It is possible to make Sufism a pastime, one interest among others, but that does not make one a dervish. It is fine to read widely and become acquainted with various traditions, but to be a Sufi is much more than to have a preference for reading Sufi books or listening to Sufi music.

The price of being a dervish is one's whole life, a total commitment of one's life energies. Fortunately, in our tradition it does not mean the abandonment of a productive and socially useful livelihood, nor the renunciation of marriage and family, but it does mean that everything we are involved with will be understood and arranged from the perspective of our essential spiritual intention. Certain lifestyles may not be consistent with our intention; certain forms of livelihood may not be appropriate in light of the more stringent requirements of remembering God with each breath. We may find that we are not asked to sacrifice everything, that the Way does not contradict our essential humanity. We may discover that God is the Friend, a patient, generous and compassionate Friend, but gradually we learn that we ourselves must withhold nothing.

To become a dervish we pledge ourselves to a shaikh and a lineage. This reaches hand over hand all the way to Allāh. Our pledge, our obedience, our commitment is to Allāh, and the shaikh is a link. Why should there be any intermediary at all? This is a very good question. Actually there is no intermediary if the shaikh is a real shaikh and if one's pledge is sincere. The shaikh actually is the evidence of God's mercy and generosity, making grace more tangible, more immediate. The shaikh does not gather power or privilege for himself or herself but is the servant of the yearning of the dervish's heart. The shaikh may also be the challenger of the dervish's egoism, calling us to surpass our timidity, our fears, our comfortable complacency. The shaikh may be the one to say, "Come into this fire; it will not burn you."

No shaikh is perfect, and it is particularly in his *function* as shaikh that he may sometimes disappear and become a pure medium for divine grace or wisdom. It is the dervish who helps to create the shaikh, and both are in the process of learning from the relationship. It must be remembered that before becoming a shaikh, one had to be a dervish, and one never stops being a dervish.

One day Mevlānā and Shams were sitting together in spiritual intimacy and conversation. A messenger entered with the news that a certain shaikh in a distant village had died. The community was asking that a shaikh be sent to succeed their late teacher. Mevlānā said, "Send so-and-so and let him be your new shaikh." After the messenger had left, however, Shams turned to Mevlānā and said, "We're lucky they only asked for a shaikh. If they had asked for a dervish, one of us would have had to go!"

Spiritual seekers are typically people who have learned to question conventional reality. Most spiritual seekers have experienced a loss of "blind faith" and are in search of answers to legitimate questions. Our postmodern culture has also suffered a loss of faith, resulting in a pervasive cynicism and inability to approach Truth innocently. While we should look quite critically at any spiritual path or teacher before committing ourselves, we shouldn't allow the cynicism and rebelliousness of our times to prevent us from seeing what humility and trust can offer. Once we have decided to play the master game of self-transformation, we must do it wholeheartedly.

In my own case it took quite a while for me to understand the value of cultivating a relationship with a teacher. Although I didn't realize it at the time, I was a typical product of my own culture, which has a fundamental mistrust of and disrespect for leadership and authority. Perhaps I was simply too rebellious and critical. Now I can look back on my own relationships with my teachers with some remorse for the disappointments and pain I caused them through my insensitivity and lack of awareness. It is easy to forget that the shaikh is a servant more than a master.

The shaikh holds the keys to a treasure the seeker cannot really understand. He may be able to unlock the treasure within the dervish's heart, but how likely is he to do this for someone who is half-hearted, ungrateful, or full of resistance, who lacks humility or respect? The dervish's intention should always be to allow a sincere love for the shaikh to grow and deepen. Sometimes the outer respect is the best that can be offered, but we must realize that we can fool ourselves more easily than we can deceive others and especially our shaikh.

What is required in this relationship is *rabita*, a connection of love, which allows everything that the mature one has to pass to the other person. When there is real love between a shaikh and a dervish, the dervish comes into resonance with the wisdom and light of the shaikh, and the shaikh carries some of the burden of the dervish. A shaikh needs to be strong enough to do this, and this is possible only with the help of God and the lineage, especially the *Pir,* the Completed

Human Being from whom the particular order derives its *baraka*, or grace.

There is more than one kind of real shaikh, in addition to the self-appointed teachers who can do some good and much harm. There are shaikhs who serve a kind of managerial function in dervish circles. They need to have a certain natural authority, experience, and knowledge; they must be trusted not to use the position to gain any kind of advantage for themselves. In their managerial capacity they are useful in the preparatory work of dervish training, provided they are backed up by a real source of *baraka*.

Then there are those shaikhs who have the permission of the unseen world, who have true spiritual authority. Such a shaikh not only has experience, wisdom, and knowledge, but also serves as a channel for the transformative energies of the tradition, both in group activities like the zikr and in relationship to individual dervishes. In order for this individual connection to work at its highest potential, the dervish needs to cultivate a spiritual connection with the shaikh. The shaikh is a "wireless transformer" connected to the powerhouse of the Pir.

In the storybook version of shaikh and dervish, the dervish is involved in a period of closely supervised experiences under the watchful eyes of the shaikh. While it would be wonderful to have such a shaikh in one's life to listen to one's problems and answer one's questions, such a situation is rare.

A Sufi shaikh is likely to have a family and a profession and rarely has the time to give such personal attention to many people. Unless one somehow shares in his mission, works by his side, or has reached a high degree of surrender and can give all one's time to the service of the shaikh, one's relationship will more likely be through attending regular meetings and keeping the heart connection active at other times.

Given the rarity of real shaikhs, especially in the Western world, one should be thankful if one has found a connection even at a distance to an effective Sufi lineage. In reality, the dervish's connection is beyond the tangible matrix of space and time, beyond even the conscious mind. What needs to flow to the student will flow if the student knows how to cultivate that connection and has surrendered to it. In the physical world we are under many limitations of time and space. In some cases you may see your shaikh in the tangible world only rarely. In the world of the conscious mind, you may cultivate a positive bond and even converse inwardly with your teacher. At the subconscious level of the heart, however, the shaikh's benevolent energy will be working on you continuously. As Yunus Emre says, "Ever since the glance of the mature one fell upon me, nothing has been a problem." There are many legitimate issues regarding authority and its abuse that have occurred as Westerners have uncritically accepted other traditions, especially those untied from their traditional ethical moorings. In some cases we have been led to believe that outrageous and abusive behavior from the teacher is part of the training. One cannot follow an absolute rule, but generally the stronger tactics are reserved for the strong and devoted dervishes, and only after the greatest bond of love has been made certain. Rūmī's own teacher, Shams of Tabrīz, was a stringent master and once said, "My wrath causes a seventy-year-long unbeliever to become a believer, and a believer to become a saint!"

We should bear in mind, however, that abusive conduct was never the method of Muhammad. On the contrary, he showed profound respect to people, always being the first to say hello, jumping up to greet the humblest people. When Muhammad set this example, he was teaching a lesson for generations to come.

Shaikhs may also challenge a person's conditioning or belief structure, may even appear to be doing something unethical or harmful, as in the case of Khidr and Moses in the Qur'ān (Surah Kahf). Khidr is the immortal "green man" who appears to those who need his guidance. Moses is considered by tradition to be one of the four strongest prophets. Yet when he attempted to accompany Khidr on a journey, he was subjected to circumstances that he could not fathom, especially since they seemed to contradict his notion of justice and morality. Eventually the true significance and background of the questionable events was revealed to Moses by Khidr. If the shaikh appears to do or require something that contradicts one's idea of the good, or moral norms, or the religious law, the reason for this should be made clear before too long, as it was in the case of Moses and Khidr. No real shaikh, however, would keep a student in a state of prolonged moral ambivalence.

The relationship between a shaikh and a dervish is one of the most sacred bonds any human being can experience. To find a real shaikh, and to be accepted by one, is a great gift. Shaikhs are taught that if one of their dervishes were to be excluded from the gates of paradise, the shaikh, too, must remain outside. If a shaikh accepts you into his heart and you can accept the shaikh into yours, it is in order that hand in hand you both will go to God. Value that relationship as you would an infant placed in your arms: in the beginning it may require great care and sacrifice, perhaps even sleepless nights, but eventually, after tests, difficulties, and joys, that infant relationship may mature into a being of strength and great beauty, and the generations of the Way will continue.

In the End Is Our Beginning

A STORY

This story, remembered by our friend Shaikh Daud Bellak, was told on several occasions in our Shaikh Suleyman Dede's house when visitors were present and there was much discussion about the Way.

A LONG TIME AGO, IN A MEVLEVI COMMUNITY (*tekke*), THERE was a certain student (*murīd*) of the Master Jelal whose duty it was to collect wood from the forest for the fires of the kitchen.

Each morning he would leave for the forest, and eventually he returned with arms full of wood he had collected—long and short, bent and gnarled, thick and thin. Time went on, and each day he carried out his assigned task with dedication and the sacred names upon his lips.

One day the Shaikh of the tekke called to the murīd from his window, where he had seen the student dervish doing his work. "Mehmet!" called the Shaikh. "What are you carrying?"

"I am bringing wood for the kitchen fires," came the reply. The Shaikh then asked him to come closer.

"Let us see the wood," requested the Shaikh, and the murīd showed him his morning's work. "These sticks are bent and distorted," said the Shaikh. "We want only straight wood for our kitchen fire. From now on when you collect your wood, you must ensure that each piece of wood is straight and not twisted like these!"

"Eyvallāh!" replied the murīd, and went on about his work.[1] From that day onward, nothing but straight wood was brought into the kitchen and used in the fire.

The years passed by, and the murīd grew in the Way, always carrying out his duties in the tekke with a good heart. His beard had begun to turn gray and his step was slower. One day the Shaikh called him to his rooms.

"Your *chille* [period of training; literally: ordeal] here is finished," he said, "and you must now leave and find your way in the world. May God guide your steps."

"Eyvallāh!" replied the murīd, and he kissed the Shaikh's hand in farewell.

The years passed by, until one day the murīd returned to the tekke. His clothes were tattered, his hair was matted, and his back was bent. He came to the door of the Shaikh's garden and, finding it open, entered the small courtyard. He knocked at the door, and the Shaikh's wife came to greet him.

"My goodness, how you have changed!" she exclaimed. "I hardly recognized you!"

"It has been very difficult," he said, "but I must now see my Shaikh."

"He has gone out for a while but will not be long. He is now nearly blind and walks with difficulty, with a stick." The murīd asked her permission to sit in the sun and rest until the Shaikh's return, then lay down and fell asleep.

A little later, with a faltering step and the tap-tap-tap of his stick, the elderly Shaikh entered his courtyard. His stick struck the sleeping murīd, and the Shaikh called out, "Who's there, who is it?" The murīd fell upon his face and, kissing the feet of his Shaikh, cried out with tears and pain, "O my Lord, my Master, it is I, your murīd whom you sent away those many years ago!"

---

[1] One day Daud had asked Dede: "What is the meaning of *Eyvallāh*?" He replied: "One *Eyvallāh* is one *il Allāh*." (*Il Allāh* is the second part of the foremost Islamic phrase: *la illāha il Allāh*: There is no god but God.)

The elderly man helped the murīd to his feet, kissed his cheeks, and said, "Ahh, my son, come sit here and tell me."

The murīd burst into tears again, saying, "These years have been wretched. I am broken, there is nowhere for me in this world, God has taken away my voice, I can earn no living, and now I am old and have nowhere to go. Please, I beg of you, allow me to come again to the tekke that I may spend my last days in peace and die here!"

"Ahh, my son, my son," replied the Shaikh. "Now your chille is finished and you may go. God will make your way open."

And the murīd left again, but now his voice had acquired a new quality. Eventually he became one of the great preachers of God's Holy Word and lived in the Light for many years.

There is a saying in our tradition: *Chillemiz hic bitmiyor; biterken gine basliyor.* "Our chille never ends; in the end is our beginning."

Spiritual Conversation

PIRITUAL CONVERSATION, OR *SOHBET*, IS THE HEART OF group practice. It is the connecting point of all the other activities: individual practice, group remembrance, music, study, social life, ethics. It is the primary relationship with the shaikh and the context in which people come to know one another. It is the activity that connects and makes sense of all others.

Sohbet is not sermon or lecture, but discourse, storytelling, encounter, and spiritual courtship. It is how God's lovers share and intensify their love.

There are Sufi circles in which sohbet is the primary practice. Among the Melameti, the people of "blame," who have minimized the importance of practices, including ritual prayer and group zikr, conversation with "a mature one" becomes the means of sharing the state of attainment. Much of the Sufi education takes place through communication that results in a profound sharing of minds. In some circles that I have witnessed, the shaikh offers a monologue of storytelling, poetry, quotations from the Holy Books[1], moral advice, and

---

[1] The Sufi tradition explicitly recognizes four Holy Books: the Torah, Psalms, Gospel (words spoken by Jesus), and Qur'ān. It is also understood that the Divine has communicated with countless communities, giving their revelations a sacred status even if the communication may have been corrupted over time.

143

spiritual encouragement, while the group members absorb the knowledge and the energy it contains. Rūmī's *Discourses* (*Fīhi mā fīhi*) are a
wonderful record of this kind of teaching. This kind of sohbet is most
often a rambling monologue that sometimes goes on into the early
hours of the morning.

When this kind of conversation is effective, it is because the speaker
is tapping into the subconscious complexes of the listeners and unty-
ing the psychological and/or spiritual knots that exist there. Often the
listener feels as if the shaikh is speaking to them quite personally, and,
of course, whether he is conscious of it or not, this is what is happening. Actually, the shaikh need not be conscious of it—that would take
more awareness and energy than is necessary to do the job. It is
enough that he become relatively empty and centered in the present,
and then what is reflected in the mirror of his heart, what enters his
consciousness, will be a reflection of what is in the hearts of the listeners.

Because the shaikh, if he is a real shaikh, has reached a state of inner
harmony and connection with Spirit, this state will dissolve many
problems and bring peace to the hearts of the listeners. Certain problems simply cease to exist at a certain level of consciousness. It is said
that a shaikh can untie the knots of the students, but those very same
knots may be retied out of unconscious habit. Gradually, however, as
people have been steeped in the knowledge and baraka of the tradition, the state transmitted in sohbet endures.

There is another level of sohbet—an encounter in which true dialogue is possible—that can be superior to the typical monologue. We
shall assume that all the qualities of the earlier form of sohbet are in
place—a mature shaikh and receptive listeners—and add to this a
more developed pedagogy whose purpose is to elicit communication
and understanding. In this case, instead of being merely passive recipients of the state and wisdom of the shaikh, there is an attempt to
develop a degree of understanding and self-expression in the students.
Such teachers follow more of a Socratic method, exploring a specific
theme, responding to questions, and questioning the students themselves. In this method, the questions asked must be grounded in awakened observation of oneself and life, not in theories and

generalizations. The teacher may introduce a theme from time to time, or suggest a line of inquiry or observation that will highlight certain experiences in the student's life. The sharing of experience in the group then adds to each person's knowledge and experience of a theme. The teacher's role in this approach is to subtly direct the student's attention to neglected areas of inquiry and to offer encouragement and support.

These questions and answers reiterate that the Sufi process of transformation is one in which a student learns a state of pure being from one who is in that state, but eventually progresses to the point of living and being from his or her own self, a self that is relatively free of self-images and from attachments to interests, activities, and dependencies that remove one from the presence of God. The student gradually grows into a kind of autonomy of pure being, no longer dependent on the guide, while along the way he or she has the joy of companionship with other souls who are also maturing in this pure being.

Some schools of Sufism place a higher value on understanding than on mere modeling of behavior or attainment of states. Of course, not all people need this level of education or are necessarily capable of it, but where it is possible, the kind of development that is produced is higher, in the sense that people who have matured under these circumstances not only attain a certain level of being but can also help others to understand and attain the same level. I believe there is a great need for this kind of pedagogy, especially among those people, East or West, who have been educated in a modern university system. For one thing, they have more questions and must receive the answers if their intellects are to be satisfied and allowed to rest. One could even say they have a right to have their questions answered. Unfortunately, this kind of pedagogy is all too rare in the Sufi circles of the East, many of which were designed to serve a kind of people in which individuality was not highly developed. We can see evidence, however, in some classical texts of this kind of relationship, especially among the Khwāja-gan[2] of Central Asia.

---

[2] A Sufi lineage that existed in Central Asia from the eleventh until the fifteenth century. See J. G. Bennett, *The Masters of Wisdom* (Santa Fe, N.M.: Bennett Books, 1996).

It has been my experience that Westerners need quite a bit of preparation to engage in true sohbet. The principles of sohbet run counter to much of the individualism and "speak your truth" mentality that our culture often encourages. To "speak your truth" is, of course, the aim in sohbet, but learning to discern whether speech and inquiry come from the intellect and opinion or from the heart is a necessary prerequisite.

In order to realize the potential of true sohbet, it is necessary to maintain an active listening and keep oneself out of the way in order to learn to attend. Without the proper quality of attention, it would be easy to drift off. Sohbet helps to develop a sustained attentiveness in the processing of ideas. Something vast opens up and connections begin to be made; one can absorb a lot of essential material. Sometimes we have to work to contain our enthusiasm to monopolize the group's attention. We learn to weigh what really is important.

The way this is most often accomplished involves a clear understanding within the group that we have not come together for an exchange of opinions. It is necessary, first of all, to begin in a state of presence, usually after some preparatory inner work: meditation, inner exercises, and the like.

The conversation is understood to be conducted or led by the shaikh, or whoever by agreement leads instead. Usually a theme or subject is specified, and when it is, the group should remember what it is. Sometimes the themes come from the inspired literature of the tradition or the Holy Books. Sometimes they are related to very practical tasks of how to develop greater presence in life. This is not an occasion for free association and moving unintentionally from one topic to another, unless that is specifically called for.

By having a theme, a line of inquiry, it becomes possible to go deeply into the subject. All paths should eventually lead to the center, and that is also the significant point. Especially nowadays, people need to develop the ability to follow a line of inquiry. There is a moment when you have enough knowledge so that you are not just absorbing material but are bringing critical faculties to bear. Different individuals will contribute different experiences and points of view, and this, too, is part of the value of working in a group. It is the shaikh, however, who should invite people to speak as they indicate a wish to contribute. He may choose to respond to the student's words, or someone else may respond, but always after having received the recognition of the shaikh or sohbet leader.

One important ground rule is that the time be used for the sharing of actual experience with the theme at hand, avoiding conjecture, generalizations, philosophizing, intellectualizing. The point is always to learn to speak from the heart, from the depths of one's sincerity, and not from the superficial personality.

A certain dynamic tension is created in this process. Some people may find this process unnecessarily formal. Some will chafe under what they imagine to be the repressiveness of the setup. Usually, such people are themselves self-repressing types who project upon the situation or the shaikh responsibility for what they are feeling.

It should always be made clear that everyone is welcome to speak and eloquence is not necessarily what is to be strived for as much as honesty and concreteness. Certain kinds of people will feel inhibited by the imagined requirement that certain subjects are "correct" and others are not, but there is no subject that is taboo.

It is true that there is a formality in sohbet, a subtle discipline that is encouraged. It is equally true that this discipline includes a nonjudgmental perspective. Everyone in the circle should be in such a state of presence that any falseness will be all too obvious. Presence creates a mirror in which our actions are more clearly reflected, and yet everything possible should be done to prevent an artificial self-consciousness, a second-guessing of oneself, from developing. The best way to do this is to remind everyone that this conversation happens in a context of love and friendship. The root meaning of *sohbet* is *hubb*, love or affection.

There is also a place for more informal sharing within a Sufi group. We have found it useful to regularly break into smaller groups in which people can share their hearts as equal human beings with as little formality as possible. We also have tea together and a light social time at the end of an evening meeting. There is a need for more than one kind of sharing.

Sohbet is a tool of self-knowledge. It is the structure and process that allow this even more than the content. People learn to keep their attention on the process at hand, to keep ego out of the way. Sohbet develops great powers of active listening. Something quite extraordinary develops in a circle of spiritual friends who can maintain this subtle discipline of conversation. Sometimes there are long silences, as there is no felt need to fill the emptiness. Sometimes the shaikh poses questions and stimulates people to deeper levels of inquiry. Ideally, sohbet is a multileveled experience. A skilled leader will meet people where they are but will also direct them toward the highest level of understanding possible. Spiritual conversation does not address itself to the lowest common denominator. Ours is very much a tradition in which the power of the word as a living source of grace is acknowledged.

The Courtesy of the Path

THE SUFIS CREATED A SYSTEM OF HUMAN DEVELOPMENT grounded in love and using the power of love to awaken and transform human beings. Rūmī taught that it is everyone's potential to master the art of loving. Love is the answer to the problem of human existence.

The way to God passes through servanthood. The point is to love and be connected with others in that love. The form of Sufi work is typically a group, or spiritual guild. The Sufis created a milieu in which human love was so strong that it naturally elevated itself to the level of cosmic love. All forms of love eventually lead to spiritual love. "*'Āshq olsun,*" they say in Turkish: "May it become love." The Sufis cultivated a kindness and refinement in which love fermented into a fine wine. They encouraged service to humanity as an expression of the love they felt. They accepted a rigorous discipline in order to keep the fire of love burning strongly.

> The porter runs to the heavy load and takes it from others,
> knowing burdens are the foundation of ease
> and bitter things the forerunners of pleasure.
> See the porters struggle over the load!
> It's the way of those who see the truth of things.

Paradise is surrounded by what we dislike;
the fires of hell are surrounded by what we desire.

—RŪMĪ, M, II, 1834–37

One of the most important guiding principles in the Sufi way of life is *adab,* which can be translated as courtesy, respect, appropriate behavior. Adab is not mere formality; it helps to create the context in which we develop our humanness. Every situation and relationship has its own adab: between students on the path, in relation to family members and elders, in relation to one's shaikh. Every level of being also has its adab, including coming into the presence of Truth (al-Haqq).

Muhammad said: "None of you will have authentic faith until your hearts are made right, nor will your hearts be made right until your tongues be made right, nor will your tongues be made right until your actions be made right."

As one begins to become aware of the benefits and possibilities of adab, it becomes strikingly clear how much has been lost in contemporary culture in the name of some hypothetical personal freedom and individuality. When a dervish steps over the threshold into a Sufi tekke, he leaves the "world" (*dunyā*) and its concerns behind. He never steps *on* the threshold, but over it. The tekke is the school of love. We come there to observe, listen, and learn, and to practice service—not to pursue the ambitions of the world, not to satisfy or promote our own egos, nor to consume exciting "spiritual" experiences.

It is recommended to arrive at the tekke in a state of ablution—this can consist of taking a shower shortly beforehand. It's good to have a clean breath and body. One might even consider what one eats before a gathering. If some have the fragrance of musk and roses, while others smell of garlic and onions, the atmosphere suffers. Wearing modest, clean, and simple clothes is a sign of self-respect. We are coming to a place and occasion of worship—not to a sporting event or a nightclub.

It is important that we arrive at least a little before the actual time of the meeting—ten minutes early is recommended. Americans may need to learn that it is not *necessary* to give an obligatory hug to everyone—especially before the meeting, when there may be little time. Once the meeting has begun, our focus is on the process that has begun. Latecomers should find a place to sit if there is room in the circle—but without disturbance of anyone's meditation. At the end of zikr, we greet the people to our right and left by kissing their hands and giving thanks. It is intended, however, for this to be a simple greeting, not an extended meditation.

Anyone sponsoring a newcomer to the tekke should first, if possible, introduce him or her to the appropriate people. Traditionally there was what was called the *meydanji-bashi*, who would be both the keeper of the sacred space and a kind of host who would assist newcomers further, if necessary, and also introduce them to the shaikh and his wife.

The life of the tekke brings us into relationship with people whom we might not choose to be with in the everyday world, and yet slowly we come to understand that every relationship is important and has been provided as an opportunity to know ourselves and purify our hearts. This circle of lovers is learning to manifest the reality of Oneness (tawhīd), the reality of brotherhood/sisterhood/fellowship. We must treat each other not just as family but even better than most families treat each other. It may be that at the tekke we learn how to treat our own family as they ought to be treated.

We learn to observe, to control our impulses when that is called for, and to lose our "selves" when that is called for. We learn to behave as if everyone else is of a higher station than ourselves. Our conversation is centered on God and coming into harmony with God and each other. Gossip or backbiting is one of the worst actions any seeker can indulge in—not only the speaking of it but the listening to it as well. Backbiting was defined by the Prophet Muhammad as saying anything behind a person's back that would displease them (whether it is true or not). He said that backbiting or gossip is worse than ten adulteries, or like eating a corpse!

Since we are attempting to bring ourselves into alignment with Reality, we will face many tests, and it is inevitable that there will be some interpersonal tensions from time to time. Adab helps us to avoid some of the destructive behaviors that could disturb or even destroy relationships in a Sufi *halka* (circle).

A special relationship exists between the dervish and his or her shaikh. The respect and affection that develops results in consideration and attentiveness to the shaikh, especially during meetings. The shaikh is the one who sets the tone of the circle and guides the discourse. Ideally, in his function as shaikh he is like an empty center who responds to the innermost needs of the circle. He perceives the spiritual winds, trims the sails, and sets the course of the boat.

We may not always agree with our shaikh. Tradition advises that we take and apply what is useful or meaningful but do not forget those words we could not entirely agree with or understand, and keep them accessible. It may be that one day, far from the dervish circle and the shaikh, we will find in the words that were rejected something important.

According to my observations of Arab, Turk, Persian, Pakistani, Indonesian, African, and Western Sufis, adab seems to be one of the constants of Sufi interaction. I have tried to distill some principles from the various forms of adab that I have witnessed in various Sufi gatherings. Our possibilities together on this path would be served by increasing our awareness of some of these principles:

To be straightforward with sincerity and truthfulness.

To be aware of and have regret for our own faults, rather than finding fault with others.

To be free from the preoccupation with and worry, vanity, and ambition over the world and the worldly.

To be indifferent to the praise or blame of the general public.

To do what one does for Allāh's sake—not out of desire for reward or fear of punishment.

To adopt an appropriate humility and invisibility in public and in the meetings of the dervishes.

To serve the good of one's brothers and sisters with all one's physical and other resources.

To seek to heal any wound one may have caused to another, and to correct any misunderstanding within three days, if possible.

To know that no good will come out of the expression of anger or *excessive* hilarity.

To be patient with difficulties.

To be indifferent to favor or benefit for oneself, for "receiving one's due."

To be free of spiritual envy and ambition, including the desires to lead or teach.

To strive to increase one's knowledge of Sufism (including Qur'ān, Hadīth, and the wisdom of the saints).

To be willing to struggle with one's ego as much as it prevents one from following proper adab, and to realize that the greatest ally is Love.

To have a shaikh whom one loves and is loved by, and to cultivate this relationship.

To accept suggestions and even criticism from one's shaikh with gratitude and nondefensiveness. (The proper response is always "Eyvallāh"—"All good comes from God.")

To keep no secrets from one's shaikh.

To not reveal any extraordinary states that occur during one's worship or practice, except to one's shaikh.

To consult one's shaikh over major decisions in life, including journeys.

To do neither less nor more than the practices suggested by one's shaikh (although to ask for more is always permitted).

To seek instead to make one's practices more and more inwardly sincere, rather than outwardly apparent.

To realize that one's shaikh is a human being with his or her own limitations; he or she has some states that are inspired and some states that are not. Yet if there is enough love between dervish and shaikh, the limitations of personality will be gracefully overcome.

As a friend of ours, Shaikh Tosun Bayrak al-Jerrahi, said, "As difficult as it may be to find a perfect shaikh, it is more difficult to be a minimal dervish."

In one of the earliest Sufi texts, *Kashf al-Mahjūb* by Hujwīrī, Abū Hafs Haddād Nayshāburi is quoted: "Sufism, in its entirety, consists of various forms of adab. Each moment, each station, and each state has its proper action. To express the behavior appropriate to each moment is to attain the measure of the great Sufis. Whoever fails in this adab cannot imagine nearness to God, nor that God might accept his behavior."

What Is a Muhib, 'Āshiq, Murīd, or Shaikh?

A STORY

O NE DAY MEVLĀNĀ WAS SITTING WITH HIS CIRCLE IN spiritual conversation when a certain man appeared. By his rustic clothing he looked as if he had come from some poor village. He had never been in such a circle, but he showed appreciation for the themes being discussed. Mevlānā kindly asked him whether he had come with a question.

"My master, I have heard so many conflicting things about *shaikhs, dervishes, muhibs, 'āshiqs,* and *murīds.* Could you possibly clarify the meaning of these words?"

"Very well," Mevlānā said. "Please sit right here, and when the time is right and if the permission is given by God, I will try to say something." Well, as the conversation, or sohbet, continued, suddenly Mevlānā interrupted and said to one of his students, "My son, we have a treasure being held for us in Spain. Would you go there and fetch it for us?"

Now, of course, back in the thirteenth century, a trip to Spain was an unimaginable undertaking, full of dangers and uncertainties. Not suprisingly, this dervish balked at the idea and said, "Master, I have no idea where Spain is. How could I manage to find my way there?"

"Oh Lord, you are right. These are the ancient times, when such a thing is nearly impossible. Never mind." And so he continued with the sohbet. But after a while he said to another dervish, "My son, we have a legacy in Spain. Would you go there and bring it back?"

"My shaikh," the dervish answered, "haven't you already said such a thing is nearly impossible?"

"Oh yes, that's right. These are the ancient times, and such a thing would be extremely difficult. Forgive me."

Finally, after some time, Mevlānā turned to the rustic villager and said, "Will you go and get it?"

The poor villager only said, "Eyvallāh, so be it, Effendi," then stood and asked permission to leave. All the while he was thinking, "Mevlānā is a great man. He must have a good reason to ask such a thing of me."

And so in complete trust he set off on his way. Almost immediately a rider came and offered him a ride as far as the seacoast. There he found a ship headed for Spain, and he was able to sign on as a crew member. When, finally, he arrived in Spain, he wandered through several cities, and one day he met a man who seemed very excited.

"Thanks be to God," he said, "at last you are here. I have been expecting you."

Very overcome, our man said, "Why me?"

"Well, aren't you the one Mevlānā sent to get the treasure? If so, let's go home right now."

There in his home the strange man brought out two coffers of gold belonging to Mevlānā and threw in a bit of gold for the return trip as well, but not without suggesting that the traveler take a few days' rest before returning.

Bewildered, our man asked, "Can you please explain what is going on?"

"Years ago I was the captain of a ship," related the strange man. "One day my ship encountered a great storm far at sea. We did everything humanly possible to keep afloat, but it was not looking good. Facing this hopeless situation, I began to pray. Suddenly I remembered that I was once told about a great saint who lived in faraway Anatolia, a friend of God who could succor those who call upon him.

Even though I did not know him personally, I called from the depths of my heart. Immediately the ship seemed to steady itself; the sea calmed a little bit. I raised my head in gratitude, and high upon the mast I saw a man clad in a green turban who seemed to be whirling majestically high above me. I did not need to ask. I knew him to be the saint I had called. Not knowing what else I could offer, I promised him this gold, and since that day I have kept it safely for him. Last night I saw him in a dream, and he showed you to me and told me that I should give this treasure to you. This morning as I left my house, you were the first person I met."

The villager from Anatolia accepted the hospitality of this captain and friend of Mevlānā's, and a deep friendship began to develop. On the following afternoon, however, while walking through the streets of this town, the villager glimpsed a beautiful young woman, so beautiful that he was overcome with speechlessness. Not knowing what else to do, he went back to the captain and told him that he had fallen head over heels in love with this beauty. "Please help me to win this woman's hand."

After some inquiries, they ascertained that she was the daughter of one of the richest men in town. Considering his own situation as a poor foreigner in Spain, he realized there was very little hope to present his proposal to the father. But finally the captain, whose heart was as big as the ocean itself, went to the girl's father and made the situation of the desperate young man clear.

The father, looking for a way to escape the proposal of the poor young man, thought that if he were to demand a certain amount of gold as a dowry, this poor young man would realize the hopelessness of the situation and give up his dream of marriage. And so the message was conveyed.

Our Anatolian friend, however, did have within his possession the treasure that he was meant to return to Mevlānā, and so, forgetting all in his great passion, he brought the gold to the father. A promise is a promise, and there was no way that this honorable man could refuse the young Turk any longer. Preparations for a great wedding began. And so a great wedding took place.

After the wedding, however, on their first night of intimacy, our friend heard a voice in the darkness: "My son, did we send you to this foreign land only to enjoy these pleasures? Haven't you forgotten something?" Horrified, remembering his task, he clung to his beautiful new wife, knowing, however, that he must return immediately.

"Darling, I have made a big mistake. I had forgotten the very reason I made this long journey, and I have lost Mevlānā's gold."

"Did that voice we heard belong to the true owner of the gold?" his wife asked.

"So, you heard it, too? That is the truth," he answered.

"I will go to my father and ask him for the gold," she said without hesitation.

Out of his great love for his daughter the father gave her the gold without any questions, and the two of them set off for Anatolia. Their journey was long and difficult, but by the grace of God, they arrived back in Anatolia at the dergāh of Mevlānā.

He asked her to wait at the threshold while he entered the hall where Mevlānā was speaking with a circle of dervishes. He quietly took a place in the corner so as not to disturb the conversation. After a while Mevlānā turned toward our friend and said, "My son, do you remember? You had posed a question? Now we can answer it.

"A muhib, a friend, is anyone who loves the Way, the School, and the Teacher, even though he may not be an initiate. He supports the Way by whatever means are at his disposal—with money, if he has it, or with his possessions, his time, or whatever is called for. And yet he does not choose to be a full member of our circle. The captain in Spain was such a muhib.

"A murīd, a disciple, is someone who, when the shaikh makes a request, tries his best to fulfill it—even if the request is 'Go to Spain!' That is what you were in this case.

"An 'āshiq, a lover, is someone who is drawn to the fire and simply goes toward it, without knowing why or how it will end. Your wife, in this case, is such an 'āshiq.

"And I guess a shaikh is someone who can assume this role while knowing that God really does it all."

TRADITION
AND SOURCES

The Living Word

O NCE I ASKED A CERTAIN SUFI SHAIKH IF HE HAD ANY advice about how to read the Qur'ān. His answer has remained imprinted in my mind and heart: "When you read it as if you are reading the word of God, it will open its secrets to you."

What could it mean to call a spiritual text the word of God? Long ago I stopped believing in such absolutes. If ever I had "blind faith," it was shattered by my early teens when I began to read the existentialists—Nietzsche, Camus, Heidegger. By my college years I was at home with Lao Tzu, Padmasambhava, and Hui Neng. Only much later did I finally meet the masters of Sufism: 'Attār, Ibn 'Arabī, and Jalāluddīn Rūmī. None of the writings of these masters, though supremely inspired, could have been described as "the word of God."

And, in fact, these Sufi writings were sometimes presented as teachings for initiates that transcended the exoteric religious teaching presented by prophets for the masses. The assumption was that mystics of a certain attainment showed respect to the outer religion of their society but became universal beings, inwardly free of all forms. In certain spiritual circles, the great Sufis were selectively quoted with an emphasis on their most unitive states, in which they uttered truths that seemed to support the formless, eclectic "truth" that many people in the West had arrived at after some experience with meditation or other mind-altering experiences.

Didn't Rūmī, for instance, say: "What shall I do, O Muslims, for I do not recognize myself? I am neither Christian, nor Jew, nor Magian, nor Muslim." And the great Turkish bard Yunus Emre could say: "Truth is an ocean; the sacred law is a ship. But the sea can always smash the ship, and many have never plunged into the Ocean."[1]

What was not obvious was that the statements of the classical Sufis presupposed an acceptance of the stabilizing principles of Islamic practice and the revelation of the Qur'ān. Their radical and ecstatic utterances were intended within their own context to urge people beyond an identification with unexamined assumptions and forms. Nevertheless, they themselves considered the "way of Muhammad," *as they understood it,* to be their own true path, and the Qur'ānic revelation as a pure, inexhaustible spring of wisdom and guidance.

In fact, it is in these writers that we meet the Qur'ān in its most accessible form. We find them continually quoting from or alluding to the Qur'ān, and we begin to have a sense of the depths of meaning to be found in this Book. Some Sufi shaikhs even recommend that students first approach the Qur'ān through the writings of the "friends of God," the *walīullāh,* before one approaches the Qur'ān directly. I suspect two reasons for this. Mevlānā Rūmī said, "The Qur'ān is a shy bride." It is better to meet her through a close friend. Equally true, the Qur'ān is a mirror; what we will see in this mirror will be a reflection of ourselves, and this reflection may include our own shadow.

It is not uncommon for first-time Western readers to see the Divine wrath in this mirror, and there is no doubt that the Qur'ān is full of warning. It tirelessly warns of the dire consequences for those who transgress "against their own souls" and "spread corruption upon the earth." The Qur'ān is a book that comprehends the whole of human life, and if we look at the history of human life on this earth, we must admit the terrible consequences of human selfishness and cruelty.

Revelation, being the complete and unsentimental Truth, must delineate both the mercy and the wrath. And yet a Hadīth Qudsī says, *My Mercy is greater than My Wrath.* In fact, from the highest point of view, there is even more "mercy" in the wrath than there is wrath.

---

[1] Yunus Emre, *The Drop That Became the Sea* (Putney, Vt.: Threshold Books, 1987).

The stringency of the wrath, which is the lawful consequences of turning our backs to Reality, may turn us in the direction of Truth, may reconnect us with our Source.

I can think of many reasons why the Qur'ān might be important to us today. To begin with, it is one of the two most influential books in human history. Because this Book plays a more central role within Islam than does any sacred text in any other religion, it has probably surpassed the Bible in the degree to which it has been read, memorized, and accepted as a guide to everyday life.

The Qur'ān is considered the foremost miracle of Islam. Fourteen centuries ago the Qur'ān and the Prophet who received it magnetized a backward and feuding people until their spiritual conviction and commitment to social justice spread through most of the known world in little more than a century.

For the next thousand years the principles derived from the Qur'ān and the example of Muhammad created a relatively unified society, characterized by a high level of personal sanctity and social justice. It was a world culture in which religious pluralism was accepted, women obtained more rights than in most cultures, class exploitation was lessened, science flourished side by side with religion, and mysticism permeated everyday life. Contrary to popular conceptions, it was a society relatively free of interpersonal and sectarian violence. One has only to compare the conditions in that society with the relatively abysmal conditions in most of the world to see that something extraordinary had been established. The influence of the Qur'ān set in motion a spiritual and social transformation of a magnitude that has not been surpassed by any ideology in the history of human life.

Nevertheless, the last few centuries have seen a gradual degeneration and stagnation within most Islamic societies, which was further accelerated by negative impacts both during and following the colonialist period. Furthermore, since the centrality and authenticity of the Qur'ān have been accepted by every major Sufi master—from Bistāmī to Hallāj, from Ibn 'Arabī to Shams of Tabrīz and Rūmī, from Hazrat Inayat Khan to Bawa Muhaiyadeen—this book deserves the careful attention of anyone drawn to the Sufi path.

Finally, the Qur'ān is a book of spiritual guidance that offers knowledge of the structure of reality and the purpose of human life. It challenges the human being to become fully human and conscious of God. The level of personal work that it asks of the average human being is very high. It outlines a way of life and spiritual practice that would put the Divine Reality into the center of human consciousness.

The influence of the Qur'ān has been a major uplifting agency in human affairs. It asks us to become people *"whom neither business nor possessions can divert from the remembrance of God, nor from regular prayer, nor from the practice of regular charity, and who remain ever vigilant regarding that day when hearts and eyes will be transformed"* [Surah Ibrahīm (14):37].

The Qur'ān should be approached and judged on its own terms.

> *Will they not, then, try to understand this Qur'ān? Had it issued from any but God, they would surely have found in it many inner contradictions.* [SURAH AN-NISĀ' (4):82]

> *It is He who sent down to you in truth the Book, confirming what went before it. He sent down the Law [of Moses] and the Gospel before this as a guide to mankind. And [now] He has revealed the Criterion.* [SURAH AL-'IMRĀN (3):3]

> *And if you doubt any part of what We have bestowed from on high, step by step, upon Our servant, then produce a surah of similar merit, and call upon any other than God to bear witness for you—if what you say is true.* [SURAH AL-BAQARAH (2):23]

As the selections above suggest, the Qur'ān is a book without internal contradictions. It is from the same source as previous revelations, including those of Moses and Jesus. Finally, for those who can hear it and understand it in Arabic, the tongue of its revelation, the Qur'ān is expressed in a language of unsurpassed depth and beauty.

To begin to appreciate what the Qur'ān is, it is necessary to first of all understand how it was revealed, for the circumstances of its revelation are unique. Virtually every other religious canon can be shown to be the product of various human minds telling a story, or commenting upon the experience of an enlightened being. We have such texts within Islam as well. A few may contain the words of the prophet or enlightened one of the religion in question, although most of these are likely to be spuriously mixed with words of known or unknown attribution, as in the case of the Gospels, for instance. The Hadīth, or sayings of Muhammad, having been subjected to the most rigorous historical criteria; nevertheless they cannot be proven to be wholly free of fabrication or distortion. The Qur'ān itself is in a unique position both in terms of how it was preserved and, even more important, how it was received.

Muhammad at age forty was a respected member of the Quraysh tribe of Mecca and a manager of caravans owned by his wife Khadīja. He was an independent seeker in a commercial, tribal society that placed very little value on spirituality. From time to time he would seclude himself in a cave on Mount Hīrā for the purpose of spiritual retreat. One night a handsome being appeared and said to him, "Recite."

"But I cannot," Muhammad replied.

Again the being commanded him, and again Muhammad declined. Finally, the being took him in a crushing embrace, released him, and said, "Recite, in the name of your Lord, who created mankind from a speck. . . ."

Muhammad was terrified by the experience and rushed home to his wife. "Cover me," he pleaded, "for I may be losing my mind." Khadīja reassured him that a man such as he did not lose his mind. She consulted with her uncle Waraqa, a wise man with an inclination toward Christian belief. Upon hearing the exact words given by the strange being in the cave, Waraqa believed that Muhammad had been visited by the Archangel Gabriel and had received a revelation like the prophets of earlier times.

This first revelation to Muhammad was followed by a silence of many months, and then the revelations began to be more regular. The effect on Muhammad was overwhelming—he would sweat, he would cover himself; sometimes the revelations would come while he was riding a camel, and the camel would fall to its knees, unable to hold him in that state.

The chapters of the revelation would usually come to Muhammad in response to the circumstances of his life. It was as if a dialogue had begun between one man and the Intelligence of the Universes. It was a dialogue both specifically addressed to Muhammad and of universal application at the same time. It was in a language of inimitable beauty and power, such that people would frequently weep upon hearing it.

The Qur'ān is a revelation that was given in the clear light of historical time. It came through Muhammad but was clearly not from Muhammad. He was, after all, a man who, despite his widely recognized sincerity and trustworthiness, was unlettered and had very little exposure to or knowledge of any of the religious traditions of the world. Nevertheless, the Qur'ān has a quality of its own, of a different literary order than the sayings of the Prophet himself, which have been preserved and which also form an important part of the Islamic tradition. The Qur'ān resonates in the heart with an archetypal call to recognize the order and beneficence of the seen and unseen worlds, promising happiness and peace for those whose hearts can hear, and unhappiness and ruin for those who spread corruption and injustice on the face of the earth. It is a plea to human beings to recognize the good and to cease destroying their own souls.

The Qur'ān is said to have been transmitted from Allāh by the Archangel Gabriel, who is understood to be the archetypal intelligence of humanity. Human language strains and is almost torn apart by the power of this revelation. The first-time reader is confronted with a text more avant-garde, in a sense, than anything the world has produced in this century. Its nonlinearity leads one into a timeless universe; its multiplicity of ideas, images, and symbols all point and refer to a master Truth of Divine Beneficence. It offers to the restless human mind a vast landscape of detail and meaning that gradually leads to the realization of the unity of Being. It shifts our concerns from the multiplicity to one underlying Compassionate Reality.

THE WORD

The Word can be understood as that which establishes and confirms the relationship between the Divine and the human. What the Divine speaks to humanity concerns Reality and Truth. It is given to human beings as a clear guidance amid the tests of this earthly life. The Revelation is meant to be reflected upon, taken into ourselves, and then: *His Word will find its fulfillment in sincerity and justice* [Surah al-An'ām (6):115].

> *Aren't you aware how God sets forth the likeness of a good word? It is firmly rooted like a good tree, its branches reaching toward the sky, yielding its fruit at all times by the permission of its Sustainer.*
>
> *And in this way God sets forth likenesses for human beings, so that they might reflect upon the truth.*
>
> *And the likeness of a corrupt word is that of a corrupt tree, torn up upon the face of the earth, unable to endure.*
>
> *God grants firmness to those who have attained faith through the word that is unshakably true in the life of this world as well as in the life to come; but the wrongdoers are allowed to stray, and God does as He wills.* [SURAH IBRAHĪM (14):24–27]

The Word will also stand against those who deny what is Real, the lawful order, and, as the Qur'ān often reminds, will be a proof against them. Muhammad Asad, the translator of the passage above, suggests that "the Word" often means "promise," that "the Word" is the promise of the Divine to humanity.

> In its wider meaning, the term *kalimah* ("word") denotes any conceptual statement or proposition. Thus a "good word" circumscribes any proposition (or idea) that is intrinsically true and—because it implies a call to what is good in the oral sense—is ultimately beneficent and enduring; and since a call to moral righteousness is the innermost purport of every one of God's messages, the term "good word" applies to them as well. Similarly, "the corrupt word" mentioned in verse 26 applies to the opposite of what the divine message aims at: namely, to every idea that is intrinsically false or morally evil and, therefore, spiritually harmful.[2]

---

[2] Muhammad Asad, *The Message of the Qur'ān* (Gibraltar: Dar al-Andalus, 1980), p. 376.

Although it is unlikely that Muhammad had any direct contact with the Torah or the New Testament, "the Word of God" as presented in the Qur'ān is remarkably consistent with the notion of the "word" as expressed in both of these: "Man does not live by bread alone, but by every word that proceeds from the mouth of God." Furthermore, in the Qur'ān, Jesus himself is referred to as "*a* word" from God.

According to Seyyed Hossein Nasr:

> The Word of God in Islam is the Qur'ān; in Christianity it is Christ. The vehicle of the Divine Message in Christianity is the Virgin Mary; in Islam it is the soul of the Prophet. The Prophet must be unlettered for the same reason that the Virgin Mary must be virgin. The human vehicle of a Divine Message must be pure and untainted. The Divine Word can only be written on the pure and 'untouched' tablet of human receptivity. If this Word is in the form of flesh the purity is symbolized by the virginity of the mother who gives birth to the Word, and if it is in the form of a book this purity is symbolized by the unlettered nature of the person who is chosen to announce the Word among men. . . The unlettered nature of the Prophet demonstrates how the human recipient is completely passive before the Divine. Were this purity and virginity of the soul not to exist, the Divine Word would in a sense become tainted with purely human knowledge and not be presented to mankind in its pristine purity.[3]

The Qur'ān refers to itself as *guidance for humanity* [Surah al-Baqara (2):185]. Its task is to awaken faith in and awareness of the Unseen Beneficence. Allāh, the One God of all religions, is the Master Truth of existence. The Qur'ān speaks often and in many contexts about God, and all of these contexts must be interiorized into a wholeness in order to do justice to the Qur'ān's message. The Qur'ān works by drawing our attention to certain evident facts—primarily the beauty, order, and intelligence evidenced in human nature and the natural

---

[3] Seyyid Hossein Nasr, *Ideals and Realities of Islam* (London, George Allen & Unwin, 1966), p. 43.

world—and turning these facts into "reminders" of the existence of a benevolent Unseen Intelligence.

The Qur'ān has the ability to communicate to the majority of human beings through concrete images and an essentially uncomplicated message. Beyond its apparent simplicity it has served as a source of inspiration to the deepest souls and commanded the interest of the greatest intellects of all time. This ability to touch the minds and hearts of all kinds of human beings is one sign of its divine origin.

The verses of the Qur'ān are called *ayats*, literally "signs." The same word is used in describing the perceptions that will be offered outwardly and inwardly to the person of faith.

> *In time We shall make them fully understand Our signs in the farthest horizons and within themselves, so that it will become clear to them that this [revelation] is indeed the truth. Is it not enough to know that your Sustainer is a witness to everything?*
> [SURAH FUSSILAT (41):53]

The apprehension of these signs depends not only upon our faculty of reason but also upon the cognitive powers of the heart. The Qur'ān mentions the kind of human being *"who is humble before the Unseen and brings a heart that can respond"* [Surah Qāf (50):33].

And it says further that *"It is a reminder to whoever has a heart and surrenders their ears to witnessing"* [Surah Qāf (50):37].

TONAL PRESENCE

The Qur'ān's power to touch the heart of human beings resides in its tonal qualities as much as in its meaning. Within the milieu of Islamic practice, this is how one would be most likely to meet the Revelation—as recitation that carries the majesty of the Divine and as sound that penetrates to the interior of the human being, to the most intimate chamber of the soul.

Reading the Qur'ān in translation is not really reading the Qur'ān at all, but a mere paraphrase of its meanings. This problem is compounded by the tendency of Qur'anic translations to take their cues from the theologized conventions of biblical translation. These conventions are arguably insufficient to translate even the Gospels, because they transpose the simple and direct Greek of the New Testament into a theological language that developed centuries later. To try to make the Qur'ān sound like the Bible is to dress it in missionary clothes.

Even some of the best translations are subject to striking distortion of this type, as for example, these lines from Yusuf Ali's translation: *"Our religion is the baptism of Allāh: And who can baptize better than Allāh? And it is He Whom we worship"* [Surah al-Baqarah (2): 138]. Compare this with Muhammad Asad's translation: *"Say: 'Our life takes its hue from God! And who could give a better hue to life than God, if we but truly worship Him?'"*

Fortunately for those who are engaged in Islamic practice, there is the requirement in the ritual prayer to include short selections of one's own choice from the Qur'ān in Arabic. In this way the worshiper acquires a store of tonal meanings that begin to live within. This is the Living Word of the Qur'ān, a divine resonance in the heart of the faithful human being—the Qur'ānization of memory.

The idea of a sacred language is relatively foreign and unfamiliar to the modern secular world. The text of the New Testament, for instance, would not generally be thought to have more efficacy in its original Greek than in a modern vernacular language. The language in which Jesus himself delivered his message, Aramaic, has practically disappeared from the face of the earth. The Church used Latin as a sacred language for centuries, but now that has been eroded. Likewise, the sacred texts of Buddhism may be in Sanskrit, Pali, Chinese, Tibetan, or Japanese. These faiths depend instead on a sacred individual as the primary spiritual manifestation, namely Jesus or Buddha, more than they do on a sacred text and language.

Hinduism, Judaism, and Islam, on the other hand, are faiths based on sacred books and sacred languages in which a Divine Presence operates through language itself. In Islam there is a grace, a baraka, that is embodied in the language of the Qur'ān. To recite or write the Qur'ān is a sacred act. The divine text gradually becomes the universe in which one lives, its words providing a spiritual nourishment.

The essence of revelation is to remind us of our origin and nature after we have forgotten. It is the remedy for our ontological amnesia. All of God's qualities have been kneaded into the bread of the human being with the pure water of God's love. The water that made the bread possible has been forgotten. Mevlānā Rūmī said:

> God has sent prophets and saints, like great clear waters, in order that the dark and murky waters touched by the clear waters might free themselves of their coincidental murkiness and discoloration. The murky water then "remembers." When it sees itself clear, it realizes that it was originally clear and that its murkiness and discoloration are coincidental. It recalls how it was before the advent of these coincidentals and says, *"This is what we were formerly sustained by"* [Surah al-Baqarah (2):25]. Prophets and saints, therefore, are "reminders" of one's past condition. They do not put anything new into one's substance. Now every murky water that recognizes that great water and says, "I am from and of this," mingles with it. But murky waters, which do not recognize that water and think they are different or of another type, withdraw so into their murkiness and discoloration that they are unable to mingle with the sea. They become ever more estranged from the sea.[4]

The Qur'ān challenges us not only to acknowledge the Reality that it proposes, but to live the kind of life that is in harmony with that Reality. From the standpoint of our own time and place, the Reality and human ideal presented by the Qur'ān must seem a remote possibility. To the extent that human beings have allowed their humanness to degenerate, the "word," the "promise" must seem unlikely, farfetched, or even barely intelligible. Is it possible that a "word" has been given to humanity that stands firm and unshakable amid all the vicissitudes of time and place? That shaikh's advice about reading the Qur'ān as if it were the Word of God continues to resonate. I return

---

[4] Rūmī, *Fīhi mā fīhi*, Discourse 8.

again and again to the pages of this Book, which itself claims not to contain any "crookedness." If I can find any crookedness in it, any inner contradiction, I might be able to say that here is an interesting text, an interesting product of the human imagination, but not a communication from the heart of Reality Itself.

It has begun to have an effect upon me, as it has had on so many others much wiser than myself, of drawing me deeper and deeper into its Reality. The Qur'ān establishes a profound and noble paradigm of the human being, of what human possibilities are. It also establishes the nature of Reality as fundamentally compassionate and generous toward all of creation, but most of all to the human being, its beloved representative upon the earth. Its light shines throughout history, revealing what is straight and true in all traditions, not because we have submitted in dogmatic compliance to its propositions, but because of the enduring Truth of its message. While I once thought that I could be the judge of Revelation, gradually I found that Revelation offers the criterion to discern what is essentially human and real. For more than two decades I have continued to return to this spring of wisdom with the question, "Can this Book really be what it claims to be? Does it offer the criterion for distinguishing what is really the most direct Way to well-being, to social justice, and to becoming fully human?"

To approach the Qur'ān requires that we prepare ourselves to be receptive to it. It requires that we get in touch with the deeper dimensions of our own being. Mevlānā Rūmī has this to say about approaching the Qur'ān:

> The Qur'ān is like a shy bride. Although you pull aside her veil, she will not show you her face. The reason you have no pleasure or discovery in all your study of it is that it rejects your attempt to pull off its veil. It tricks you and shows itself to you as ugly, as if to say, "I am not that beauty." It is capable of showing any face it wants. If, on the other hand, you do not tug at the veil, but you acquiesce, give water to its sown field, do it service from afar and try to do what pleases it without pulling at its veil, it will show you its face.

*Seek the people of God, enter among my servants; and enter my
paradise* [SURAH AL-FAJR (89):29–30].

God does not speak to just anyone, as kings in this world do
not speak to every weaver. They appoint viziers and deputies
through whom people can reach them. So also has God selected
a certain servant to the end that whoever seeks God can find
Him through that servant. All the prophets have come for the
sole reason that they are the way.[5]

In order to truly and adequately apprehend the Qur'ān, we must bring
ourselves to that state that Muhammad and his companions were in
as this revelation was being received. In other words, we must be as if
we were living in the first twenty-three years during which it was revealed. If the Qur'ān can contribute to our discovering within ourselves that same Source that first revealed this Book to Muhammad,
then it will have accomplished the essential work of all spirituality—to
reconnect the isolated human being with the Intelligence and Love of
the universes.

*Thus, step by step, We bestow from on high through this Qur'ān
all that gives health* [to the spirit] *and is a grace to those who
have faith.* . . . [SURAH AL-ISRĀ' (17):83]

---

[5] Ibid.

The Example of Muhammad

T HE WAY OF SUFISM IS SECURED ON THE FOUNDATION OF the spiritual virtues and practices of the Prophet Muhammad. This Way has had its interpreters in every age, and yet it was complete from the time of Muhammad. The Sufi way actualized and fulfilled certain qualities that had been latent in what was revealed through Muhammad, and the literary, musical, aesthetic, and interpersonal refinement of the Mevlevi Way, in particular, testify to the inexhaustible treasure of Muhammadan spirituality.

Most Westerners who are drawn to Sufism were first attracted by its qualities and were only gradually led to understand how the qualities of Sufism are the fruit of the Qur'ānic revelation and the example of Muhammad. Sufism is a wide and universal door that leads out of the prison of human vanity and conjecture to an expansive spiritual reality. After this reality has been tasted through experience, it is possible to grasp how completely it is testified to by the revelation of the Qur'ān and the life of Muhammad.

Sufism has been relatively free of the embellishments of theological speculation. By theological speculation I mean those notions that require belief in theological constructs that are not verified by experience. For instance, Sufism does not require us to believe that our salvation depends on our belief in the intercession of Muhammad, or the divinely revealed origin of the Qur'ān, or the exclusive efficacy of

Islamic practices. What Sufism proposes is that God's Mercy has shown itself in various revelations to humankind by various messengers. The Qur'ān is an example of this, and its historical soundness can be verified by the most rigorous standards. The spiritual path of Muhammad can be put to the test by any individual, and one can find out for oneself whether or not its practices remove the veils of human conditioning and open the heart to new spiritual realities. All of this depends on practice and effort, not on adherence to belief.

Love is both mystery and knowledge. Furthermore, it is a mystery that has spoken to us about itself in the form of those revelations and exemplars that have profoundly altered the course and quality of human history.

Without the character of Muhammad, who was called "the living Qur'ān," the early Muslim community would not have possessed the magnetic and inspired qualities that gave birth to a high level of culture. Within a few generations, this impulse of Islam spread from the backwater of Arabia to become a vast civilization—a civilization based on a universal ideology of human equality, social justice, and divine remembrance.

Without the character of Muhammad, the whole spirit of Sufism is inconceivable. The study of the Prophet's sayings and actions has always been central to the curriculum of Sufism.

'Alī, one of the Prophet's closest companions and one of the first links in the chain of Sufism, preserved this saying:

> Meditation in God is my capital.
> Reason and sound logic are the root of my action.
> Love is the foundation of my existence.
> Enthusiasm is the vehicle of my life.
> Contemplation of Allāh is my companion.
> Faith is the source of my power.
> Sorrow is my friend.
> Knowledge is my weapon.
> Patience is my clothing and virtue.
> Submission to the Divine Will is my pride.
> Truth is my salvation.

Worship is my practice.
And in prayer lies the coolness of my eye
and my peace of mind.

Muhammad's character exemplified a life of love and became a model
for all who were called Sufis. These Sufis in their turn continued this
impulse into an ever more explicit expression of love.

What Human history has no greater example of a figure who was both a
contemplative and a social revolutionary. On the one hand Muhammad devoted himself to meditation, vigils, and fasts; he opened his
heart to the Invisible and there he heard Gabriel's voice; he listened to
the guidance that was given for the various circumstances he encountered; and he transmitted a revelation and way of life for the benefit
of humanity. After that revelation began, he also found himself responsible for a growing community, and eventually a nation, which in
an unbelievably short period of time became a unified and energized
culture that swept across the world. For someone even cursorily acquainted with the facts, it would be difficult to deny that any other
single human being has affected so great a number of people so deeply
and in so many aspects of their lives. The way revealed through Muhammad and the Qur'ān enlists from its more than one billion faithful
a remarkable degree of commitment and energy: prayer and ablutions
five times a day, a month-long fast, a universal pilgrimage, a single
ritual prayer and Holy Book accepted by all Muslims, a practical and
specific rule of social law governing business, social life, the family,
and the individual.

What stands out in the prophet's life are a combination of qualities
that include sanctity, wisdom, faith, integrity, strength, justice, generosity, magnanimity, nobility, humanity, and modesty. It was these
qualities that shaped the spiritual climate of Islam. Because Muhammad's speech and actions were remembered and preserved more exactly than perhaps any other historical personality, in the hearts of
Muslims his life became a norm for all of human life.

And yet Muhammad could not be confused with God. He listened
to what the Divine revealed even when it criticized his own actions.
Even after he was the ruler of a state, he lived a life of voluntary

poverty. He allowed his grandchildren to climb upon his back when he prostrated himself in prayer. He swept his own house and mended his own clothes. Once when an uncouth visitor relieved himself in the mosque, Muhammad himself cleaned it up without complaint. As beautiful as his character and behavior were, he did not claim infallibility for himself. He was known to ask God's forgiveness many times a day. He can, however, be considered perfect in one important aspect: He passed on exactly what was entrusted to him by God. He could do this, at least in part, because He was a *tabula rasa* on which God wrote His qualities. He was basically uneducated, but truthful and sincere, and could transmit the divine message without confusing it with his own ideas. He completely lacked ambition or opportunism. He was a direct instrument of God, and he faithfully fulfilled his purpose.

He showed by his own example the strength to affirm the Divine Truth within the soul and in the world. And yet his strength was balanced by magnanimity, liberality, generosity, and forgiveness. Melted in the Divine Being, detached from the ego and the world, he was a living example of the serenity of nonexistence. We do not melt in God without love; we do not survive in God without the humility of submission. Muhammad once expressed his own situation, and the situation of all human beings who realize their true Selves: "I am He and He is I, except that I am he who I am and He is He who He is." The Prophet, as a true human being, is a threshold between two worlds.

Sayings of Muhammad

Selected and Translated by Kabir Helminski

Islam began as something strange,
and it will become thus again,
as it was at the beginning.
Blessed, therefore, are the strangers.

The strangers are those who
restore what the people have corrupted of God's law,
as well as those
who revive what has been destroyed of it.

You will not enter paradise until you believe,
and you will not
believe until you love one another.
Let me guide you to something
in the doing of which you will love one another.
Give a greeting to everyone among you.

I was delegated as a prophet to perfect moral virtues.

Good character is half of faith.

God is merciful to those who show mercy to others.

Power consists not in being able to strike another,
but in being able to control oneself when anger arises.

Honor your children, and thus improve their manners.

The three best things:
to be humble amid the vicissitudes of fortune;
to pardon when powerful;
and to be generous with no strings attached.

Whoever does not express his gratitude to people
will never be grateful to God.

The best people are those who are most useful to others.

Living among others is a cause for blessing,
while seclusion is the cause of torment.

Happy is the person who finds fault with himself instead of
finding fault with others.

From morning until night and from night until morning,
keep your heart free from malice toward anyone.

A perfect Muslim is one
from whose tongue and hands mankind is safe.

Islam is purity of speech and hospitality.

Every religion has a distinctive virtue,
and the distinctive virtue of Islam is modesty.

Greet those whom you know and those whom you don't know.

When asked what was most excellent in a human being,
he answered: "A friendly disposition."

The best of God's servants are those who, when seen,
remind you of God;
and the worst of God's servants are those who spread tales
to do mischief and separate friends,
and look for the faults of the good.

Whoever believes in one God and the Hereafter,
let him speak what is good or remain silent.

He is the best Muslim whose disposition
is most liked by his own family.

Respect the guest, and do not inconvenience your neighbors.

The faithful are as one person.
If a man complains of a pain in his head,
his whole body complains; and if his eye complains,
his whole body complains.

He is not of us who is not affectionate to the little ones and
does not respect the reputation of the old.

Truly, the farthest seat from me on the day of resurrection will
be the garrulous, those who talk glibly,
and those who talk tall.
And who is it that talk tall? The vainglorious.

God is gentle and loves gentleness.

Inscribed on the Prophet's sword:
Forgive him who wrongs you;
join him who cuts you off; do good to him who does evil to you;
and speak the truth even if it be against yourself.

Whoever restrains his anger when he has the power to show it,
God will give him a great reward.

Backbiting is more grievous than adultery, and God will not
forgive the backbiter until the one wronged has forgiven him.

Keep yourselves far from envy, because it eats up and takes away
good actions as fire consumes and burns the wood.

What actions are most excellent?
To gladden the heart of a human being,
to feed the hungry, to help the afflicted,
to lighten the sorrow of the sorrowful,
and to remove the wrongs of the injured.

The Sacredness of Everyday Life

A SPIRITUALITY ADEQUATE TO OUR TIMES WOULD HAVE TO establish the sacredness of everyday life in the face of increasing challenges to our humanness. The acceleration of time, the coercion of mass media, the commercialization of human relationships, and the artificial environment that technology is creating—all serve to create conditions that present new and unforeseen challenges to the human soul. While we seem to be advancing technologically, the capacities for sustained attention, for spiritual aspiration, for deeper relationships, and for spiritual presence seem to be diminishing.

Amid all this noise, are we becoming deaf to the overtones of transcendence? With so much entertainment at our fingertips, is humanity's range of experience actually shrinking? Are we becoming trapped in appearances, oblivious to the essential ground of Being?

Sufism is a path formed from the cumulative experience and wisdom of generations of human beings who have attempted to live according to what they consider a divine way of life and to empirically resolve the conflicts of existence. Sufism aims at the highest spiritual attainment within the context of everyday life. Sufism has been called "the path of return." It is fundamentally a movement of consciousness from the state of separation, or exile, to a reunion with our Source. In essence, if we trace our own consciousness back to its Source, we will

find that we have never been separate. We will experience the dissolving of that which never was in that which has always been.

There is a Hadith Qudsi that aptly expresses the intimate union of
the self and its Source:

> As My servant continues to draw near to Me through
>   voluntary practices,
> I become the Hearing with which he or she hears,
> the Seeing with which he or she sees,
> the hand with which he or she touches,
> the feet with which he or she walks.

It should be clear from this saying that a mysterious cooperation is
acknowledged between the human and the Divine. It is less a matter
of the human knowing God than of God being discovered in all the
sensibilities of the human. From the perspective of Truth, I cannot
know God, but God is both the knower and the known. Only God
knows God.

Practically speaking, what are the human capacities required to experience the sacredness of everyday life?

We have a *heart*, by which is meant an organ of perception through
which the reality of Spirit can be apprehended. We cannot begin the
spiritual journey unless the "eye of the heart" is at least slightly open.
It is for the heart to know that Reality which is not immediately apparent to the intellect or the senses. Every other organ of perception dis-
cerns through its own limited window; only the heart sees from all
sides at once and can perceive Oneness.

It is necessary to distinguish the heart from our common emotions
that are rooted in our egoism and that mostly obscure the knowing of
the heart. The spiritual process from this point of view is removing
the distorting factors of egoism that veil the heart. This is often described as "polishing the mirror of the heart." Muhammad said,
"There is a polish for everything, and the polish for the heart is the
remembrance of God." The "remembrance of God" is not primarily
an intellectual activity but a state in which consciousness expands into
a sense of God's "presence." In other words, it could be understood
as a state of individual presence in relation to an Infinite Presence.

In addition to the heart, a human being has the faculty of *reason*, the ability to consciously reflect. Reason helps us to assimilate the sacred knowledge and apply it to our own circumstances. This knowledge includes all the practical principles of how to live a more human life, which include prayer, fasting, contemplation, and service. It includes all the modeling that has been offered by the realized men and women of the tradition. Reason helps us to apply the stories of their lives to our own lives. Thus, reason helps us to deal with our own conditioned thinking and to undo the knots in our subconscious. Reason helps us to purify the subconscious by replacing ego-based assumptions with the principles of Oneness.

The third element is *will*. We can do nothing unless we find the will to do it. The spiritual journey requires a commitment of will strong enough to overcome all distractions, unconsciousness, and compulsions of everyday life. It requires a master desire, a prioritizing of one's life energies. Awakening the will requires a knowledge of how to ask for guidance, how to form an intention, how to activate our inner resources, and how to sustain our intention. For this we need both the motivation of the heart—the core of our being—and the guidance of reason.

No mature shaikh, in my experience, would encourage seekers to abandon themselves to the Divine Will without first having experienced a "prior education" in which a healthy personal will was developed—an education involving the development of reason, the practice of courtesy, ethics, and right livelihood.

There is a mystery connected with human will. A very strong case can be made that human beings only have the illusion of will and, in fact, possess little or no will of their own. Abu Bakr, that sincere companion of the Prophet Muhammad, said, "Glory be to God, who has not given any of His creatures a means of attaining knowledge of Him except through the inability to attain knowledge of Him." According to what Abu Bakr says, the process of attaining union is the initiative and action of God in the heart of His creature. What appears to be our will is actually His. This, of course, is also logically consistent with the notion of Oneness. The tradition teaches that there is and always has been only one "religion," and it is *surrender* to God, Reality,

Truth. Although this Reality is a universal truth beyond forms, in sharing how any tradition works, it is necessary to describe the container as well as what is contained. And so I would like to describe some elements of a typical Sufi practice.

A DAILY PRACTICE

There is a time before the first light of the new day when "the angels draw near to earth" to listen to the prayers of those who are awake. We understand this to mean that the "angelic powers" within ourselves are more available at this time. A few days each month I may undertake to fast. In this tradition a fast begins before the first light of dawn and continues until sunset. Fasting is a "meditation for the body." Just as in meditation we empty the mind of thought, in fasting we empty the body of food and experience a new receptivity. Having eaten before sunrise, I will abstain from all food and drink until after sunset. This practice teaches how food can be a veil over the feelings. Fasting is a time of transparency, of fragility, of hunger. Withholding the self-numbing tastes of food, I find myself aware of levels of emotional pain I have denied, and I become vulnerable to my own undigested emotions. I may observe that a part of me does not want to fast. The ego is a sharp lawyer, and I laugh at all the excuses that come to mind.

If I were in Turkey, or Indonesia, or Morocco, I would probably hear the voice of the muezzin at the first light of day, a voice of both majesty and mercy: "God is the most great. . . . There are no other gods than God. . . . Muhammad is a messenger of God. . . . Come to fulfillment. . . . Come to prayer. . . . Prayer is better than sleep. . . . God is the most great. . . . There are no other gods than God."

I wash my hands and refresh my face with flowing water. I rinse my mouth and ears and neck and hair. I let the water flow over my ankles and feet. I purify this body to stand before the Infinite. I face the *qibla*, the direction of prayer, located at the Ka'bah, the house of Abraham in Mecca, the point toward which one-fifth of humanity orients its worship. Mecca is actually the point where humanity faces itself. At any moment of the day, hundreds of millions of people are turned to this point, this black stone, symbolic of the Divine Essence.

I stand as a human being on earth, hands clasped at my solar plexus, asking for the strength to be more human. I bow from the waist as a servant of creation, remembering that each human being is God's *khalīfe*, His representative or caretaker on earth. After bowing, I stand again. I prostrate myself, head to the ground, and am grateful for this simple posture, which has guided me to a bodily experience of surrender—as the finite before the Infinite, as the conditioned before the Unconditioned, as the natural before the Supernatural, existence annihilated in Eternity. Then I sit back on my heels in a kneeling posture. Once more I put my head to the ground in surrender, annihilating even that annihilation, erasing that erasure, and stand once more as a human being. Muhammad once said, "The best of you are those who are most useful to others." And the Qur'ān mentions *"those who remember God standing, and sitting, and lying down, and whom neither business nor profits distract from the remembrance of God."* Our way is not to abandon human responsibilities in order to seek God. For at least fourteen hundred years Sufis have followed a path on which the highest spiritual attainments were realized while living a human life with a socially useful livelihood within the context of family and community. Muhammad said, "Marriage is half of faith." Right livelihood, too, is worship, whether I am in a counseling session, or repairing the plumbing, or working with a computer.

Each of us is inspired with a longing to do something. Each of us has some part to play in maintaining the "tent of material existence," as Mevlānā called this world. Some of us make the tent poles, some the ropes, some the canvas. But the greatest fulfillment comes to the one who has a Beloved and meets the Beloved within this tent of material existence.

How many times during a day am I faced with a choice between what "I" want and what is truly needed? Or between what I want and the way things actually are? I am given the opportunity to surrender again and again. But to know what surrender entails, I need both my heart and my reason, and I use one to check the other. If I can see where surrender lies, then I use will to help my ego get out of the way.

The master truth of this whole path is very simple. It has been expressed in the words of Jesus: "Those who exalt themselves will be brought low, and those who bring themselves low shall be exalted." Love cannot coexist with the desire for status, exclusivity, power, and control. The power of God can only become obvious in those who have relinquished the need and desire for worldly power and status. As Muhammad said, "The best among you are those who, when seen, remind you of God."

Meanwhile, there is time to live one's life. We do not owe Ultimate Reality some extraordinary sacrifice, but we do need to integrate our remembrance of our Source into every moment of our lives.

Twice more during the daylight hours, I let the refreshing waters flow over my skin; I stand and bow and kneel and touch my head to the ground. The practice is physical, emotional, mental, and spiritual. The physical dimension involves a pattern of exercise, a yoga, in which all the major joints are gracefully and mindfully exercised. The prayer also follows a discipline of time that is coordinated with the position of the sun throughout the day. There is an emotional dimension that in various moments encompasses humility, self-acceptance, reverence, trust, and awe. The mental dimension consists of the conscious intention, a presence of mind without which the prayer is just a mechanical ritual. With this presence the mind is consciously employed in the recitation of sacred language, and the choosing of certain lines from the Qur'ān that seem meaningful or appropriate. Using the mind consciously and intentionally prevents absentmindedness. This state of presence and surrender itself is deepened and enriched. The flow of the day is punctuated by these intense, wholehearted exercises of devotion and remembrance. The prayer occupies a very short but concentrated period of time, and I find myself longing for these moments in which I find wholeness in surrender. Humans can create rituals and ceremonies; but the essential practices of a sacred tradition are most often handed down from a higher world. The Arabic word for "revelation," *tanzil,* means something that has been sent down. What may be revealed to a prophet by an archangel, to a Sufi Pir by the Prophet in a dream, or to a tribal wise person in a vision quest, then becomes the sacred practice of a particular people or lineage. Such practices were not the creations of a conjecturing intellect; they were received with the permission of the Unseen. In other words, Reality creates its own forms of address and worship.

Yet it remains for the human being to complete these forms with his or her own substance. Prayer without presence of heart is an empty form. But when Presence takes over, then prayer is an Ocean and you are a wave, prayer is Wind and you are dust, prayer is the Hand and you are a glove.

After the sun has set, before having a full meal, I break the fast with some water and dates. I am the wave again upon the Ocean. And I am not alone, because in this tradition one rarely eats alone. I may be with my family or with friends, and it seems we are all waves upon this ocean of Mercy with its movement, laughter, and life. The Qur'ān promises:

> *In time We shall make them fully understand Our signs upon the farthest horizons and within themselves, so that it will become clear to them that this is indeed the Truth. Is it not enough to know that your Sustainer is a witness to everything?* [Surah Fussilat (41):53]

And the great poet and philosopher of science Muhammad Iqbal has written: "The denier is lost in the horizons. As for the one with faith, the horizons are lost in him or her." The heavens and the earth cannot contain the Real. Only the heart of a faithful human can contain the infinite horizons of the Real. God's names are infinite. I select one of His names and call that name hundreds, maybe thousands, of times, until in some way I take on the hue of that Name. I pray and *am* the prayer. I know and am all that I know. As the Prophet said, "Whoever knows himself knows his Lord." But no one can know God, because God is the only Knower. Again in the darkness of night I let fresh water flow over these sensitive areas of the body. I stand again before the Infinite, and bow as a servant, and prostrate myself in surrender, and kneel in gratitude, and prostrate myself again, and rise, not knowing whether I am inside myself or outside myself. Oneness is near, not far.

To fully become what we are meant to be, we must undergo a

fundamental transformation: to become free from self(ishness) and unified with the Truth. The highest Truth is that knower and known are One. Furthermore, this is the Truth that we must not only know about; it is the Truth we must consciously become.

While expressing the Truth in this way may seem distant or abstract, especially from the perspective afforded by our world today, the Truth itself is that which we cannot live without. It is the key to our happiness and well-being, and ultimately, we must suspect, to our very survival on this earth.

Anything less than the Truth of Oneness leaves us in a maze of conflicting desires, fragmented awareness, and separative actions. It should be obvious that if we are in disarray within ourselves, if our reason, heart, and will are without a harmonious center, we will find it very difficult to relate to and function harmoniously with others and with our environment.

As I persevere in this daily practice, the moments are increasing when it is possible to know the reconciliation of all opposites, of rigor and gentleness, of freedom and submission, of outer and inner, of self-hood and selfless being, of conditioned and unconditioned, of human and divine, of knower and known—the inseparable oneness of all and everything.

We Mevlevis have our "turn," the whirling ceremony, which is a form of worship particular to our lineage but whose origins are veiled in the countless centuries of the Great Spirit tradition of the Asian heartland. In the turn, movement and stillness are combined. One foot is anchored like an axis, while the other is stepping 360 degrees around that axis. The arms are outstretched: the right with the palm up in a receptive gesture, the left turned down, bestowing. Energy flows from one to the other, through the human heart. In the course of fulfilling this movement, we are drawn to our inmost center, the point where we are closest to God. The body must be in balance. The mind must be empty but aware. The heart must be surrendered and open. The soul is in harmony with its Source.

I am coming little by little to understand that there is a way of being human that encompasses all levels of being at once, that the physical, emotional, mental, intuitive, and transcendent aspects of the human being can be experienced as a whole, a single pattern of meaning. The binding force that connects everything is "Love," but I do not think that we understand this Love just because we have named it. It confounds our conceptual understanding, and yet it is the very essence of what we are.

THE NEEDS
OF OUR TIME

What Is a Truly Universal
Spirituality?

I
S IT POSSIBLE FOR HUMANITY, OR EVEN A PORTION OF IT, TO embrace a truly universal spirituality? If so, what would a universal spirituality be based on? And would such a spirituality be able to offer a path to complete spiritual realization?

The answers to these questions have become more urgent as the world becomes smaller through technologies of communication and transportation. While we can appreciate the need for greater understanding and acceptance of our differences and greater recognition of our common humanity, should this spell the end of religion as we know it? Is it time for a spirituality that is founded upon universal principles or upon a scientific spiritual psychology? Can we dispense with forms if we have found the essence? Can we separate spirituality from religion?

Various people have attempted to identify the spiritual values common to the various sacred traditions. Yet even if we could agree on a list of spiritual values, we would have only abstractions. Once we go beyond abstractions, we enter not only the realm of spiritual metaphor but also cosmology, mythos, human exemplars, ceremony, and practice. We are on relatively safe ground as long as we only espouse generalities and abstractions; but as soon as we approach the images and stories that could motivate and inspire the human heart, we have entered into the possibility of conflict and disagreement.

Most people who opt for the universal approach to spirituality really have in mind taking a little bit of this and a little bit of that. It is a particularly modern and Western (and especially American) notion that we can customize our spirituality, or that we can choose our portion as if we were at a salad bar.

Historically, the significance of religion has more often been that it united human beings in a common purpose and destiny. In most traditional cultures, which placed so much emphasis on unity and continuity, the modern preoccupation with personalizing a religion or path would have seemed insane.

There is another kind of universality that proceeds from within a particular tradition when someone decides that he or she does not wish to be bound by forms and beliefs and so attempts a "formless" spirituality. In the few cases of this kind that I have observed, there is always the inescapable necessity of carrying the assumptions and perspective of the original tradition into the formless version. In one Buddhist version of this approach, the point seemed to be to reach a state of perfection through continuous awareness. This universal and formless path was simply Buddhism stripped of its name, rituals, and hierarchy. In a Middle Eastern version of the formless path, the idea was to merge into Love by sharing in the being of a particular person who was supposed to have become one with Love. In other words, it was Sufism without ceremony, prayer, or revelation. More often than not these kinds of attempts at universality result in one-man traditions that have a tendency to cut themselves off from a wider sense of tradition and community in the name of universality. In the name of transcending forms, beliefs, and identifications, they seem to acquire many of the characteristics of a cult—especially a focus on a single charismatic figure without whom the whole enterprise would dissolve.

Yet another form of universality, and to my mind the most authentic form of it, is the result of committing oneself wholeheartedly to a particular tradition, while honoring the goodwill and truth within other paths. Eventually, if one goes far enough on one of the real paths to God—and these are usually paths that have been sanctioned by a lineage of enlightened beings—then one arrives at a truly universal perspective because one has used a particular tradition to transcend the egoism that *needs* identifications and exclusive beliefs. A striking example of this kind of spiritual attainment is Ibn ʿArabī, the great formulator of Sufism, who said, "My heart has become receptive of every form. It is a meadow for gazelles, a monastery for monks, an abode for idols, the Kaʿbah of the pilgrim, the tablets of the Torah, the Qurʾān. My religion is Love—wherever the camels of Love's caravan turn, Love is my belief, my faith."

He could say that because he could see, from his vantage point, the relativity of all beliefs, and the Reality behind all beliefs, although this did not deter him from a very strict practice and a very intimate relationship with the Qurʾān and sayings of the Prophet. This was his framework, this was his path; but it did not prevent him from seeing the universality and the Truth in all ways. He could even see some value in denial and doubt.

Ibn ʿArabī was not a practitioner of a universal faith, but one who was wholly in harmony with Islam and from whom issued an expression of that tradition that influenced subsequent generations until the present day. It is true that with his depth of apprehension he gave very original and, to some, shocking interpretations of the Qurʾān. For him the way of Islam was revealed to be the very matrix of Truth in a unique sense, yet through it he became a universal human being.

Among those who have identified themselves with the teachings of Sufism, there have been in this century, mostly in the Western World, a significant number who have espoused a universalistic Sufism, one no longer embedded in the religion of Islam, although availing itself of some of the terminology, metaphors, and practices of Islamic Sufism. On the other hand, outside the West we find the vast majority of Sufis, despite their tolerance and liberality, firmly rooted in Islam. For the contemporary student of Sufism, the relationship between Sufism and Islam offers ample opportunity for confusion, ambiguity, paradox, and argument. In the end it is related to the questions raised in the preceding paragraph—namely the relationship between spirituality and religion.

To what extent is it desirable and possible to distill the spirituality from a religious tradition, receiving what is most pure and essential while leaving behind the dregs of cultural relativity and historical bias? In a sense this is a task that must be done by every generation: restoring the essential message, the living impulse, the spirit of a tradition.

Some would go further, proposing that we either break with the past completely or, in a sense, create a new way based on former traditions. Rajneesh (now known as Osho) was an example of the former, claiming to represent a new beginning. Various gnostic, Rosicrucian, and even "Sufi" groups fit the second category, offering new rituals, symbols, and practices. Having experienced some of these activities, the question to be asked is: Apart from the subjective apprehension of their aesthetic or intellectual qualities, do these practices have the signs and characteristics of being a gift from a higher world, or the signs and characteristics of a human-invented ritual, symbol, or practice?

For example, tribal shamans may perform some strange and even bizarre acts, and yet these may have their own power, if received from the unseen world. We, however, in our desperation for authentic spiritual experience, may attempt to design rituals of our own to fill a metaphysical vacuum. While, on the one hand, this can be an innocent and entertaining activity, it may fall short of offering a comprehensive way of life and path to realization.

A truly universal spirituality is one that is not *limited* by any form. It's not a universality that's made by taking a little bit of this and a little bit of that. It's not a designer religion, which is what people often mean by universality. The ego sometimes says, " I'd like a little bit of this, a little bit of that, and over here this may be difficult, so I won't take this now. I'll take some of this," and we put together our own shlocker-mocker workshop of spirituality, which suits the ego perfectly.

If we look at the origin of the practices and ceremonies of classical Sufism, we see that virtually all of them have been inspired, not invented. The ablutions and ritual prayer of Islam were taught to Muhammad by the Angel Gabriel through visionary experience. At various times in history the Pirs of various Sufi orders have been instructed through dreams or visions to perform certain rituals in certain ways. A good example of this was the initiation of the Halveti-Jerrahi

Order, which happened in the following way. Nureddin Jerrahi is said to have received confirmation of having reached a certain spiritual station and the mandate to begin a new branch of the Halveti when the Prophet Muhammad appeared to him in a dream. But this was not the end of it. The following morning, various shaikhs began showing up at his door offering different aspects of what was to become the zikr ceremony and characteristic dress of the Halveti-Jerrahis—all these shaikhs, moreover, had seen the Prophet in a dream and had been told specifically what they should contribute. In this way, the rituals and practices of most Sufi orders have been gifts from the Unseen.

Within the Mevlevi tradition we are fortunate to have, in addition to the classical practices of Islam, the whirling ceremony, a form of worship whose origins are hidden in the immemorial Great Spirit tradition of Central Asia, but which took on a unique cosmological/ alchemical symbolism in its Mevlevi form, which traces back to Shams of Tabrīz and Rūmī's son, Sultan Veled.

Furthermore, the treasure contained within the *Mathnawī* and *Divan* of Jalāluddīn Rūmī can be considered the most significant body of inspired literature originating from a single human being. While it cannot be considered a "revelation" in the same sense as the Qur'ān, it is nevertheless a literature of the highest level of inspiration and aesthetic beauty that fulfills what is revealed in the Qur'ān.

Inevitably, when Mevlānā is introduced to people in the West, most writers feel duty-bound to mention that while he lived and wrote within the framework of Islam, his spirituality was not dogmatic. Of course. Mevlānā was another universal human being, and yet it deserves to be mentioned that all his life he was devoted to the prayers, Qur'ānic recitation, fasting, and night vigils that were the common practice of all classical Sufis.

The issue of the relationship of Sufism to Islam can be better understood if we consider the centrality of the Qur'ān and the example of Muhammad. In brief, Muhammad was an unlettered but intelligent recipient of a communication that bears all the marks of having come from a very deep or high source. He was like an empty tablet, at first the unsuspecting recipient of language so powerful that its effects upon Muhammad were obvious to all when it descended upon him. The voice of the Qur'ān is certainly not the voice of Muhammad.

If we take the Qur'ān at its own word, it claims to be *"a mercy toward mankind," "a guidance," "containing no distortion,"* and *"providing all that is healthy for the soul."* It claims to be a message from the *"Lord of the universes,"* who is also the God of all religions. It *"confirms what is true of past revelations,"* and offers a critique of where those revelations have been distorted.

Its intent is to remind us of the master truth of existence, the reality of an Unseen Beneficence, who is intelligent, aware, and powerful enough to embrace every detail of existence. It is this Love (ar-Rahmān), this Truth (al-Haqq), in which we are to place our complete faith, rather than worshiping secondary causes or ascribing other gods as equals to the One God. We can find this God *"nearer than our own jugular vein,"* and yet this God is *"beyond anything we can say"* about it.

Most spiritual seekers in these times would assert their freedom from religious "dogmas," preferring, instead, an experiential spirituality. No spiritual practice, however, is entirely free of assumptions, premises, cosmology, metaphysics, and myth. By dogma, however, is probably meant those assertions of opinion based exclusively on some human authority—usually an authority claiming to speak for God Himself.

The Qur'ān is virtually free of dogma—and by dogma, here, I mean the assertion of belief or opinion without evidence. In the category of dogma I would place those ideas that either (1) define or particularize Absolute Reality with concepts, or (2) ascribe an exclusive agency of salvation to one religion (the notion that God "has a religion and it is . . . ," as is encountered in most fundamentalisms), or (3) claim a unique and unverifiable divine power for a particular individual.

The Qur'ān is not unique in its relative freedom from dogma. The words of Jesus in the Gospels are likewise free from dogma and theology—although this has not hindered the formation of dogmas and theologies based upon these words. All faiths necessarily assert or propose some model of the Divine. These can be as general as "God is Love." Or as particular as "God is an invisible purple armadillo."

Whereas the first assertion may be supported with "And you can verify this for yourself if . . . ," the second assertion is likely to be supported by "Because we say so" or "Tradition says so."

Once one has accepted that there is a Reality that is apparent neither to the senses nor to the intellect alone but can be apprehended by another knowing faculty within the human being, and that this Reality might be able to communicate with humanity by offering the same message to various messengers, then one can take a critical look at the Qur'ān, the circumstances of its revelation, and Muhammad and decide for oneself whether this offers a truthful and helpful description of the human situation. One may find that it even helps to sort out the essential truths from the relative accretions in other traditions. In other words, it may point us to the universal spirituality itself.

From a certain point of view one need not even become a Muslim, in the sociological sense, to live in harmony with or value the Qur'ān's guidance and message. Since, for instance, Jesus is viewed in Islam as a prophet of God, just as Muhammad is, there can be no essential conflict between the way of Jesus and the way of Muhammad. Any Christian who sincerely follows the message of Jesus is in fact a "Muslim" from the point of view of the Qur'ān. Muslims, however, might question whether certain Christian dogmas represent the true teachings of Jesus, but that is another matter. Anyone who takes the message of the Qur'ān seriously must accept all the previous messengers of God—both those we know and those we don't know.

Those who have encountered and lived with the message of the Qur'ān must acknowledge that God's Compassion, Generosity, and Mercy operate through all religions, and in fact through all the phenomena of existence. God's qualities rain down upon the faithful of all faiths and even upon those who deny this Reality.

On the other hand, the Qur'ān can be viewed as a clear, undistorted communication from the Divine Intelligence offering the guidance needed to reach our full human potential, God-consciousness, and social harmony.

Having glimpsed the universal spirituality revealed in the Qur'ān, what remains significant and compelling for the Sufi is the particular grace operating through the specific forms of the Islamic revelation: ritual prayer, fasting, the human example of the Prophet Muhammad, and the guidance of the Qur'ān, as well as the Sufi practices that have been developed over the centuries. At the same time, it is possible and necessary to love and find common cause with all people of good will.

Soul Loss and Soul Making

I T IS A COMMON ENOUGH NOTION THAT MODERN HUMANITY is suffering from a loss of soul that can be traced to the quantification and intellectualization of reality. The development of soul depends on our understanding of what the soul is and what its possibilities are. What has to be restored is the presence of soul and its imaginative powers, but souls can be sick or healthy; souls can be created in this vale of soul-making, and souls can also be lost.

The prevailing Western culture, especially of the last century or so, has recognized only two forms of knowledge: the concrete/sensory and the abstract/conceptual. We have sense impressions, and we have ideas. The Qur'ānic proposition *"Wheresoever you look is the Face of God"* would be viewed as neither a statement of sensory fact nor as a valid hypothesis deduced from sensory experience but as a statement of the religious imagination. According to our cultural prejudices, whether the statement is inspiring or entertaining, it is imaginary, and what is imaginary is not real.

That existence can be imagined to be the "Face of God" signifies a way of perceiving that depends on a psychospiritual power that has more or less atrophied in modern humans. We have to rediscover it in order to know the value of the knowledge it offers. This psychospiritual power has been called the "active imagination," and its field of perception is neither the world of abstract impersonal concepts nor the world of sensory data, but the imaginal world (*mundus imaginalis* in Latin, or *'ālami mithāl* in Arabic).

Active imagination is a term used by classical Sufis who represented a metaphysics of pure monotheism in which God alone is real, while the "I" that separates itself from this unified Reality is unreal.

The *mundus imaginalis,* or *'ālami mithāl,* is a level of reality in which "meanings" are embodied as images that have a kind of autonomous existence. The imaginal world is an "interworld" in which visions, which are simultaneously meanings, are experienced by a psychospiritual faculty, the active imagination, or what Sufis would simply call the "heart." It is important to realize that this level of perception was reliably available only to those souls that were to some extent "purified." In its mature functioning it was certainly not a conceptual, intellectual, or merely symbolic experience, but a visionary one of the kind that many Western psychospiritual explorers touch only rarely in their lives, but which is the natural medium of mature mystics. It is not uncommon for a Sufi to ask another, "Did it happen in the tangible world or in *meaning (māna)?*" Whether the experience of the active imagination is in a dream or in wakefulness, it has the quality of profound significance.

For some, whom I will call the psychological polytheists, the *mundus imaginalis* is the playground of "the gods." They have appropriated the concept of the interworld for very limited purposes. The *mundus imaginalis* is not to be unlocked by either fantasy or intellect, but by the purified heart, understood here as a subtle but penetrating cognitive faculty of mind beyond intellect.

When it is proposed that modern man has lost his soul, one meaning is that we have lost our ability to perceive through the active imagination, which operates in an intermediate world, an interworld between the senses and the world of ideas. This active imagination is the imaginative, perceptive faculty of the soul, which cannot be explained because it is itself the revealer of meaning and significance. The active imagination does not produce some arbitrary concept standing between us and "reality" but functions directly as an organ of perception and knowledge just as real as—if not more real than—

the sense organs. And its property will be that of transmuting and raising sensory data to the purity of the subtle, spiritual world.

Through the active imagination the things and beings of the earth are made spiritually luminous. This imagination does not construct something unreal; it unveils the hidden reality. It helps us to return the facts of this world to their spiritual significance, to see beyond the apparent and to manifest the hidden. Every form is a concealer of truth and a possible distraction, on the one hand, and a revealer of truth and a sign of God, on the other. Reading God's signs is an aspect of our communication with God. We can read God's signs if we learn to return the signs to their original source, to first principles.

The function of this power of the soul lies in restoring a space that sacralizes the ephemeral, earthly state of being. It unites the earthly manifestation with its counterpart on the imaginal level, and raises it to incandescence. Isn't this what is sought by most of those who are drawn to paganism, mythologies, and mystical eroticism?

REINVENTING THE SOUL

One of the dubious ideas that has gained some currency is a reinvention of the meaning of "soul." The word has traditionally meant one's essential, spiritual identity, one's deepest self. Yet according to this reinvented view, soul is somehow *contrasted* with or opposed to Spirit.

In some forms of this view, the soul has become a catchall term for deep, moist, feminine, imagistic energies that love to taunt, distract, and otherwise harass the rigid, self-serious ego and the well-meaning but rather dry and all-too-highbrow spirit. Yet this "soul," at the same time, is also understood as the key to meaning, love, religious concern. Sometimes it seems that all that is left over for poor old spirit is but an impersonal bird's-eye view of all the messy stuff of life.

It is difficult to argue with concepts and categories as amorphous and self-contradictory as this. Is the matter of soul so beyond definition, beyond principles, that we can only make poetic lunges at meaning that lead to no particular conclusion? It may be that soul cannot be confined by anyone's definitions and is fundamentally a mystery.

Nevertheless, the idea of "soul" has a history within Western spiritual tradition.

The Neoplatonic heritage to which most Western spiritual thinkers must trace their idea of soul can be read very differently. According to Plotinus, for instance, the human soul was originally free and super-sensuous but turned its gaze earthward and bodyward and so fell into this earthly existence. Having lost its original freedom, it will find its fulfillment in "remembering" its condition prior to this involvement with flesh and material. The true self, which consists of *logos* and *nous*, pure knowing and reflection, later became obscured or veiled by the animal appetites and attachment to material existence. As a prepara-tion for visionary contemplation, this true soul must first go beyond the conceptualizations of the philosophers and then must purify itself of the contamination of the body and its sensuality. Even this, how-ever, is not the final stage. Union with the Divine can be known only through *ecstasy*, namely when the soul is taken out of itself and reaches identity with . . . Spirit.

It is not among the realized saints of Spirit that we find dryness and denial of the earthly, but among certain intellectuals and religious professionals. The saints, by contrast, are the first to meet the salt of the earth on their own terms. This is what Spirit does, in addition to lifting the human being up. It is not Spirit that denies the validity of earthly existence, both its pleasures and suffering, but that indulgent hedonism which is more likely to be the outcome of psychological polytheism's Felliniesque concept of soulfulness.

Psychological polytheism conceives the psyche's basic structure to be an inscape of personified images. Through the lack of a true center, this view diminishes and trivializes the human soul by reducing it to the terms and level of the social disease of our time: psychic fragmenta-tion. Mysticism would propose that this structure is not the psyche's basic nature, but only a superficial layer of the psyche. Beyond this psychological menagerie lies a deeper selfhood, which alone can give order and meaning to life.

Doesn't it strike anyone as strange that the psyche should be com-posed of an inner pantheon of ancient literary creations, as if such a pantheon were an objective personification of the human psyche? Why select one mythology out of all the world's many mythologies and give it central importance, especially considering that it was probably supplanted many times over by later "myths" that were more alive and of much wider application. The return to mythology is a narrowing of our consciousness into an archaic and idiosyncratic soap opera, which is not to say that some human psychological truth can't be found in it. But just because the human psyche creates characters does not necessarily mean that the human psyche is determined by the characters it created.

Yet a pure monotheism need not be monolithic or abstract. Zoroastrian monotheism, for instance, has its angels: an angel of the earth, angels of the mineral and vegetable worlds, an angel of feminine wisdom, an angelic counterpart for each human soul. Islam, the matrix within which ecstatic Sufism arose, has its divine attributes, which fall into the two categories of *jamal* and *jalal,* or gentleness and rigor, intimacy and awe, hope and fear. Although Plotinus did not reject polytheism out of hand, he saw the "gods" as manifestations of the One Divine. Historically, however, his successors deviated further and further until their polytheism degenerated into superstition, magic, and theurgy, which are distractions from the One Spirit and Unity of all existence. Psychological polytheism could contribute to a similar degeneration.

What distinguishes psychological polytheism from monotheism is not its willingness to admit diversity; rather, it is that polytheism has no center. Polytheism is a not an uncommon state in the modern world, an unconscious and chaotic idolatry of appearances, a fragmentation and disintegration of the psyche, which is a living hell. It is the state of the one whose identity is always shifting, a dissociation of voices and images absorbed from the mass media, an identity without integration. A comedian like Robin Williams, who can shift personae in midsentence, is an entertaining example of psychological fragmentation; at least he makes us laugh. Some would have us believe that we are nothing but a menagerie of animals and mythological figures, and that any integration around a center is a ploy and fantasy of the ego.

One of C. G. Jung's contributions to our understanding of the psyche is the discovery of autonomous complexes or archetypes that create drives and produce images and stories that seem to have lives of their own. These archetypes are relatively independent of the conscious ego and are sometimes opposed to it. Jung, however, believed in a central and essential archetype, the Self, which is the unifying principle of all other archetypes. For Jung, all archetypes were in service of the Self, and the end of conscious development is a harmony between ego and Self.

It is true that our greatest disease in this postmodern era is "the loss of soul," but this is not necessarily because we have denied the image-making capacities of the psyche (our culture is dominated by images), nor because we have denied ourselves a soulful sensuality (we live in the era of unrepression), nor because we live at such a spiritually transcendent height. We have lost our soul, our interiority, within the artificial and unnatural conditions that we have accepted as everyday life and within which it requires an extraordinary sense of purpose to sustain that interiority. We have set in motion forces that have their own oppressive momentum oblivious to the rhythms of the human soul. As a result, we have surrendered to compulsive and stressful living, and have seen our attention fragmented. More and more, these unnatural conditions have driven us toward more unconscious sensuality and materialism in a blind effort to grasp something real.

PSYCHIC FRAGMENTATION AND
SPIRITUAL MINIMALISM

As we are pulled into the future, our developing technologies shrink time and space while increasing information. More and more information and fantasy is available, and it is available more easily and cheaply. Whether we gain access to this new world of fantasy, instant shopping, and pornography by cable in Atlanta or through a "satellite-wallah" in a Calcutta slum, old boundaries are dissolving and new "realities" are beckoning.

Satellite television, VCRs, and computer networks are offering us a world of entertainment and distraction, most of it created and controlled by commercial producers whose main interest is to make profits. In traditional, premodern societies, culture developed out of whatever sacred framework the tribe or community shared. Such sacred frameworks were the repository of wisdom and experience and of the needs of the unconscious. Today's mass culture is created by marketing departments that are seeking to hold people's attention by any means possible, regardless of whether what is communicated affords any personal, social, or spiritual benefit.

Our subconscious dream life has now been exteriorized through the omnipresence of surrealistic images and sounds. It could also be proposed that the entertainment environment is degrading our subconscious psyche by indiscriminately, if not perversely, catering to our appetites and egoism.

We may be creating psychic ghettos in which a poverty of human values, an unemployment of creative powers, an overcrowding of inner space, lead to gratuitous violence, atrophy of will, and addiction to mind- and heart-numbing entertainment.

Just as the sociological ghetto is the outcome of the dark side of economic exploitation and social injustice, leading to the fragmentation of the family and community, so is the new psychic ghetto of inner world decay. The perverse individualism we have accepted as normal is based not on the human being as the center of the universe, but on human egoism having usurped the wholeness of the human mind. Many human problems are rooted in the slavery of the human ego to a formless, unconscious, selfish search for individual pleasure that becomes increasingly a numbing addiction.

This tyranny of the ego is the direct result of the abandonment of the principles of transformation, sacred to all traditional wisdom cultures, involving sacrifice, love, presence, humility, and surrender to the Way of the Universe.

It may seem unfashionable, untimely, or politically incorrect to offer a prophetic voice at this time, but perhaps we need a reminder that many "civilizations" before us have perished through their own excesses, the loss of control of their own selves, their transgressions of common sense, harmony, and balance.

Not all choices and developments in an individual human life or in a society's life are necessarily the healthy, self-correcting, self-regulating powers that may sometimes be found in a healthy or nearly healthy psyche. Sometimes the subconscious (heart) has the power to guide, heal, and redirect the consciousness (ego), but this exteriorized dream world we are living in may be the nightmare of a collective mental illness. If so, what are our possibilities and choices? The conscious self can make certain decisions and choices that reflect upon the health and, might we say, purity of the unconscious. In the past, these choices would have been informed by the collective wisdom of the culture, a wisdom that included such values as humility, self-respect, patience, sacrifice, and self-awareness. But then the culture might have been the product of some wisdom and not of mere marketing.

Hearts need education and refinement just as the body needs exercise and moderation. While a large percentage of our planet's population is malnourished, a large percentage of industrial culture is overfed and toxic. Likewise, to the extent that we do not incorporate some conscious principle of transformation, some uplifting agency, our souls are malnourished and toxic, our hearts are numb, and our wills are atrophied.

Perhaps what is called for at this time, more than anything else, is a spiritual minimalism, a reliance on the principle of less is more: less distraction, less cynicism, less entertainment, less pleasure seeking for its own sake, less indiscriminate consumption of information and fantasy, and more inner silence, more concentration upon our own nature and being, more unmediated sharing of one another's simple human presence, more development of our innate human qualities of friendship, nurturing, awareness, sensitivity, humbleness, and awe.

The outer dream that surrounds us may be the manifestation of our own psychic fragmentation. It may be less an embodied vision than a broadcast, commercially sanctioned schizophrenia.

When the heart has been awakened and refined, its dreams are freed from neurotic subjectivity and become more objective, symbolic, and inspired. These are obviously not the dreams our consumer culture is dreaming. It doesn't take a brilliant observer to realize that the quality of our dreams has been becoming more morbid and perverse even in the relatively tiny span of recent decades. How will we wake from this disturbed sleep? Are these the symptoms of an illness that will finally be acknowledged? Where would we find the collective will to commit ourselves to our own recovery?

THE SOUL AS UNIFYING PRESENCE

If there is a realm of soul it is this: presence, which is an attribute of the Spirit, and which as center can integrate all the levels of the human being. Presence is a faculty that operates at all levels of being and that also makes the *mundus imaginalis* intelligible, but only if we have "presence" on that level of refinement where we are not dominated or ruled by sensual concerns—which is not the same as denying or repressing them.

The psychological polytheists often ridicule or dismiss a spirituality that focuses on the transcendent at the expense of the immanent. It is true that there are pathologies of spiritual aspiration. But the realization of the spiritual is always allied with a realization of our own humanness in humility. It is the helplessness of our human situation, our weakness in relation to our subconscious complexes, that leads us to surrender to the wholeness of the Self. While the unconscious may produce complexes that challenge the autonomy of the ego, the soul is precisely that unifying presence and interiority which experiences and reconciles our finite humanness and our spiritual transcendence. Both the ego and the unconscious complexes, on the one hand, and Spirit, on the other, are held within the embrace of presence.

All true spiritual work is based on the unity of these different aspects of our being. An alternative to the conception of the human being proposed by psychological polytheism and other regressive pathways, and one more consistent with the sacred wisdom traditions, would be the model we have already described, which is based on three essential factors combining to form a whole. The terms that must be used in English are, unfortunately, somewhat vague and imprecise. By defining our terms, however, we can give them a more exact meaning within the context of our studies.

1. The "ego" (or natural self, the realm of eros), a complex of psychological manifestations arising from the body and related to its sur-

vival. It has no limit to its desires, but it can supply the energy necessary to aspire toward completion, or individuation.

2. The "Spirit" or "spiritual self" (essential self, essence, nous), the inmost center, the divine reflection at the core of our being, which is capable of higher reason and is in direct contact with the spiritual world. This spiritual self can help to guide the natural self, limit its desires to what is just and reasonable, and, more important, help it to see the fundamental desire behind all desires: the yearning to know our Source. It can help to establish presence on all levels of our being.

3. The "soul," whose chief instrument is "the heart" (including the psychic and intuitive functions, active imagination), an interior presence that can be under the influence of either the ego or the spiritual self. When we speak about involving ourselves "heart and soul," we are speaking about this aspect of ourselves. Living from the heart, having a pure heart, refers to a deep condition of spiritualized emotion. Losing one's soul refers to a condition of having the soul dominated by material, sensual, and egoistic concerns. Such a "heart and soul" are veiled, dim, unconscious. The heart is the prize that the "animal self" and "spiritual self" struggle to win, but when it is dominated by the "animal self," it is not truly a heart at all.

4. The "individuality" (the result of the relationship of all three). When the spiritual self has been able to harmonize with the natural self, and "heart and soul" have been purified, then the human being exists as a unified whole, fully responsive to the Divine, Creative Will.

One way to conceive of this model is as three concentric layers. The outer layer is the "natural self," which contains the deeper level of the "soul," within which is contained the "Spirit." If the soul, as presence, is not in place, there cannot be a relationship between the natural self and Spirit.

We are not the first people on earth to attempt to understand the human soul and its purpose in the universe, nor are we necessarily the best prepared or the most mature. The principles of the Way are neither so mysterious nor complex. Essentially the work means transforming the ego, the desire nature. Some religious traditions have proposed weakening the ego and the body in order to experience the spiritual self, but weakening ourselves is denying what we have been given. A more complete way is to strengthen the essential, spiritual self, to purify the heart, and to bring ego and eros into harmony with the heart. Only a strong and healthy individuality can reach completion. The individuality needs strength and passion to reach spiritual completion.

Both the spiritual self and the body have their needs. The body needs to be cared for, nurtured, and trained and exercised. It should not be allowed to dominate the heart. The more the animal side dominates, the more the heart is weighed down. The more the spiritual self predominates, the more lightness and spirituality we feel, the more our desires are in harmony with the Divine Will. Such a person will be content with relatively little in the material world, whereas a person dominated by the ego's desires will never have enough sex, pleasure, money, or power.

All of existence is the manifestation of Spirit in a vastly colorful and real array. The soul and its imaginative power is that which experiences Spirit—unless, of course, it only experiences the body and its emotions.

Psychological polytheism seems to overlook the degree to which the unconscious complexes may also be related to the ego. The ego, then, in a desperate attempt to assure its own survival at the expense of the wholeness of mind, can produce unconscious complexes of nightmarish power. One suspects that what is sometimes meant by *soul* may be the deep voice of eros/ego, of hedonism, of narcissism, of simple indulgence.

Perhaps real healing and real wholeness on the individual level exist when we operate as a whole, when we are not in disabling conflict, emotionally or physically. On the spiritual level, health is realizing that we are integral to this universe, not a part of it, not a microcosm of it, but coextensive and consubstantial with the Whole, the true Center. The awakened soul is characterized by presence of heart. Through its purified imaginative powers, the awakened soul raises the earthly and ephemeral facts to the level of spiritual incandescence. By virtue of its reconciling power it brings about a loving marriage between the natural self and the Spirit.

The world is a place for fashioning the soul, in the sense that soul is not given to us automatically, despite our assumptions to the contrary. Our interiority, our presence, must be created from within the distractions and forgetfulness of everyday outer life, from within the constant clash of pleasure and pain, happiness and loss. Our soul is a *space* for our experience; it makes the difference between being nominally alive and consciously alive. It makes a real connection possible between the ego and Spirit.

> My love for You goes deeper than my own self.
> My Way amounts to this:
> I don't say I'm inside myself. I'm not.
> The I within me is deeper than myself.
>
> Anywhere I look, it's filled with You.
> Where can I put You if You're already inside?
> You are Beauty without features,
> something deeper than any signs. . . .
>
> Some get their share of revelations,
> and some go deeper than this.
> In the beautiful light of His face
> is a fire brighter than the light of day.
>
> What a suffering it is
> that's deeper than any remedy.
> The Law and the Brotherhood are paths.
> Wisdom and Truth are still deeper. . . .
>
> I've forgotten religion and piety.
> What if there's a doctrine deeper than religion?
> The works of those who leave the faith
> are blasphemy. What about a blasphemy
> deeper than faith?
>
> Yunus chanced to meet a Friend
> who showed him a door inside.[1]

---

[1] Yunus Emre, *The Drop That Became the Sea*, translated by Kabir Helminski and Refik Algan (Putney, Vt.: Threshold Books, 1986).

Ecstasy and Sobriety

WHAT IS THE PLACE OF ECSTASY IN A MATURE SPIRITUAL-
ity? Are there different states to be discerned beyond the
label of ecstasy? Can it be reconciled with sobriety? Should
ecstasy be pursued?

The poetry of Rūmī and other Sufis often exudes a fragrance of
ecstasy that has attracted generations of seekers. While this fragrance
has spread far beyond the boundaries of its original homelands, its
source is not merely cultural, historical, or geographic. The source of
this ecstatic state is experiential, spiritual, ontological. The fragrance
of ecstasy reminds some people of *home*. In the words of Mevlānā
Jalāluddīn Rūmī:

> I'm drunk and you're insane,
> who's going to lead us home?
> How many times did they say,
> "Drink just a little, only two or three at most"?
>
> In this city no one I see is conscious;
> one is worse off than the next, frenzied and insane.
>
> Dear one, come to the Tavern of Ruin
> and experience the pleasures of the soul.
> What happiness can there be apart

213

from this intimate conversation
with the Beloved, the Soul of souls?

In every corner there are drunkards, arm in arm,
while the Server pours the wine
from a royal decanter to every particle of being.

You belong to the tavern: your income is wine,
and wine is all you ever buy.
Don't give even a second away
to the concerns of the merely sober.

Have I lived among the lame for so long
that I've begun to limp myself?[1]

What is this drunkenness? What kind of sainthood is this? What was the context of this utterance? What is the role of ecstasy in Sufi spirituality? And what could these words mean in our own contemporary culture?

Rūmī's time was no less complex than our own. In his world there was neither peace nor security nor a monolithic belief system. Within the Islamic society of his time, diverse ways of seeing the world naturally flourished. Conventional religious piety, legalistic rigidity, cultic heterodoxy, philosophical cynicism, and what I will call orthodox Sufi mysticism breathed the same air.

Before our own cultural assumptions project Rūmī as a spiritual renegade who stood outside all beliefs, it is worth noting that Sufis like Rūmī never relinquished their claim to represent the heart and soul of Islam. Both Jalāluddīn Rūmī and his teacher, Shams of Tabrīz, walked in the footsteps of Muhammad, and said so clearly. When they were irreverent, it was against rigidity and hypocrisy. Within the essential boundaries of Divine Law, they found an approach to Truth by the ecstasy of Love.

We live in a time of practically institutionalized nonconformity, an unprecedented era of personal freedom and unrepression. We live in a

---

[1] From *The Rūmī Collection* (Putney, Vt.: Threshold Books, 1998).

time when ecstatic experience is compulsively sought. Ecstasy suggests being outside one's ordinary state, overcome with rapture. Today the flight from self-existence, from the burden of egoistic preoccupations, strategies, and ambitions, is accomplished through sensuality, intoxication, and mass entertainment.

Rūmī's call to drunkenness should not be confused with these dissolute or superficial intoxications. Ecstasy, like any precious commodity, will have its imitations and counterfeits. The authentic ecstasy of the Sufi is not based in emotionalism. Ecstasy is not a feeling to be pursued; rather, it is the freedom from all self-seeking pursuits.

The key to the drunkenness advocated by Rūmī and other Sufis lies in understanding the educational and transformational process of Sufism. "The Tavern of Ruin" is the Sufi dergāh in which this education is carried out. In the ideal of the dergāh, seekers came to lose the passions of the self and to experience the ecstasy of selflessness. This education was in every respect a deconstruction of the false self.

I am not aware of any book, or even chapter, in all of classical Sufi literature that is specifically addressed to the subject of ecstasy, although there are many terms in the Sufi "glossary" that relate to the subject of extraordinary spiritual experience. The Sufi technical term closest to ecstasy, *wajd,* is derived from the root meaning "to find." The great formulator of Sufism, Ibn 'Arabī, defined it as "a state formerly hidden from the heart that now confronts its perception."[2] The experience of ecstasy is the discovery (wajd) of true being (wūjūd). In this discovery the seeker is lifted to a transpersonal state of consciousness in which individual existence is seen for what it is: a provisional being, an existence dependent upon another order of Reality.

> O you whose selflessness and intoxication are Our Self,
> O you whose existence derives constantly from Ours.
> Now I will tell you without speech and with constant renewal
> The ancient mysteries: Listen!
>
> —RŪMĪ, M, III, 4682–84

---

[2] From *Al-Istilahat al-Sufiyyah,* published in Ibn 'Arabī, *What the Seeker Needs* (Putney, Vt.: Threshold Books, 1992).

It is also worth mentioning that there is a term, *tawājud,* which signifies pretending ecstasy, or attempting to summon ecstasy without ecstasy itself.

The everyday training was framed by the boundaries of Divine Law and the model of Muhammad's behavior (*sunnah*): ritual prayer, fasting, remembrance, the development of virtues (*akhlāq*). Within the Mevlevi tradition, community service, the study of sacred literature, and the cultivation of the arts (calligraphy, design, music, poetry, Qur'ānic recitation) completed the curriculum. The culmination of all of these practices might be the *semā,* a weekly event in which chanting, sacred music, mystical poetry, and various movements might lift the heart to a true spiritual ecstasy.

The practice of whirling may have its origins in the timeless shadows of Central Asian spirituality, where shamans used it to induce altered states of consciousness. We know that in the time of Mevlānā Jalāluddīn Rūmī it was already an ancient practice in use among Sufis. Shams of Tabrīz, beloved friend and initiator of Mevlānā, tells us:

> In the people of God, these (spiritual) manifestations and visions are more common during the Semā, when they have passed beyond their usual universe of existence. Semā carries them out of other worlds to the Truth. It is true that there is a kind of Semā that is forbidden; but it is blasphemy to say that the Semā performed by God's people is a sin. That hand which moves without the Divine exuberance will burn in hell for sure, and the hands that rise in Semā will reach paradise—for sure. And there is a Semā that is permissible but not obligatory. This is the Semā of those Sufis and ascetics who live in a state of fasting. It brings tears and softness of heart to them. There is no doubt that they will also enter Paradise. And another Semā is religiously a must. This is the Semā of the attained ones who have reached the holy state of mind. And another is a duty applicable to all, as the daily prayers and the fast of Ramadan. Just as food and water are necessary in the time of hunger and thirst, this Semā is necessary for the spiritually mature, because it increases their joy

of life. If one of the mature ones begins to whirl in the East, another one starts moving in the West. They are aware of each other's states.[3]

Shams also tells this story: A certain shaikh said, "The Caliph has forbidden the semā." This prohibition turned into a knot within a certain dervish. He fell ill, and they took him to a specialist. He examined his pulse and looked for the cause of illness. It was like nothing he had ever learned about. He couldn't find anything wrong with him, but the dervish died. Afterward, the doctor performed an autopsy and found the knot within his chest. It had become a carnelian. The doctor kept this gem until a time when he needed some extra cash. The gem passed from hand to hand until it reached the caliph, who had the gem set into a ring. One day, that same caliph was attending a semā, watching from a balcony above, when he discovered that his clothes were covered with blood. He examined himself but could find no wound anywhere. He felt for his ring and the stone was gone. Later they traced that gem back to its original owner and the doctor told them the whole story mentioned above.

The word *semā* comes from a root meaning to listen, suggesting an occasion when music is used to uplift the soul. The form that semā and whirling took in Rūmī's day was probably informal and ecstatic, consisting of long nights of zikr, music, and poetry. After the master's death and under the guidance of his dutiful son, Sultan Veled, the semā took a more ceremonial form, as a kind of embodied cosmology.

The semā that we witness today has existed more or less unchanged for at least several centuries and probably goes back to the time of Rūmī's son, Sultan Veled. It is a ceremony of worship, a meditation in movement, in which the human being becomes pure axis, integrating all levels of being within him- or herself, including the physical, emotional, mental, and spiritual levels. To perform the semā is to be centered on the timeless and spaceless, and to experience the meaning of these words from the Holy Qur'ān: *Wheresoever you look is the face of God.* It is to be unified with others who are compelled by the same

---

[3] Shams of Tabrīz, *Maqalat.* Unpublished translation by Kabir Helminski and Refik Algan.

spiritual longing. It is to be emptied of all distracting thoughts and to be filled with the presence of God. It is itself a journey taken in a direction opposite to that of temporal time, a journey of return to the Source, through our innermost center where we are closest to the Divine.

It would be worthwhile to try to describe what occurs within individuals as they enact this ceremony year after year as part of their spiritual training, for the ceremony itself teaches its secrets over time, and no two ceremonies are experienced in the same way. The individual *semāzen*, or dervish, must be able to expand awareness to include several dimensions at once: He or she must focus on his or her own physical axis, which in this case is the left leg and foot, revolving three hundred and sixty degrees with each step, inwardly pronouncing the name of God, keeping an awareness of exactly where he or she is in space and the narrow margins of error in this tight choreography, feeling a connection through the shaikh of the ceremony to the whole lineage and also the founder of the order, Mevlānā, and most of all turning with a deep love of God. The sheer impossibility of accomplishing all of these tasks through one's own will can push one toward another possibility: that of letting a deeper will take over. In this way, the semā becomes a lesson in surrender.

The Mevlevi tradition has always been a way of both aesthetic refinement and inner development. It includes not only the writings of Mevlānā Jalāluddīn Rūmī, arguably as great a literary opus as exists on earth, but seven centuries of other Mevlevi poets and scholars as well. In addition, there is the vast tradition of Turkish classical music with its subtlety of melody and modes, which generations of Mevlevi composers made possible. And finally there is the whole Mevlevi way of life, progressive in spirit and spiritual to its core. Within the later Sufi tradition, semā was routinely forbidden to those who were dominated by their worldly selves, because the music and movements were likely to magnify whatever qualities predominated in the soul. On the other hand, Rūmī and his companions would sometimes spontaneously engage in semās lasting for days.

Such activities were radical behavior in the context of the religious orthodoxy in which the mixing of music and spirituality was suspect.

Because the original impulse and inspiration of Islam was meant to offer human beings a purified spirituality, it is understandable that there would be some resistance to the employment of secondary means of achieving interiority. This had the advantage of fostering a religious culture relatively free of poor taste, mawkish art, and spiritual materialism. Within the sacred context, visual art became abstract design and musical expression was channeled into Qur'ānic recitation. And so music and representational art were generally discouraged as a *means* to spiritual experience.

Nevertheless, among the mystics, the positive effects of semā and ecstatic experience were recognized. Hujwīrī wrote in his *Kashf al-Mahjūb*:

> The effects of semā can be very different, depending on one's degree of spiritual realization. For the penitent, semā brings remorse. For those longing for God, it increases their yearning. For the believers, it strengthens their certainty. For the disciple, it verifies what has been taught. For the lover, it helps to cut off attachments. And for the selfless Sufi, it is the basis of his loss of faith and trust in the world, enabling him to give up everything including himself.

Music, whirling, chanting, and spontaneous poetry were the expression of the state of spiritual love in those early days, but gradually these practices were formalized and ritualized, becoming a means toward the state of spiritual love rather than the spontaneous expression of it.

The majority of human beings cannot grasp the mysteries and pleasures of selfless ecstatic experience. And so it has been necessary that the work of mystics and ecstatics be guarded and protected from the intrusion and meddling of those whom the Sufis call "raw."

> Listen to the words of Sanā'i from behind the veil:
> "Rest your head where you have drunk the wine!"
> Any drunk who strays from the tavern
> becomes the fool and the laughingstock of children.
> He stumbles in the mud at the sides of the road

and every fool laughs at him.
He continues on his way, the children following behind,
ignorant of his drunkenness and the taste of wine.
All of mankind are children,
except for those who are drunk with God.
No one is mature who is not free of self-will.

—RŪMĪ, 1, 4326–30

To misunderstand or exaggerate the place of ecstasy in Sufism is to diminish and distort the wholeness and balance that characterize the Path. I once heard Sufism defined by an outsider as "a body of techniques for producing ecstasy," but ecstasy is not the goal, even if it sometimes is a by-product.

There is a creative tension in Sufism between enlightenment and maturity. By enlightenment we mean those higher states of consciousness that bring light and life into the soul. By maturity we mean that overall development of character and virtue, including the ability to express oneself and participate effectively in the life around us. The ultimate expression of maturity is "servanthood," not in the menial sense but in the way of dauntless friendship and generosity. And yet the servant assumes a kind of "ordinariness," an invisibility within society.

In the whirling ritual of the Mevlevi, there are symbolic actions that suggest the balance of ecstasy and the containment of ecstasy. The ceremony is punctuated by "stops," in which the participants come to stillness, hands upon their shoulders, forming the Arabic letter *alif*, which is also the number one. Instead of pursuing ecstasy, they are called back from the brink of ecstasy to testify to the oneness of God. The dervish recalls his or her "nonexistence." God is everything. The ultimate state for the human being is conscious servanthood, which continually recalls the Being of God as the Source of everything. It is utter humility and abandonment of self. A second feature is when the shaikh whirls near the end of the ceremony. He turns slowly and majestically in the center of the floor, his right hand holding open his robes just slightly. This gesture is a reminder of the early days when people uncontrollably tore their robes in a state of abandonment.

While it is true that many who are attracted to the path of Sufism are ecstatics by nature, just as many are sober and practical. Rūmī's teacher, Shams, said of his own teacher, Shaikh Selabaf, that he attained intoxication but never reached sobriety! Within the tradition it is no secret that spiritual maturity is a state of sobriety that encompasses intoxication.

There have always been and will always be a percentage of the mystically inclined who may be somewhat dissolute. Faced with the hypocrisies of conventional social life and the traumas of periodically arising social disruption and mass insanity, it isn't surprising that more sensitive souls would turn to transcendence in whatever form might be available. It is no less true today. And yet the widespread misinformation, especially in contemporary Islamic societies, that Sufis are irresponsible, indulgent, or dissolute belies the facts: in the history of Islamic cultures, a majority of the most creative and accomplished minds and the most sanctified souls have been affiliated with Sufi orders.

The ecstasy that is sought for the purposes of escaping the burden of egoism cannot emancipate us from that egoism, because it is a direct expression of it. The real spiritual ecstasy may occasionally come to those who have learned the lessons and art of sacrifice. Ecstasy is strangely associated with agony. To the outside observer the signs of ecstatic transport may even look like torment. To the extent that any self-awareness remains, to the extent that there is an experiencer of the experience, there is the possibility of bewilderment, unfulfilled longing, and even awesome dread.

One of the most sobering examples of ecstasy may be in the movie *Schindler's List*, near the end when Schindler realizes the actual "cost" of a limousine he has selfishly held on to throughout the war. In a moment, he admits to himself that several lives could have been saved with the money this car would have brought. In this excruciating moment, we witness the coming together of intense personal remorse with the exaltation of seeing things as they really are. Schindler's pain was the precious experience of unconditional love. His "ecstasy" is that he was transported beyond his conventional self to a new and higher realization of the possibilities of freedom from self, of servanthood. This paradoxical shifting of form and ground, of agony and bliss, of individuality and selflessness may be the essence of the ecstatic experience.

Conventional religion becomes mere ritual and moral obligation without the reality of higher states of being. This characterized the spiritual bankruptcy that many people recognized within our own Western culture through the mid-twentieth century. Mysticism, on the other hand, can become a narcissistic obsession with higher states of consciousness—a tendency witnessed especially since the late sixties. How can balance be achieved? Is this the question our culture is asking at the moment?

The original and pure Islam called the average human being toward the depths of mystical experience by inviting to contemplative prayer five times a day. The ritual was meant to awaken a state of presence. Muhammad said, "One moment of conscious reflection (*tafakkur*) is more valuable than seventy years of [unmindful] ritual prayer." But Islam also calls the mystic to rejoin the human community by melting into the bioenergetic ritual of surrender, by being grounded in the ranks of congregational prayer, by participating in the equalizing spirit of collective worship.

Sufism, as with any complete spirituality, is the integration or synthesis of the mystical and the prophetic consciousness, of ecstasy and practicality, of enlightenment and maturity. The mystic is inclined to explore states of consciousness, the prophet to bring earthly life more into harmony with higher states of consciousness. A Sufi is one who has attained "functional nonexistence," a grounded selflessness, a practical enlightenment.

> God! God! Don't expect the qualities of wine
> From the self-existent.
> Behold its all-encompassing Gentleness
> in the eyes of the drunk!
>
> —RŪMĪ, D, 23311

This Drunkenness Began
in Some Other Tavern

VETERANS OF THE CONSCIOUSNESS REVOLUTION MIGHT recall with pathos the battles waged against the conventional consciousness of the day. The enemy, so to speak, was the self-righteous state of mind, which believed it had a monopoly on reality and which at the same time had a shadow of cruelty and insanity. Tens of millions of people opened up their minds, let an uncensored truth into consciousness, and saw for themselves that most of modern life looked patently insane when seen against the backdrop of nature and eternity. For all its misguided power, conventional consciousness was still naively ridiculous. In those days, altering one's state of consciousness was a cleansing from the unrealities of social conditioning. It was not only revolutionary, it may have been an evolutionary necessity. Perhaps it allowed enough people to see the disastrous fate society was hurtling toward and to begin to change that direction.

Those who used certain substances to expand or deepen consciousness usually distinguished between other substances that merely offered sedation (heroin, barbiturates) or illusory well-being (cocaine, amphetamines). But many believed that certain substances could contribute to spiritual awareness.

Just as some human beings are compelled to explore the physical world as scientists, geographers, or naturalists, others are compelled to explore states of consciousness. These explorers of the mind work primarily with the equipment that nature has provided: the subjective human nervous system. These geographers and naturalists of the mind can be divided into two categories: first, those purists who work entirely with the nervous system, and second, those who rely on substances that modify the functioning of the nervous system.

I cannot judge whether psychoactive substances have been helpful to certain native peoples using animistic or shamanistic practices within an ancient cultural context and living in isolation from other societies. Do we have something to learn from them? Definitely. Should we try to live like them? I don't see how it would be either possible or desirable to apply their solutions to our environment, which is, after all, the contemporary multicultural, technological world.

A more important question, however, within the context of our current "culture," is whether drugs are useful or helpful in attaining our full humanity, our spiritual completion, or whether they are more likely to reduce our possibilities of such attainment. Since certain drugs are prevalent in the world today and hold an attraction, especially for the young, we cannot afford to stick our heads in the sand and ignore this question. More than anything else, we need a spirituality that can preserve and develop our humanity in the face of the challenges that our environment offers.

We exist as if we are imprisoned in a small part of the mind, the conscious mind, which is veiled or partitioned from the relatively infinite supraconscious mind. This supraconscious mind is considered by Sufi teaching to be the source of meaning and value that flows into consciousness. We are condemned to function in this small room of our conscious mind, occasionally receiving hints, messages, intimations of a vast world beyond.

There is more than one way to leave this room. One day someone finds that by taking a certain pill, he is miraculously transported outside the room to an extraordinary world. Unfortunately, he also finds that outside the room he has a much reduced capacity of reasoning, intention, and memory. Because whole parts of his being are meanwhile shut down, he cannot participate wholly in those worlds. He is much like a tourist on a chartered bus who can view the scenes that he passes through but is rather limited in his interaction with the landscape and its inhabitants. During his occasional tours, this psychic tourist glimpses the grand architecture or natural beauty of the world outside the bus; while the rest of his time is spent inside this small room, *which does not change.*

The world outside his room, the world glimpsed from this chartered bus, begins to be his place of temporary escape. He begins to live in two worlds, but the experiences of one world seem to preclude the experiences of the other world. One day the prisoner receives a book through a small window in the prison cell. The book's message could be summarized thus:

Your state of imprisonment is not a natural or necessary condition at all. In fact, you have a home beyond the walls of your prison, and you are meant to be free. You may regain your home and your freedom by relying on the capacity of your own nervous system and developing it in various ways, so that you can prepare yourself for the journey and the conditions of the outside world. You must be willing to leave behind your former life of imprisonment and find a way to undo the unique lock on your cell. The most likely chance for this is to be in contact with someone "on the outside" who can help you, and there are people willing to help those with a real wish to be free.

The prison is nothing but a habit of mind reinforced by the conditioning and general atrophy of the human nervous system. Let us say that the mind has its surface and its depth. The surface of the mind also has very useful functions: attention, decision, intention, recollection, forethought, and judgment, which collectively we might call higher reason. The surface of the mind can be further cluttered by acquired attitudes, beliefs, and opinions, as well as mechanical thoughts, associations, and reactions. The depth of the mind is the source of meaning and significance. Infinite resources and qualities are stored there in potential, as well as the means for creative action and problem solving of all kinds. The supraconscious also has subtle faculties or senses that are directly connected with the Divine Will. These correspond to the physical senses, but they are the means of perception

of the spiritual world. The subconscious also has its clutter of incul-
cated beliefs, compulsions, obsessions, and buried memories of emotional traumas. In the imprisoned state of mind, our contact with the
subconscious and supraconscious is very indirect and vague, because
the surface of the mind is totally in control.

Certain substances disable the surface of the mind (including attention, decision, intention, recollection, forethought, judgment, and reason), allowing the more or less random contents of the subconscious
mind to flood in. What fun! . . . for a while. A price is paid for the
disabling of will, which is one of the most essential characteristics of
our humanness. The crippling of will is a reduction of the holistic
functioning of our human capacities. Meanwhile the subconscious has
not necessarily been purified, and so it may yield up bizarre/subjective
as well as holy/objective impressions.

Intoxication could be viewed as psychic masturbation. Masturbation can be defined as trying to do something when you don't have
everything needed to do it. Contacting the supraconscious realms of
significance without our full equipment is like making love without a
partner. Not only is it less physically satisfying, it bypasses the emotional and spiritual dimensions of relationship. One can understand
the many reasons why people do it: loneliness, impatience, narcissism.
Masturbation creates a tension between the actual and the fantasy. It
leaves people askew and ultimately crippled.

Can psychoactive substances ever yield psychological or spiritual
benefit? A qualified "yes" suggests itself here. An experience produced
by external substances may give enough of a taste of a higher state of
being to motivate someone toward awakening that state on a more
permanent and stable basis, especially in the absence of the mature
spiritual guidance that certain traditions could offer. It is important to
keep in mind that the shift of perspective offered by certain drugs can
also be accomplished through various other means, one of which is
contact with someone who has attained a higher state of being. While
such an experience may be a bit less dramatic or extreme than a drug
experience, it nevertheless is less likely to cause a psychological imbalance. Such imbalances can also be caused by teachers who with limited
knowledge induce certain states in their students that may, if indulged

in, make them less fit for ordinary life and less capable of reaching completion.

In a mature spirituality a distinction is made between temporary states, on the one hand, and station or level of being, on the other. In less mature approaches there may be the tendency to rely on ecstatogenic techniques, narcotics of the path for the spiritually addicted. Certainly many people from the drug culture have been attracted to spiritual paths because they seemed to offer these altered states of consciousness. But mature traditions speak of a sobriety that encompasses and surpasses the ecstasy of intoxication.

In the higher forms of Sufism there is a fastidious purification of experience from all subjective (that is, personal) concerns. Shams of Tabrīz said, "Some of our friends find their joy in cannabis. This is the fantasy of the devil. With us, there is no place for the fantasy of the angels. How much less is there a place for the fantasies of the devil! We don't even accept the illusions of the angels, so what can the illusions of the devil be? Why don't our friends take pleasure in that clean and infinite universe of ours? This universe embraces them and makes them drunk without ever making them aware of it. Everyone is in unanimous agreement that this universe is not an illicit substance."[1]

The question might be asked: In working with the nervous system "alone," isn't one, in fact, producing the same substances (e.g., endorphins, neurotransmitters) through breathing and meditation exercises that are stimulated through certain drugs? And if this is so, couldn't one say that the person who uses a pill or "brain machine" in a disciplined way might not also produce the same results but in much less time?

This question is a little bit like asking: If it's possible to stimulate certain states in a laboratory monkey that are similar to the states that the monkey will meet in the jungle, can the monkey of the laboratory achieve the same maturity as the monkey who develops in the jungle? Both may experience "all that a monkey can experience." What is the difference?

According to Sufi understanding, one can experience Truth-Reality-God in "essence" or through "the attributes." The monkey who ma-

---

[1] Shams of Tabrīz. *Maqalat*. Unpublished translation by Kabir Helminski and Refik Algan.

tures in the jungle is developing through an experience of the attributes. Because of its relationship with its own natural milieu, the milieu in which its species developed, the jungle monkey, though theoretically experiencing the same states as the laboratory animal, will have more richness of experience, more maturity and understanding.

Let's imagine, for example, that we could raise a human being in a "spiritual hothouse," a programmed setting from birth, and give that person all the "meditation" experience it is possible to give, but withhold all the complexity, suffering, and disappointment that ordinary human beings face. This, too, would be a kind of laboratory enlightenment. How much compassion and understanding would such a person have for the struggles of an ordinary human being? Many attributes of our own essence seem to develop only when we are faced with certain kinds of challenges and difficulties. Sometimes the remedy is contained in the poison. In the illness is the cure and the means of immunity.

This is a complex subject. We can consider some principles and not get caught in absolutes.

The strongest argument in my own mind against any artificial means of spiritual exploration is that a price seems to be paid. The price is the weakening or disabling of important functions of the mind that could integrate the experience of the expanded states. For this reason, I would rather trust a tradition that offers a gradual approach that integrates expanded consciousness with practical and social skills.

A second consideration is that seeking "states," through whatever means, is at best an entertainment, and very likely a form of aggrandizing the ego. Can we see the trap involved in looking for some shortcut or high that will do it for us? Does the Beloved, as it were, want a conscious lover or an inebriated one?

A third consideration is an issue of faith, and by faith I mean a certainty in the existence and support of a Beneficent Reality. Can we accept that this equipment we have been furnished with and this life that we face are the best possible conditions for consciously knowing this Reality? Perhaps if we can surrender to *what is*, we will meet Truth, face to face.

Maybe we are meant to walk out of our prison with all our faculties intact and functioning. Maybe we are given exactly the equipment we need to know the universe. If we do not know how to use the equipment, that is another matter. We can learn. Through the conscious work on the nervous system, including purification from chemical and psychological toxins, understanding the finer energy system and the science of breath, we can prepare this physical vehicle for contact with all levels of reality.

Most important, we can open to Reality through our most human qualities: humbleness, gratitude, and love. These are not so much emotional states as cognitive capacities. We can live and function within the infinite ecology that lies outside the prison of conventional "reality" and, yes, paradoxically, right in front of us. *"Wheresoever you look is the face of God."*

> It's late and its raining, my friends,
> let's go home. Let's leave these ruins
> we've haunted like owls.
> Even though these beautiful images beckon,
> let's go home. And all the reasons offered
> by the sensible, dull, and sorrowful
> can't darken our hearts now,
> nor can all this phantom loveplay,
> this imaginary paradise, hold us back.
> Some see the grain but not the harvest.
> Don't ask too many hows or whys. Let beasts graze.
> Come home to the real celebration and music.
> The Friend has built a house for the naked and the pure.
>
> —RŪMĪ[2]

---

[2] *Love Is a Stranger*, translated by Kabir Helminski (Putney, Vt.: Threshold Books, 1993), p. 24.

NUANCES

The Hū of the Human

The sign of the faithless (*kāfir*) is that he is lost
    in the horizons.
The sign of the one with faith (*mu'min*)
is that the horizons are lost within him.

—MUHAMMAD IQBAL

A TRUE HUMAN BEING, ONE WHO *KNOWS* THE SECRET OF his or her humanness, is very rare. Many walk in the form of a human being while manifesting the qualities of animals, dominated by the desires of an animal. Many manifest the qualities of machines—very fine, well-programmed machines. Many manifest the qualities of actors, reading familiar lines, or improvising a little now and then. It might be possible to walk through a crowded city and see few, if any, human beings. No one completely loses his or her humanness by forgetting it or being ignorant of it, but a person who fully knows his or her humanness is extremely rare.

Much is said about our human condition in the Qur'ān. The voice of this revelation is addressed to the human being from the Creator of humanness. The path of classical Sufism is founded upon this view of the human being.

It is notable that God is said to have certain qualities: life, will, action, speech, seeing, hearing. It may seem strange to describe God

233

with the qualities of a human being. Or is it? Maybe it is the human being who has the qualities of God? These qualities are the inner form of the human being. These qualities are the seeing within seeing, the hearing within hearing, the life within life. The indwelling presence of God is signified by the word, *Hū*, the pronoun of Divine Presence.

The human is the eye of God and the hearing, speech, will, and life of God. The human being is not a face, although humanness shows through the face, especially through the eyes. The human being is the being who can finally say, "I am nothing." It is the depth within the human being that can perceive and say this. This is the highest truth, but how do we arrive at this truth?

We can begin by considering the creation of the human being as it is expressed in the Qur'ān.

> *And lo, your Sustainer said to the angels: "Behold, I am about to establish a representative on earth."*
>
> *And they said: "While we glorify You, and praise You, and keep Your name sacred, will You place there those who will spread corruption and shed blood?"*
>
> *And God answered, "In truth I know something you do not know."*
>
> *And God gave unto the Human (Adam) all the names of things; then God brought Adam before the angels and said to them, "Tell me the names of these, if what you say is true."*
>
> *The angels replied: "You are infinite in Your glory! And we have no knowledge other than what You have given us. Truly, You are the All-knowing and Wise."*
>
> *God said, "Adam, tell them the names of these things."*
>
> *And as soon as Adam had told them the names, God said, "Didn't I say to you, 'Truly, I alone know the hidden reality of the heavens and the earth and know all that you bring into the open and all that you would conceal?'"*
>
> *And when We told the angels, "Prostrate yourselves before Adam!" they all prostrated themselves except for Iblis, who refused and gloried in his arrogance, and thus he became one of those who deny the truth.*

And We said, "O Adam, may you and your wife live in this garden, and both of you eat freely whatever you wish from it, but do not approach this one tree."

But Satan caused them to stumble there, and thus caused the loss of their primordial state. And so We said, "Down with you, and be in conflict with one another, and have your home and your livelihood on earth for a while!"

From then on Adam received words of guidance from his Sustainer, and He accepted his repentance, for in truth, He alone is the Acceptor of Repentance, the Giver of Grace.

For although We did say, "Down with you all from this [state]," nevertheless guidance shall come to you from Me, and those who follow My guidance shall have no fear, nor shall they grieve; but those who are determined to deny the truth and giving the lie to Our messages—they are destined for the fire, and there shall they abide. [SURAH AL-BAQARAH (2):30–39]

The human being is God's representative on this earth, one who knows the true names of things. This knowing of the names is the knowing of the distinguishing characteristics of things, their innate qualities. The angels knew that such a creation would also be capable of spreading corruption and shedding blood, but after they were shown that the human being had inherited God's knowledge and language, they showed respect. Iblis, the one who could not show respect, became the sworn enemy of the human being, determined to waylay and distract humans from their own nature.

The satanic is not anti-God as much as it is anti-human. The satanic impulse is no threat to God except insofar as it threatens humanness. A sin is not a transgression against God but against humanness. To become a true human being, the divine representative and inheritor, each person faces a struggle with whatever distorts or corrupts this humanness.

We need to examine the characteristics of this struggle toward wholeness as well as the fragmentation that is our everyday life. The struggle most of us experience while contending with our own psychological fragmentation is the "horizontal" struggle of one part of ourselves in conflict with another, In this state we experience the tyranny of the ego, ruling by its often contradictory whims within a state of psychological anarchy. This struggle is especially destructive when each voice speaks within its own room, when there is no means of reconciliation, no table at which the different voices may be heard.

> Have you ever considered the kind of person
> who worships his own desires?
> —Surah al-Furqān (25):43

> They are like cattle, indeed worse.
> —Surah al-A'rāf (7):179

Here is the problem. We tend to externalize our own desires, thus creating idols to worship. We then direct all our efforts toward these idols, but because those idols are just the externalizations of our own desires, they cannot really help us. This false worship turns out to have led us nowhere.

The human being tends to be restless and unstable:

> *Truly, a human being is born with a restless disposition. When-*
> *ever misfortune touches him, he is filled with self-pity; and*
> *whenever good fortune comes to him, he selfishly withholds it.*
> [Surah al-Ma'ārij (70):19–21]

When this instability is combined with a lack of moral energy that results from losing touch with the transcendental anchoring point of human action, it is as though *"these people are being called from a distant place"* [Surah Fussilat (41):44].

Ibn 'Arabī writes:

> This world is not bad; on the contrary, it is the field of eter-
> nity. What you plant here you will reap there. This world is
> the way to eternal bliss and good, worthy to be cherished
> and worthy to be praised. What is bad is what you do with

the world when you become blind to truth and totally consumed by your desires, lust, and ambition for it. Our master the Prophet (peace and blessings upon him), in whom wisdom was as clear as crystal, was asked, "What is worldliness?" He answered, "Everything that makes you heedless and causes you to forget your Sustainer." Therefore the goods of this world are not harmful in themselves, but only when you let them render you forgetful, rebellious, and unaware of the Sustainer who has generously offered them to you. It is your sense of the world, your relationship to it, your preference of it over the One who gave it to you, that makes you insensitive and causes you to break your connection with divine truth.[1]

Nevertheless, our humanness is given very high regard in the Qur'ān. A trust, a covenant, is offered from humanity's Source, and it is the human being's role to accept the responsibility of this trust and to engage in this spiritual struggle.

> *In truth, We offered the trust* [of free will and self-awareness] *to the heavens, and the earth, and the mountains, but they refused to bear it, because they were afraid of it. Yet the human being took it up, and yet, humanity has always been prone to evil and foolishness.* [SURAH AL-AHZĀB (33):72]

And what is the significance of this trust? How are we to become what we are?

> *And so, turn your face steadfastly toward the faith, turning away from all that is false, in accordance with the natural disposition* (fitra) *which God has instilled in the human being: not to allow anything to corrupt what God has thus created; this is the ever true faith, although most people do not realize it. Turn toward God alone, and remain conscious of God, and be constant in*

---

[1] Ibn 'Arabī, *What the Seeker Needs* (Putney, Vt.: Threshold Books, 1989), pp. 21–22.

prayer, and do not be among those who reduce divinity to any-
thing less than God, nor among those who have broken the
wholeness of this faith and have become divided into parts, each
group indulging in their own opinions.
—SURAH AR-RŪM (30):30–31

While we are free to act and to choose, the consequences of our actions and choice are determined by a greater Law, a higher Order. One of the most important terms in the Qur'ān is *taqwā*, often mistranslated as "fear of God." Actually, a better translation would be "consciousness of God" or "vigilance," a fastidious attention to the consequences of one's actions.

We are being reminded to discern whatever corrupts this natural purity, whatever contradicts this harmony. It asks us to turn toward the wholeness and purity which is our nature, to be in that state of presence, and not to reduce that wholeness to anything partial by allowing the particular to make us forgetful of the Whole.

By the human soul (nafs), *and its harmony,*
and the gift of knowing right from wrong;
surely, he who purifies the soul is fortunate,
and ruined is he who corrupts it.
—SURAH ASH-SHAMS (91):7–10

This passage points us toward the inner nature—pure, benevolent, harmonious, and whole—which is the natural disposition of the human being. The human being has been created in the best of forms, but eventually by losing our connection with wholeness we have been reduced to a lower state by the circumstances of worldly life.

Consider the fig and the olive, and Mount Sinai, and this secure
land. In truth, We created the human being in the best of forms,
and thereafter We reduced him to the lowest of the low, except
for those who attain faith and do intentionally positive actions,
and for them is an unending recompense.
—SURAH AT-ṬALĀQ (65):1–6

The proximity of the images of the fig, the olive, and Mount Sinai to the description of humanness as the best of forms is not accidental. On the surface these are references to the lands of Syria-Palestine and Arabia, but at another level these images can be seen as symbolizing the distinguishing features of human nature. The fig is an image of the human brain itself; the olive could be the pupil of the eye, through which human intelligence is focused; Mount Sinai could be understood as the mound of the frontal cortex, which allows the human being the function of intentional action; and the secure land is the whole of the organism when the human being has accepted the trust of being human and is functioning as a unified whole.

This body is an instrument, a very fine instrument of perception, but the being, the perceiver itself, is what is human. The true human being embodies the divine presence, Hū. The true human being is the eyes and the ears of God. The depth of perception is what is human, and that depth is infinite, as deep as God.

The Path of Blame

THE MELĀMI DECONSTRUCTION
OF THE FALSE SELF

A FRIEND OF MINE TOLD ME THIS STORY:
"When I was young I had a shaikh, one of the greatest human beings I have ever known. I had met him quite by accident. He lived in a small shack in a poor neighborhood. I had to deliver some medicine there for my father's pharmacy. Once inside this man's quarters, I realized I was in the presence of someone quite unusual. For one thing, he possessed the relics of several great shaikhs of different orders. The day I met him he was having a conversation with two other young men about my own age. Their names were Metin and Refik. After hearing their conversation, I began to lose interest in the things that had occupied me. I wanted only to attend these conversations. The three of us were learning so much that we wished that more and more people could also hear these conversations. We begged our shaikh to allow the size of our circle to increase.

"One day we were attending the prayers at a great mosque. It was the feast of 'Āshūrā, the twelfth of Muharram. We were just leaving the mosque when our teacher paused on the steps because he noticed that a pigeon had just dropped dead from the sky. He picked up the poor bird, which was totally lifeless, held it tenderly in his hands, breathed a long *Huuuuu* . . . and the bird came back to life and flew off into the sky.

"Well, this act did not go unnoticed, and before long there were many people interested in our shaikh. Many of them asked to attend his conversations, and our circle grew. It was not long before we found that we had very little time with our beloved shaikh. He was too busy to see us, attending to the needs of so many people. Then one day, while doing the night prayer after our zikr, our shaikh let out a loud and smelly fart. People were astounded that this holy man could do such a thing. In a short period of time most of them had lost their faith in him, and our circle returned to nearly the size it had been originally.

"One night when just the three of us were sitting together, our shaikh remarked: 'You see, my sons, those who come because of a pigeon, leave because of a fart!' "

PRINCIPLES OF THE PATH OF BLAME

The Path of Blame (Melāmet) is a hidden tradition within Sufism, which is, above all, a way of relating to our egos. It is a kind of spiritual warriorship, not a violent warriorship but a subtle and exquisite psychological warriorship. This kind of psychology is rarely encountered in any of the world's religious traditions.

The Melāmiyya, the blameworthy ones, are those who see themselves as still subject to hypocrisy and subtle forms of self-importance. The Melāmi principle is simply to expose one's blameworthiness. This is very different from the "crazy wisdom" school, in which supposed spiritual teachers perform incomprehensible and reprehensible acts in the name of holiness.

The Path of Blame is not a path to be recommended to anyone who is beset with neurotic shame or guilt; it implies and requires a certain stage of ego integration and ego development. If we're not, in a certain sense, integrated at the ego level, following the Path of Blame could be unbalanced or not very useful. It is an esoteric school for those who've already graduated from a certain level of Sufi education.

This is why many people who have experience with the Sufi orders sometimes find it valuable to either move on, after a certain level of training is reached, or mix the Melāmi principles, and perhaps even involvement in a Melāmi group, with the work of their order. It's also relatively common for shaikhs of the different orders—those who have completed the work of the tarīqa—to also have an informal Melāmi affiliation. So it's an advanced teaching, in some ways. It's also a teaching that is very characteristic of the Mevlevis. Mevlevis are natural-born Melāmis in their attitudes. It is an approach to spirituality that is really suited to our place and time because of its invisibility and integration with everyday life.

Many of us who are seekers in the modern world have put behind us many identifications with conventional religion and belief systems. The Melāmi path is a path of spiritual invisibility, a noninstitutional spirituality and yet a spirituality that involves brotherhood and sisterhood, close relationships, spiritual dialogue. Melāmis wear no characteristic dress, do not identify themselves, and generally tend to keep their institutional profile virtually invisible. They consider it a virtue to preserve the feeling of an amateur spirituality rather than develop an organization.

It would appear that the Melāmis of all Sufis are the least involved with form. But that is not in fact the case. Remember, Ibn 'Arabī says that Muhammad himself was the foremost of "the people of blame." So there is no denying that there are some nominally Melāmi groups that have very little form. For instance, they don't wear robes in public, they don't create a lodge with a sign on it saying, "The Melāmi Order." They stay invisible, but the forms of worship, the forms of real adab, the sensitivity to what is proper, to what is right and what is wrong—these standards are maintained.

On the Melāmi path the struggle between the self and the Spirit becomes increasingly refined and subtle. The work and method are to be able to balance the demands of self with the demands of purity. We have two sides of our nature: our egoism is visible to all, but our inner purity, called *fitr* in the Qur'ān, is not so obvious. Fitr is our pure capacity for inner discernment, which depends on the health and purity of the heart.

The goal of the Melāmi path is to live a moral and sincere life for the sake of God alone and not to be concerned with appearances. The Melāmi does not wish to appear as a spiritual or pious person and regards any display of spirituality as a kind of hypocrisy. To be a hypocrite is to claim for oneself something that one does not possess. Since the human being is the extension of God's Compassion to the creation, there is nothing for us humans to call our own except our limitations. The Melāmi even goes so far as to avoid and escape the praise and good opinion of people by making public or even exaggerating his own shortcomings, while keeping his superior qualities hidden, or attributing them to God. The Melāmi allows himself to appear as less than he is.

So the Melāmi is willing to go so far as to even sacrifice his or her own respectability. The fundamental attitude toward the ego—our egocentricity, our false self—is that we want to deprive it of everything that feeds it. The Melāmi wishes to be free of subtle forms of egocenteredness, including criticizing another to make ourselves look or feel superior; indulging our disappointment with those we are close to because they have not met our expectations; feeling separate and withholding ourselves; inflating ourselves through our achievements or talents. We want to sacrifice the pleasure and status of our egocentricity, and at the same time be willing to sacrifice whatever we have, whatever property, whatever time, whatever resources we have, for the sake of others.

Ibn 'Arabī describes the people of blame in this way:

> The Melāmis, who are also called the ones who expose their blameworthiness, make the literal meaning of "blame" appear weak in comparison to their actions. They are the guides on the path leading to Allāh. The Master of the Universe is among them, none other than the messenger of Allāh, the Prophet Muhammad, peace and blessings upon him.
>
> These are the ones who have established upon the face of the world Allāh's injunctions of what is right and what is wrong. They have shown them in actions. They have ex-

plained the reasons they have left what belongs to the world to the world and what belongs to the hereafter to the hereafter. They look upon the material world as if they are outside of it, as the Lord looks upon His creation. They have not confused the Truth with the imagination of the Truth.[1]

The aim of all mystical spirituality is the dissolving of the human self in the being of God. This is our ultimate aim, and we know that it is our vanity and our pride that creates the false self. The edifice of the false self is built on the framework of our vanity and pride. We construct a self-image with a certain amount of pretense and defensiveness. So how do we purify ourselves of the pretense and defensiveness of the self-image, of the edifice of the false self? The Melāmi approach is to be willing to commit artful acts of sabotage against one's false self. Reflect on Ibn 'Arabī's words: "The people of blame are the ones who expose their blameworthiness." We all have blameworthiness, so if we could simply be open about the truth of our own being and not have any pretense about who we are or what we are, we would be much better off. There are examples in the history of the Melāmiyya of people who did unusual things that attracted blame to themselves. One doesn't defend oneself; one doesn't try to explain oneself. If someone thinks a certain way about you, it may be useful and even healthy for you to be totally nondefensive about yourself. Showing a total nondefensiveness is healthy if your true identity is strong enough.

One of the most beautiful examples of the Melāmi attitude was this saying by Nur al-'Arabī: "If you're walking down the street and you see a drunkard staggering, don't say, *Alhamdulillāh*, 'Thank God I'm not a drunkard like him,' but stagger a little bit yourself." Should we actually stagger on the street? Of course not, but perhaps we can recognize that there is a bit of a drunkard in us; that I'm really not so different from this drunkard. Maybe he's drunk with his wine and I'm drunk with something else, with my pride or daydreams, for instance.

---

[1] Ibn 'Arabī, *Futūhāt al-Makiyyah*, II, 16.5. Quoted in William Chittick, *The Sufi Path of Knowledge* (Albany, N.Y.: SUNY Press, 1989), pp. 372–73.

So I might realize that actually I'm staggering, too. Unless I'm on the straight path, I'm staggering.

So the path of blame is a psychology for learning to consciously and artfully undermine this sense of the false self, the pretense, the identification, the attachment to our ego, and to be doing this always on subtler and subtler levels. And the Melāmi even learns to enjoy teasing his or her own ego. How different this is from the touchiness of our egos when we feel we are slighted in some way, not given our due, or not recognized as we think we ought to be recognized; immediately we are wounded, our egos are wounded. But the Melāmi learns to embrace blame. He learns to see those who criticize him or don't think highly of him as his friends, as serving a useful purpose in his development. He sees the ego—in the sense of the false self—as the partner of *shaytān*, the devil himself, which is the principle of deception; so he's willing to use any means whatsoever to undermine this false self.

The path of blame has always been characteristic of and woven into the Mevlevi line, and the Mevlevis have been friends with the Melāmis. If only we could understand that it's a way of sincerity and that we all need to know that such a way exists. It is quite unique; nowhere else is this relationship to the ego, this undermining of the false self, made this explicit.

The spiritual basis of the Melāmi path is described by the three steps or three stages of fanā. The first: there are no actions but God's actions. Second: there are no qualities but God's qualities. And third: there is no existence but God's existence.

First we begin to realize on many levels, both intellectually and experientially, that there is one Agent that has given us life and set us in motion. Even though we appear to be acting and making choices in our lives, we may come to the realization that something else is operating in this whole process. Even the dance between the opposing sides of our being, between ego and spirit, is arranged for the benefit of our self-realization. And Mevlānā conveys the truth of this when he tells the story of the young dervish who was chanting, "Allāh, Allāh, Allāh," along the side of the road, and a certain cynic passed by and said, "Well, we hear you calling Allāh, but we do not hear Allāh's answer, do we?" And the poor man, who thought he was doing it all himself, that *he* was making the call and that *his* call was unanswered, fell into depression and self-doubt. Eventually, God sent an angel with a message: "Your Lord wants you to know that your calling Him *is* His response to you; your calling Him is His call being made through you." This is the annihilation, the fanā of actions.

The next stage is the annihilation of qualities. Sometimes we experience a moment of patience and, as if that were not enough, we become proud, saying, "I'm patient"; or we experience a moment of generosity, and our egocentric viewpoint, which finds it so difficult to escape itself, grabs onto that experience and says, 'It's mine." If we cannot see how we do this, we cannot be sincere and we cannot begin to dissolve the false self. If we do not face the power this false self has over us, all of our spiritual efforts will be various strategies for ego development, and the ultimate result will only be ashes and disillusionment. Yet maybe in those ashes and disillusionment we once again will rise like a phoenix and begin the quest again, because we all have experienced those ashes already, we've all experienced that disillusionment with the ploys of our ego masquerading as spiritual work.

The final stage is the realization that even our own essence does not belong to us. At the core of ourselves is an individualization of Universal Spirit, a reflection of God. In so far as we exist at all, we exist as servants in relation to Spirit. Everything we are is derived from God, and we have only a relative existence in ourselves.

A Melāmi shaikh said to me: "In whatever form we find ourselves, we take that form. There are thousands of caftans of different colors, and no matter which caftan we wear, we take that color. If we are with Mevlevis, we are Mevlevis; if we are in the Church, we are Christians. We take the adab, the behavior of the community we find ourselves in, and we accept it, we see it as good. We don't even like to be called Melāmis, but people call us this, so we say, 'Fine.' We don't defend ourselves. Actually, we could say that this is the beautiful profession practiced by Muhammad, but we don't want to say that either, because then we might fall into the trap of trying to show the people that we are better than others, because we are giving the Prophet's name to what we are trying to do. We believe that every one of us in this world needs a profession to make a living, but we think that this profession is like one wing of a bird. And if it doesn't have two wings to fly, then spirituality is needed in order for this bird to fly. So, we need another profession, a spiritual profession, which is the profession that Muhammad and all the other prophets had. We have to use both professions. Our spirituality should not take us too far away from the world. We try to be right in the middle of it all, but in a state of prayer."

And so the best teacher may be the most hidden; the best virtue may be the virtue that is not aware of itself. The aim of all spirituality can only be the dissolving of the human self in the Being of God.

Become What You Are

PARTICULARLY IN NORTH AMERICA, BUT MORE OR LESS ALL over the modern world, we have societies that are based on the individual. The individual is taken as the center of reality, the most important unit of reality, and this assumption pervades everything. But in the modern world, meaning the world of the last few centuries for the West, this individual who is the center of reality is an individual unlike the person of traditional societies and of many Eastern societies. It is an individual cut off from the transcendent; a crippled individual, a separated individual, and sometimes an emotionally toxic and wounded individual; and yet it is this individual to whom we refer everything, and who is taken as the norm of reality.

Any authentic spirituality, whether it is Sufi or something else, any spirituality that has not degenerated into a device that serves our egoism or our separation, any true spirituality teaches that our humanness is a treasure. It was our teachers in the Mevlevi Way, particularly, who impressed us with what an incredible thing the human being is. "Become what you are" was one of the favorite sayings of our shaikh, Suleyman Dede.

So what we are trying to develop is our humanness, our *sacred humanness*. This work is about the integration of humanness with transcendence—making them completely one. This is our way; this is the way of Muhammad. This is the way of the prophets, and we're trying to learn what that way is. And if I were to say that spirituality is the ultimate development of our egoism, I wouldn't be far from the truth; because our spiritual development depends on developing something in us that is very strong and very clear. Egocentricity, however, is not that strong and clear center, not that clarity of being, not that real "I." Egocentricity is our tendency to be fragmented this way and that way, to be seduced from ourselves.

ANNIHILATION OF THE FALSE SELF

People get confused if we talk about fanā as the annihilation of the self. We should talk, instead, about the annihilation of the unreal, the dissolving of the false self, namely the dissolving of all our habits of disatisfaction, resentment, and resistance—if only I had a different job, if only I had a different body, if only I had a different partner, if only I had a different brain. Fanā, annihilation, is the letting go of all this, the ability to be completely human, to be in touch with something other than that which distracts us or waylays us from our humanness. The conception of the devil, or satan (shaytān), in our tradition is that which waylays us from our humanness. It's quite specifically spoken of in the Qur'ān, for instance, in Sura Yūsuf: "*Truly the devil is an avowed enemy of the human being.*" So we can think of the shaytān as that which reduces our humanness. We want to get out of our heads the notion that the spiritual and the human are pointing in different directions. It's not that way at all, but it is necessary to find out what our humanness is.

One aspect of being human is the capacity to make a sacrifice. The ego, of course, can sacrifice, too. The ego can sacrifice by saying: I'm going to work eighty hours a week, and I'm going to save my money, and I'm going to take a trip to Paris, and maybe I'll be discovered and meet some really attractive person; but for now I'm going to sacrifice and work eighty hours a week and put my money in the bank. That's one kind of sacrifice. But what is the sacrifice of a real human being? Parents sacrifice for their children; there is an unselfishness in it, because there is great love. And yet, as beautiful as it is to love your children, still there is a kind of egoism in it, because, after all, our children are from us.

The ultimate state, we might suppose, is to be able to sacrifice for other human beings without seeing them all personally, and yet feeling love for them as for all manifestations of life. We may not be able to do this yet, but maybe the circle of our love is widening and maybe, for instance, our love is not limited by the mere likes and dislikes of our personality. Maybe we can step beyond the temporary likes and dislikes of our personality, to look beyond and to see the being behind the mask, rather than seeing another person merely through the distorting lens of our own subjective egoism.

This is what a Sufi circle also is for. Once I asked some of our friends: What's the most important part of this work? Is it our zikrs? Is it our singing together, is it our worship, is it our cooking together, is it our conversations? And someone said, "It's our love," which runs through all of these. On the path of love we call upon this love as much as we can remember to and as much as we occasionally may touch the reality of it. We call it to our aid to help transform our egoism, because the ego itself, the commanding self, the nafs al-ammāra, is so clever, so powerful, so continually self-serving. In our way we try to remember to call this love to our service. And sometimes we feel at that same moment a resistance in us. The resistance is that other pole. Spirit knows, and still there's something in us that resists the Light. Ego resists any constraints, even the common courtesy of the path. Sometimes, instead of seeing it as the most natural thing, instead of seeing courtesy, adab, as being the freedom from resistance, and as respect, gentleness, and gracefulness, this self projects onto it restraint, constraint, repression, artificiality.

SELF-DEVELOPMENT AND SELF-TRANSCENDENCE

In our way we are always trying to do two things at once: one is to develop the self and all of its gifts to the highest level. In this work, in all sorts of ways, we are trying to bring people out, to bring out their humanness, to bring out their qualities, fearlessly, to get people integrated as strong human beings. No shaikh wants weak and meek dervishes.

So practices, opportunities, and responsibilities are given to people all the time, to bring people forth, to bring that integrated self forth with all of the divine qualities. And in this case what egoism amounts to is our fear, our resistance, our self-doubt, our withholding of ourselves. This is the egoism that has to be annihilated.

At the same time and in complete balance with that, we must develop self-transcendence. Self-integration and self-transcendence have to be unified. On the one hand we are learning to manifest being with clarity, with all the qualities that the moment requires, and at the same time we wish to remain free of that false sense of "I," not to unconsciously say me, myself, I.

The human being has two purposes in life: one is to develop his or her creative expression to the utmost, and the other is to put that in the service of something greater than him- or herself. The teaching of Sufism seeks to remind us what is *worth* surrendering to. We are always serving something or someone. So what do we serve? Is it that tyrant within ourselves?

There is no fulfillment in serving the self alone, but ultimately fulfillment comes in having something much greater to surrender to. And the Friend is asking for our nonexistence, certainly, but not for a nonexistent person. The Beloved is not asking for a nobody in the personality sense. We must become everything that we are meant to be; we must actualize all the gifts we have, and yet it can't be done willfully, by sheer dint of will and effort; we don't develop that way.

Among the greatest gifts we have been given are the names of God, the qualities of God in the form of specific divine names that we use in our practice. The divine names are the vocabulary of the Supreme Poet. Their power is such that when we enter into those divine names through a zikr, for instance, it's as if we are putting a fine Damascus sword into the fire and holding it there until it is red-hot. If you then ask yourself, "Is this sword steel or is it fire?" you realize it has the qualities of both. Are you human or are you divine? Are you material or are you spiritual? Are you in existence or are you in nonexistence? Are you in time or out of time? Are you *you*?

We may not be able to truly see ourselves and how we are developing and changing spiritually. We are in the hands of Life; and Life, al-Hayy, is also one of God's names. Without this Life, what would this material existence be? If you were to take the Life out of this situation, we'd quickly become rotting corpses. This Life is a mystery; it's not explained yet, and it will never be explained—how it enters the world, how it gives and takes, how it establishes relationships, how it makes us interdependent with the substances of existence. And we know that the ultimate source of Life is Love.

Look what became of Mevlānā Rūmī when he was educated by Love, when he was set afire by Love. He became an intoxicated slave of God. He spent his nights awake doing hundreds of prostrations in prayer, and not out of effort or willfulness.

The shaikhs of this tradition will tell you, "Become the Mevlānā of *your* time"; so if a shaikh says, "I'm the Mevlānā of the time," don't listen to him, but if he says, "Become the Mevlānā of your time," listen, and trust him. Become what you are.

The Education of the Heart

OBJECTIVE KNOWLEDGE AND
SPIRITUAL NUANCE

THE DIVINE REALITY HOLDS US ALL IN ITS MERCY, AND yet the needs of humanity at this unprecedented time are very great. Our humanness is more challenged than ever before. We are swimming in a tide of unconsciousness, consumerism, mind-numbing distraction, aimless subjectivity, neurotic individualism, and philosophical fragmentation. The artificial conditions of modern industrial and postindustrial societies are accelerating time, increasing stress, isolating individuals, reducing our human interactions, corroding our hearts, and fragmenting every aspect of our existence. We have lost the sense and purpose of life. As we have lost our wholeness, we have fashioned a world that is not a garden but a place where people are enslaved, where the beauties of nature are pillaged, and where unjust and unnecessary wars destroy what the human heart would create.

The fragmentation that we see on the level of society is, of course, only mirroring what we are inside. The compulsive ego is not a unified tyranny but a many-headed monster, a shape-shifting phantom. The fragmentation of the self is the fundamental cause of all our problems, and this fragmentation is the direct result of our loss of an objective knowledge of the self and Reality.

We are living in a time when the knowledge of all the world's spiritual traditions is available to more and more human beings. We can no longer easily maintain the kind of blind faith and insularity that suited human beings of former times.

For many people this is an experience of the relativity of all approaches to the Divine. Many people are struggling with the question: from where will we draw our certainty, our faith, our commitment to spiritual discipline? One of the most pressing questions of our time is: Do we live in a postreligious, postdenominational era? And if we do, from where will we draw our discipline and practice?

We can see two major trends operating in the world. One is toward a generic, self-service, subjective spirituality. Another is toward the rigid one-dimensional fundamentalisms.

Will the majority of humanity now settle for a generic, mass-media spirituality drawn from the ever-increasing self-help literature, most of which is preoccupied with ego themes and feeds upon itself rather than from any authentic source?

Or will spirituality be hijacked by those who would offer rigid simplifications or indoctrination into a one-dimensional reality? Such a religion cannot offer the human heart what it longs for. The human heart is an instrument of fine gradations and subtlety. It is an instrument that is commensurate with the qualities of the Divine Reality. We need a spirituality of subtle nuance, as well as objectivity. We need a religion that is as much art as it is law.

Recently I have been asking this question of many people: What would be a spirituality adequate to the times we live in? Twenty-years ago, perhaps, we may have been hearing about the need for a formless, universal, nondogmatic spirituality. Today, many people who have experimented with a formless and eclectic spirituality are asking different questions. While they still seek a spirituality beyond dogmatism, they are beginning to ask questions like:

By what criteria will we be able to make the right choices in life?
How will I establish some structure in my own life while living in
   a society that seems to have lost its bearings?

What will help us to sort through the mass of information and opinions that we're continually bombarded by?

As Sufis we know that the objective knowledge we require cannot be constructed by human intellect alone. Intellect can perform many useful functions; it can divide, critique, and negate, but intellect is not the source of inspired knowledge about the purpose of life. Intellectual conjecture too often leads only to a labyrinth of opinion. Sufism is not merely the product of human conjecture. It is based upon the divine revelations, the Holy Books, which have been handed down to humanity and which offer the essential knowledge we need to develop our humanness. Admittedly most of these revelations have been distorted to various degrees. And even when we have a revelation, such as the Qur'ān, whose integrity has been preserved, there is the problem of understanding what it has to say. So much cultural distortion gets in the way, and our own selves get in the way.

But the Qur'ān does offer us an essential spiritual vocabulary and certain essential propositions. It provides the essential bearings and a context for human experience. It provides the anatomy of Reality.

Muhammad said, "Seek knowledge as far as China." The human being is asked to be an active seeker of knowledge, not the passive recipient of dogma. But the knowledge we seek must not only be a quantitative, factual knowledge, but a qualitative, spiritual knowledge as well. The human heart occupies an important place in the anatomy of Reality. "The heavens and the earth cannot contain Me; only the heart of my faithful servant can contain Me." We need an education of the heart to receive this qualitative knowledge. The heart is not merely a vague metaphor for some undefined capacity for feeling. The heart is an objective, cognitive power beyond intellect. It is the organ of perception that can know the world of spiritual qualities. It is the heart that can love, that can praise, that can forgive, that can feel the Majesty of God. Only the human heart can say yes, can affirm wholeness, and can know the Infinite. Guided by its inner discernment, the heart can apprehend what is Real.

But the human heart in most cases has suffered so much artificial conditioning that it has become a distorted and distorting instrument.

In order for the heart to be an adequate cognitive instrument, it needs reconditioning. The reconditioning of the heart is a task that must be guided by objective principles. We have the means to offer the world a true psychology of the human being, a true science of the soul, a true education of the heart. We have been provided a reliable guide to the questions of life in the form of divine revelation and in the example of complete human beings, beginning with the Prophets and continuing through the renewers of that message, the masters of the tradition, the friends of God.

This does not mean that we have a convenient body of dogma to answer every question. It means, rather, that we have objective and reliable principles that have been handed down from a higher Source and from a lineage of complete human beings. It still remains for us to verify and apply this knowledge. Is this not the meaning of the following passage?

> Soon We will show them Our Signs in the farthest horizons and in their own souls until it becomes manifest to them that this is the Truth. Is it not enough that your Sustainer witnesses all things? [SURAH MU'MINŪN (23):53]

Because we are alive within a unified, conscious Reality, possessing will, intelligence, conscious purpose, and love, everything is a sign to be read, revealing the meanings and purpose of this Reality. We are encouraged to look to the signs with our hearts. We have been given a revealed text composed of ayahs (signs), and we are promised that we will be shown over time the Truth of these signs in ourselves and in the farthest horizons.

> Here are Signs self-evident in the hearts of those endowed with knowledge: and none but the unjust reject Our Signs. [SURAH AL-'ANKABŪT (29):49]

In the spiritual psychology of Sufism that was described earlier, the heart (qalb) is the midpoint between self (nafs) and Spirit (rūh). The heart is suspended between these two equally powerful and attractive forces. If the heart gives itself to nafs alone, it does not receive what it needs for its own healthy life. It becomes first veiled, then hardened, and finally diseased. If the heart opens itself to the influence of Spirit, it begins to receive the spiritualizing energies and to distribute them to every aspect of the human being and to the wider world. But unfortunately the heart is virtually helpless between these two forces of nafs and rūh.

What power put our tender hearts in this seemingly merciless situation and why? Could it be that we find ourselves in this dilemma in order that we might learn to call out in our weakness, to ask for help, to make a clear call to the Infinite?

The real and essential needs of the human being have not changed very much over the centuries. Who would disagree, for instance, with al-Ghazālī's assessment eight centuries ago that "human perfection resides in this, that the love of God should conquer a man's heart and possess it wholly, and even if it does not possess it wholly, it should predominate in the heart over the love of all things."[1]

What has changed is the form and pressure of those forces that could displace the love of God from the heart. And what may change further is that human beings may lose the whole notion of love of God as the criteria of human perfection and well-being.

To be a Sufi is to be a lover, but not just any kind of lover. We need knowledge to discern what to love and what love asks of us, in order that we might become Love itself. Mevlānā Rūmī says: "There is no greater love than love with no object."

> *Truly, those who are faithful and do righteous deeds, the Compassionate will endow with love.* [SURAH MARYAM (19):96]

With this spirituality of nuance and with the objective principles of the Revelation, we will find the true Faith, or essential Surrender, in unexpected places: in great literature as well as in children's books, in nature and ecology, in the honest attempt to deal with social prob-

---

[1] Al-Ghazālī, *The Alchemy of Happiness*, translated by Claude Field (New York. M. E. Sharpe, 1991), p. 79.

lems. If there is a primordial religion, it is the objective Reality within everything. It is not primarily a religion characterized by a particular dress or architecture or customary behavior.

We can read the signs in the unfolding of human history. In this unique and unprecedented time, all of humanity is becoming conscious of important and fundamental rights and obligations:

> We may be learning how to live within the laws of God's ecology.
> We may be learning how to maintain open societies where human rights are guaranteed.
> We may be learning how to allow a true partnership between man and woman.
> We may be learning to find our connection with the Hū, the Divine Immanence within.

We are not people of the past, living solely in our recollection of a former purity. We need to have the courage to be of this moment. Muhammad said, "He whose one day is like the next is not of us."

Because tradition can easily crystallize into social conditioning, we might keep in mind that our tradition has been one of transcending identification with forms and concepts. *La illāha il Allāh* (There is no god but God) is a self-transcending affirmation that does not define God but allows us to move from one level of reality to the next, always transcending our limited conceptions, our idols. The Sufi path is an organizing pattern of energy. It has never been a static tradition; it is a dynamic way, not a position; it is living, not dead. It is impartial illumination, not egoistic opinion.

We need to understand the Revelation with all of the knowledge and human experience that is now at our disposal. If the Qur'ān is what it claims to be, it must inspire us anew to find the most real and appropriate solutions to the challenges the human spirit faces. The reality of the message of Muhammad has been in serious trouble before, but it can be revived, God willing.

Sufism is not the state of having preexisting answers to every question; it is understanding our place in this expansive reality and thus being open to the moment, responsive to the Divine Intelligence. As

Mevlānā says: "The Sufi's book is not of ink and letters; it is nothing but a heart white as snow."

Rigid opinion and negative judgment darken the heart. The contracted, critical part of the mind is the distorting lens that magnifies our identifications and differences, creating a world of self-importance, disharmony, and imbalance. Opinion veils the heart. Opinion says: "I know, and you do not." It minimizes our own fallibility and searches for the errors of others. It makes ourselves into competitors with each other and finally competitors with God, the only Knower. Opinion tends toward intellectual arrogance, an occupational disease of esotericists. It leads to false claims that make orders, shaikhs, and religion more important than God. Cultic behavior can undermine any group that does not place itself under the purest auspices of Love and illumination. The illuminated heart is content and at peace with God.

An illuminated heart is rare; opinion is all too common. The illuminated heart sees the Divine Reality, the Balance in all things; it sees with the impartial light of Allāh. Illumination says: "Let's see what God does; what God does is always beautiful."

It is essential to work for the unity of humankind, to safeguard the planet for future generations, to show a way in which humanity can free itself from egoism and fear. The seeking of personal salvation needs to be sacrificed in order to make the message clear.

We must remember the facts of our situation: the potential for devastation, the economic injustice, the secret powers that shape our lives. Humanity is on the brink of catastrophe, and we have been asleep. What, therefore, is the most effective means of issuing a call to awakening?

It is time to break out of our prisons of private pleasure and security, to use all our powers of presence and communication to remind all human beings of the essential reality of the heart and of the unity that can be achieved if we live from the heart. When the heart fills with the breath of fanā, we can float on the stormy seas of life. We do not own ourselves anymore; we are only the servants of Hū. This Hū is the divine immanence burning within us. In order to be a servant of this Hū, we have to make fundamental changes in our lives, to live a heroic generosity, a spiritual chivalry, and to create enduring relationships for the sake of God alone.

> *And verily your people are a single people and I am your Sustainer: therefore be awake to Me and no other. But people have fragmented their purpose among themselves into sects: each party rejoices in that which is with itself.* [Surah al-Mu'minūn (23):52–53]

Real human solidarity may be rare, but it is natural and human to forget our self-interest in love, to cultivate enduring relationships over worldly interests and accomplishments, to build something in the spiritual dimension, something real and eternal.

This material existence is a canvas that we paint with the qualities of our own selves. What we see on this canvas is what we have created. If we do not make these changes, we will continue to see a desperate, depressed humanity and a ravaged environment. If we don't find the jewel of the Divine Reality within our hearts and begin to live from it, the bazaar of this existence may be destroyed stone by stone.

With this objective knowledge and spiritual nuance we must create a culture of love. We must invite the era of enlightenment by putting spiritual education at the center of all education. We have only one kind of work to do, and it is the divine work. This is essential Sufism.

Sufism is nothing less than the path of experiencing our divine essence, our Hū, the secret of our humanness. When we appear before our Sustainer, bringing all the accomplishments of our lives, our Sustainer will say, "Bring me the Heart. If the Heart is pleased with you, I am pleased with you. Your relationship to your inmost Heart is your relationship to Me." Sufism is essentially the education of the heart. This education consists of both enlightenment and maturity. The enlightenment is the light of continuous zikr in our hearts, light upon light, *nur 'ala nur*. The maturity consists of the human attributes we choose to develop that reflect the beautiful names of God. The human heart is the most precious substance in existence. We are the people of Heart, who have heard from deep within our own hearts a voice that says: God is Great.

Refractions of a Single Light

APHORISMS

Some of these aphorisms are original, while some of them are inevitably derived from insights we have received from our teachers.

Behind the veil of appearances,
Mercy and Love prevail
over all qualities in the universe.

Life is a school of love,
and love is the only lesson
to be learned in this life.

The more we fall in love with Truth,
the more our intelligence increases.

If we don't know our own value,
even though we may know the value of everything else,
we have failed in the most essential knowledge.

The Creative Power of the universes
created human nature as its foremost
theater of manifestation.

Developing our presence, our inner being,
is developing that which is most essentially
and characteristically human.

All universes are contained within
the experience of human presence.

The human heart is the doorway to Reality.

Everything in existence is in a state of worship naturally,
except the human being,
for whom it must be a conscious choice.

The lover is in relationship with his or her Origin,
as a child with its mother.

For a human being, worship leads toward
the authentic connection with all levels of reality.

All loves are the reflection of One Love
and ultimately lead to that Love.

The gift of will is the capacity
for making a conscious choice.

The supreme act of will is to choose to be in harmony
with the Divine Will, the sum of all will.

The greatest development of self
is to be free of all selfishness.

Every breath offers a new possibility
to be aware of Spirit.

All religions worship the same One.

Real prayer is an intimate dialogue with Reality.

We do not melt in God without love.
We do not survive in God without
the poverty and humility of submission.

Humility is our awareness of
our dependence on a vast Intelligence.

The universe is infinitely intelligent,
and it is for human intelligence to recognize
just how intelligent.

Faith is our certainty regarding the Unseen Beneficence.

Experience is structured to reveal Spirit and develop soul.

Faith and denial are the two essential choices
faced by each human being.

Separation is the fundamental sin,
which has countless expressions.

When we stop complaining, we will be in paradise.

Ego is the fuel of hell.

Indulging our appetites is not
a reliable path to happiness.

Every particle of the universe can be
a distraction or a reminder.

Whatever brings people together for a good is good.

Generosity is a sign of our reliable
connection to the Abundance.

Service is a sign of our active connection to Life.

It is possible to live other than the way
we see being lived around us.

The degree of harmony in our relationships
is the degree of our skillfulness in living the Truth.

The self must get accustomed to
the experience of surrender
in order to purely be itself.

Gratitude is better than the gift.

Let us observe how we fill ourselves
and learn to be more empty.

Everything on the outside is only reminding us
of what we are inside.

Everything of real value is invisible.

Grace is always available to us,
only we are not always available to receive it.

The human being is purely a reflector
of the attributes of the One.

Nothing but limitation originates with the human being.

Sometimes the purpose of sin
is to awaken us to forgiveness.

Reality teaches through contrasts.

Time and space do not exist for the heart.

The human being cannot become God,
but God is the Reality of the human being.

For us servanthood is greater than sovereignty;
spiritual maturity is knowing the time and place for each.

We must first learn to be a child of the moment
before we can become the parent of the moment.

Hunger is the food of the wise.

Why trust or depend upon appearances?

We are responsible for our intentions, not for outcomes.

Thought is a form of action.

One cannot think properly or make use of thought
if one has not learned to stop thinking.

Meditation is listening to the silence within.

The greatest wisdom is listening
to the guidance of the heart.

The best course of action is
when reason and the heart agree.

Take care of whatever is placed in your care
as you would want to be cared for.

There is freedom in preferring others' needs to our own.

The greatest pleasure is the felicity that comes
from having lived with compassion and kindness
toward other human beings.

All of humanity is a single body.

Be aware of the drumbeat of death in the distance.

Life is a dream whose meaning will be revealed
when we awaken from life.

To die before death is the greatest freedom.

God is the light of the heavens and the earth
and the mirror of our inmost experience.

God is a vast ocean;
the human being is God in a usable portion.

God is the educator of the universes.

Be at the side of those who remember God often.

To accomplish the task of being human
is not impossible nor unlikely,
because it is what we are designed for.

Our spirituality and our humanness are not in conflict.

Love is a surrender of wills.
Lovers disappear in each other,
and from their disappearance God emerges.

Love cleanses us of false attributes
and reveals our essence.

The self is the outer covering of God.
Every outer covering is different.

"Worldliness" is nothing but the code
of drudgery, greed, and arrogance.

A needy person humiliates himself for trivial things.

A lazy person is deprived of the divine path.

There is no such thing as death.
No one is going to die. But since death is so valuable,
it has been hidden in the safe of fears.

If we can discard the words that belong to our self,
the Friend will speak through us.

Total surrender, transparency of self, is salvation.
It is the full understanding
of our insolvency, our metaphysical poverty.

When ego disappears, our burden is lighter.

Whenever we judge another,
whether he knows it or not,
we hurt God.

Though we are judged and blamed,
we will love; we must love.

The clothes of love are
knowledge, ethics, and religion.
Love is beyond all of them.

The language of conscience is sweet and good.
The language of blame is devilish.

God loves us to be together.
God is us-with-us and doesn't like loneliness.

Love surrounds us,
but only one who loves
can direct its current.

In whomever we see a spark of love, we are their servant.

Spiritual conversation is divine light.
It brings us close together and melts us in unity.

If we attempt to go this way alone,
we will only find our own egos.

Let our hymn, our communion, our prostration
be our love for each other for God's sake,
without profit or recompense.

The divine path rejects no religion.

The essence of worship is to love.

Real joy will come when we have given up name and form.
This great power has neither name nor form.

Glossary

A definition has to cover all kindred aspects of what is being defined, and should be free from all aspects which don't agree with it.

—HASAN TAHSIN BABA

A definition is a statement that includes all the friends of the defined and excludes all its enemies.

—MURAT YAGAN

T HIS "GLOSSARY" IS AN ATTEMPT TO BUILD A MORE PRECISE spiritual vocabulary in the English language. Its purpose is not to explain foreign terms, which will for the most part be explained in the text itself.

Every field of knowledge requires its own specific vocabulary, a well-defined glossary for its own needs. English is a relatively undeveloped language for the expression of spiritual realities, especially when compared with certain languages like Greek, Hebrew, Sanskrit, or Arabic. These languages not only have a long history as vehicles for the expression of spiritual realities, they have also been the recipients of revelation, by which we mean a direct communication from divine intelligence.

In order to be able to communicate with each other and to achieve a coherent knowledge at the conscious and unconscious levels, we would do well to have a spiritual vocabulary that is both precise and unified. In our definition of "humbleness," for instance, we find a relationship between this single word and the master truth of Sufism: "The awareness of our dependence on Spirit, that we are not the originators of anything but the reflectors of the attributes of Spirit; and the awareness of our need for other human beings."

Ideally, every word of our spiritual vocabulary should clarify and support other terms and remind us of the essential truths of the teaching. While it is true that the Arabic language, for instance, may have a precision, depth, and allusiveness that English lacks, we still have an obligation to use the English language as well as we can. This is made all the more urgent as English, for better or worse, seems to have become the most widely spoken language on our planet.

ABUNDANT LIFE   Living life fully and being consciously aware of becoming whole with your mind, body, soul, and ecology.

ALLĀH   The Divinity; the God of all religions, who is beyond any description or limitation.

APPROPRIATENESS   The child of love and humbleness.

ATTAINMENT   The progress in using human faculties. Something is an attainment if it can be produced at will.

ATTRIBUTE   The Divine Qualities and Meanings that are the real causative factors of the manifestation of material existence.

AWARENESS   Any perception; not necessarily "conscious."

BARAKA   Grace; Divine charm; the ability of putting into action the divine attributes of supraconscious mind.

BEING   A timeless, spaceless attribute, satisfying in itself, that can be experienced by the soul. When applied to an individual human being it is the degree of our identification with Spirit.

BEAUTY   Anything that becomes our point of contact with Love.

BELOVED   One's point of contact with Essence; it can be one person, and it can be everywhere.

CHIVALRY (*futuwwa*): Heroic sacrifice and generosity. The Sufi ethic that traces back to the family of the Prophet.

COMPLETED HUMAN BEING   Someone who has become transparent to God and thus can reflect the Divine Attributes appropriately.

COMPLETION   Being one with the Whole, realizing Truth.

CONSCIOUSNESS   The degree of our awareness, inner and outer, on as many levels of our experience as are available to us. A potentially comprehensive awareness that encompasses thinking, feeling, and bodily sensation without being limited by them.

CONTENTMENT   The awareness of one's present richness, without precluding having more.

DENIER (*kāfir*)   One who denies the reality of a beneficent Unseen Order; the original Arabic term is often poorly translated as "unbeliever."

DERGĀH   A Persian word for a Sufi training center. Synonyms: *tekke* (Turkish), *zawia* (North African), *khānaqāh* (Persian and Indian).

DERVISH   A seeker on the Sufi path; one who stands at the threshold between slavery and freedom.

DISCERNMENT (*furqān*)   An innate capacity within the human being to discern the good and the true.

DISCIPLINE   Methodical pursuit. The state of someone who does everything for a purpose.

DISPOSITION (*fitra*)   The natural disposition to the Good that God has instilled in the human being.

ECOLOGY   Relationship with our environment.

EGO (*nafs*)   The self, which we will always continue to transform and develop into ever more subtle and spiritualized states of being.

EGOISM   The self in its more compulsive manifestations. The self-righteousness of the intellect working for its own survival at the expense of the whole self. The illegitimate child of the union of mechanical thought and selfish desire.

ELDER   A mature carrier of the teaching; a light-holder of the tradition.

EMANCIPATION   Freedom from the fear of loss.

ESSENCE   1. God; that from which everything proceeds. 2. The essential nature of anything; that which is inherently and utilizably good in something.

FAITH   Hope substantiated by knowledge. Certainty regarding the reality of the Unseen Beneficence.

FANĀ   The state of having melted into the Divine Being, which is followed by or alternates with *baqā*: the state of resurrecting through the Divine Being.

FREEDOM   Having will; being free of negativity; doing what one chooses without hurting anyone.

FUTUWWAH   *See* Chivalry

GOD   The absolute source and subtlest state of everything; the sum of all will; the ultimate meaning of everything.

GRACE   The continuous overflowing of the Divine Essence that is coming to all witnesses of God. The grace we receive only depends on our ability to receive.

GRASP   Understanding reached through our mobilization of the supraconscious and subconscious minds, as well as our five senses.

HEART (*qalb*)   The subconscious/supraconscious faculty of mind; all the faculties of mind that are nonintellectual. The core of our individuality. The midpoint between self and Spirit, which allows a connection to be formed between them.

HIGHER SELF   That part of ourselves which is in contact with the Creative Power or Divine Being.

HŪ   The pronoun of Divine Presence, also understood by Sufis to be the indwelling presence of God.

HUMAN BEING (*insān*)   A vehicle for individualized Spirit; the most complete witness of Spirit within this material world.

HUMBLENESS   The awareness of our dependence on Spirit, that we are not the originators of anything but the reflectors of the attributes of Spirit; and the awareness of our need for other human beings.

IMAGINAL   *See* Interworld

INTELLECT (*aql*)   Thought, distinguished from the faculties of the supraconscious mind; mind activated by will and reason. The faculty of mind most under our immediate control.

INTENTION (*himmah*)   An aim or wish, clearly formulated in words, by which we mobilize the energy to attain that aim or wish. Having a spiritual intention is the beginning of integrity.

INTERDEPENDENCE   The recognized need of human beings for each other in order to attain the fullness of life on all levels from material to cosmic.

INTERWORLD (*barzakh*)   *Mundus imaginalis,* an intermediate visionary realm between pure meaning and material existence; the locus of imaginal experience.

KNOWING HEART   Loving mind (Turkish, *gonül*). All the faculties of the mind that transcend the intellect. The supraconscious, subtle, creative, and spiritual departments of mind.

KNOWLEDGE   Seven levels are recognized: knowing something's name; knowing through the senses; knowing about something; knowing through deeper grasp and understanding; knowing through doing; knowing through the supraconscious faculties; knowing by Spirit alone.

LATĪFAS   Capacities of the human nervous system to reflect the one Creative Energy. For example, just as the brain is the platform of intellectual mind, which is one kind of reflection of the Creative Energy, there are other, more subtle faculties, which can apprehend the infinite qualities of Being.

LEADER (*shaikh*)   Someone who is lifted up by others in order to be of service, to get a particular job done, to whom we give love, respect, and whatever necessary to get the job done.

LIFE (*hayy*)   An attribute of God. It is from eternity to eternity and forms our existence.

LOVE   The greatest transforming power; our experience of Spirit. The electromagnetic milieu in which we all exist, which exerts various forces of attraction among all that it contains.

LOWER SELF   The self based on ego.

MARRIAGE   The result or destination of our sexual maturing and fermentation.

MATURITY   Skillfulness within our particular ecology, which comes from the development and balance of latent human faculties under divine grace and guidance. It leads to fulfillment in every department of life.

MEVLĀNĀ (or Mawlana)   "Our Master"; an honorific commonly applied to Mevlānā Jalāluddīn Rūmī.

MEDITATION Listening within, a function of consciousness, not intellect.

MEEKNESS Patience developed in suffering acts of injustice.

MIND The whole field of Reality.

MYSTICISM (*tassawuf*) A faculty peculiar to the human being, which is obvious to neither the intellect nor the senses, but which depends on the refinement and receptivity of faculties within the supraconscious mind.

NOTHINGNESS The point reached by utmost subtilization. Like sugar dissolved in water, the self is not really gone.

PERSONALITY Learned habits of thought, feeling, and behavior; the social self. Personality can either manifest our essence or obscure it.

POINT OF CONTACT A person through whom we gain access to Higher Self.

PRESENCE The state of being consciously aware, in alignment with our deepest and highest capacities.

PROPHET One who brings a Code of Living, a Sacred Law. A prophet may also initiate an elite into knowledge of the Truth.

RABITA An affectionate bond formed between a dervish and shaikh in which spiritual support and protection are maintained.

RABB (Sustainer, Lord, Educator) A synonym for *Allāh*, the Rabb al-Alamīn, Lord of All Worlds.

REMEMBERING, REMEMBRANCE (*zikr*) When the state of presence comes into relationship with the Divine Being, whether in its Majesty or its Intimacy.

REVELATION A communication of the Divine Being for the sake of guidance; instructions for the realization of our true human nature from the Source of our human nature; the Holy Books (explicitly: Torah, Psalms, Gospels, Qur'ān; implicitly the sacred books of all traditions).

SACRED LAW (*Sharī'at*) A code of living based upon the Qur'ān and the example (*sunnah*) of Muhammad, whose intention is to restore and safeguard our humanness and the social order.

SECRET (*sirr*) The knowledge of which helps the human being to discern the Real from the illusory. The innermost essence of the human.

SELF   The sense of identity, that with which we are always working. At the lowest level it can be a complex of psychological manifestations arising from the body and related to its pleasure and survival. At its highest level it can be experienced as an infinitely refinable substance. *See also* Soul; Spirit

SENSING   Being grounded in an awareness of the body.

SERVICE   The functional outcome of being connected to Cosmic Energy.

SHAIKH   *See* Leader

SIN   Separation from Essence; the opposite of submission. Saying no to God.

SOUL   Individualized Spirit. The core of individuality, which can be developed and spiritualized and which forms a connection between ego and God/Spirit. *See also* Self; Spirit

SPIRIT   The first or primary manifestation of the Essence we call God. Spirit (spiritual self, essence, *rūh*) as an attribute of the human being is described as an impulse or command (*amr*) from God. Spirit is the essence of life itself. It is like a nondimensional point that is linked to the realm of Unity and has access to the realm of Attributes, the Divine Names. *See also* Self; Soul

SUBMISSION   Lower self bowing to Higher Self. Listening to the directive of Higher Self wherever we find it.

SUFI   A word first used to describe one who understands Essence beyond forms. A word whose root means pure and unadulterated.

SUFISM (*tasawwuf*)   The education of our humanness; the cultivation of divine character.

SUPRACONSCIOUS   Faculties of the human mind that are subtle and nonintellectual, a synonym for which is *heart*.

TARĪQA   The spiritual path. A Sufi order; an esoteric school with a spiritual lineage.

TRUTH   For the human being: the knowledge that I am not separate from the Whole.

THE UNSEEN   Those aspects of reality we have veiled ourselves from; the reality behind appearances made up of qualities, intelligence, and will.

WILL   The ability to *do* consciously; the faculty of conscious choice; a unique attribute of the human being.

WISDOM   Knowledge that comes from within.

WORSHIP   Loving respect for a higher spiritual Power; a yearning found in human beings.

YEARNING   One of the most valuable attributes of a seeker, which become the motivating force of the whole journey of return to God.

Index

--- ∽✿∼ ---

ABOUT THE AUTHOR

KABIR HELMINSKI is the author of *Living Presence: A Sufi Way to Mindfulness and the Essential Self*, as well as the translator of numerous books of Sufi literature and especially Rumi. He is the codirector, with his wife, Camille Helminski, of the Threshold Society, a nonprofit organization dedicated to sharing the knowledge and practice of Sufism. As the publisher of Threshold Books for some twenty years, he was largely responsible for making Rumi the most widely read poet of our time. As a producer and writer of Sufi music, he has gained recognition for numerous recordings, including his own *Garden within the Flames*. He is a representative of the Mevlevi tradition founded by Jalāluddīn Rūmī.

For more information about the Threshold Society, contact:

The Threshold Society
Box 1821
Soquel, CA 95073-1821
http://www.sufism.org